Remodeling
Country Homes

Remodeling Country Homes

LOFT

Editorial Coordination: Cristina Paredes
Texts: Montse Borràs, Cristina Paredes
Translation: Jay Noden
Art Director: Mireia Casanovas Soley
Layout and Graphic Design:
TRAMA, Estudi Gràfic
www.tramaestudi.com

2008 © **LOFT Publications**
Via Laietana 32, 4º Of. 92
08003 Barcelona, Spain
Tel.: +34 932 688 088
Fax: +34 932 687 073
loft@loftpublications.com
www.loftpublications.com

ISBN: 978-84-96936-10-2

Printed in China

LOFT affirms that it posseses all the necessary rights for the pulication of this material and has duly paid all royalties related to the authors' and photographers rights. LOFT also affirms that it has violated no property rights and has respected common law, all authors' rights and other rights that could be relevant. Finally, LOFT affirms that this book contains no obscene nor slanderous material.

The total o partial reproduction of this book without the authorization of the publishers violates the two rights reserved; any use must be requested in advance.

If you would like to propose works to include in our upcoming books, please email us at loft@loftpublications.com.

In some cases it has been impossible to locate copyright owners of the images published in this book. Please contact the publisher if you are the copyright owner of any of the images published here.

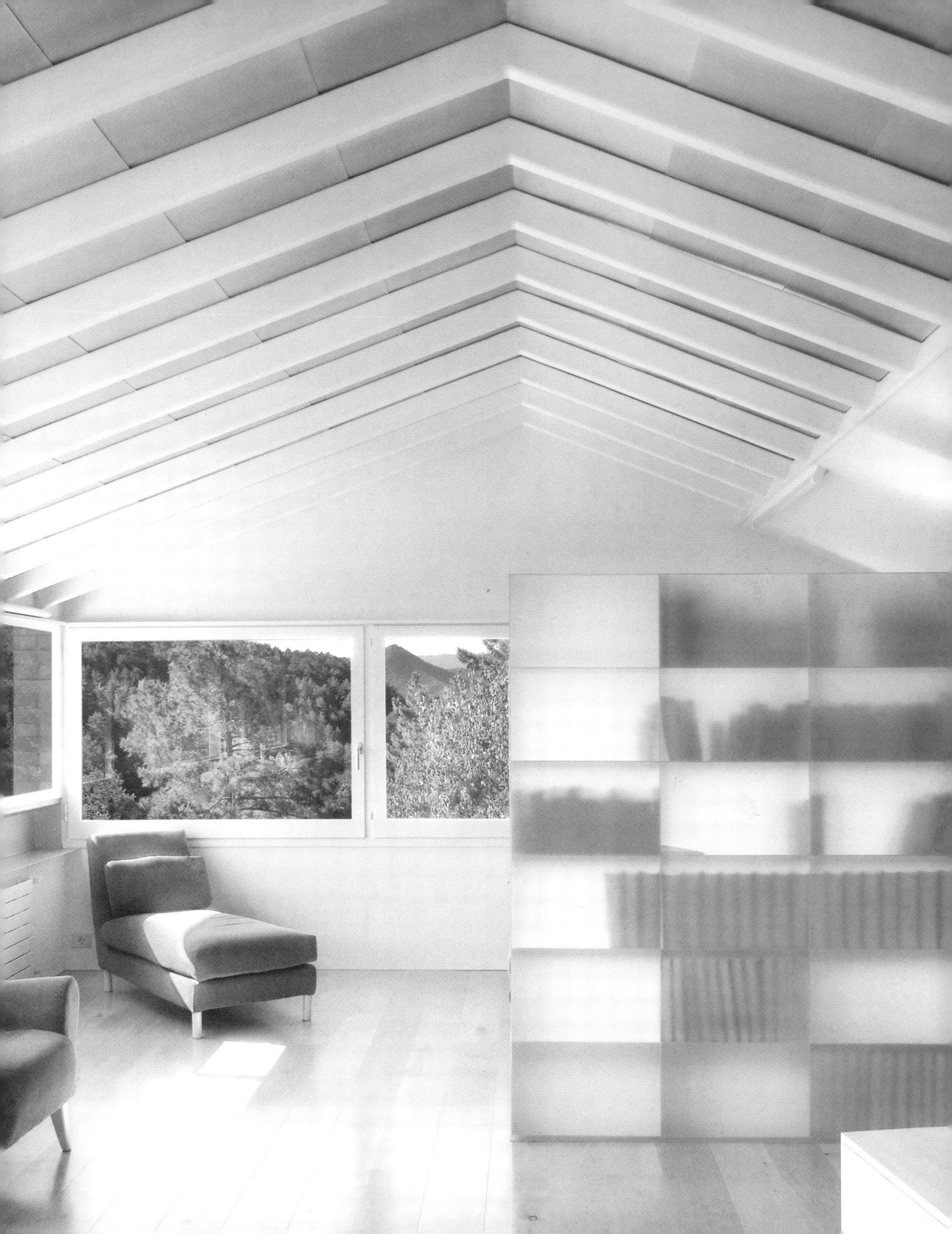

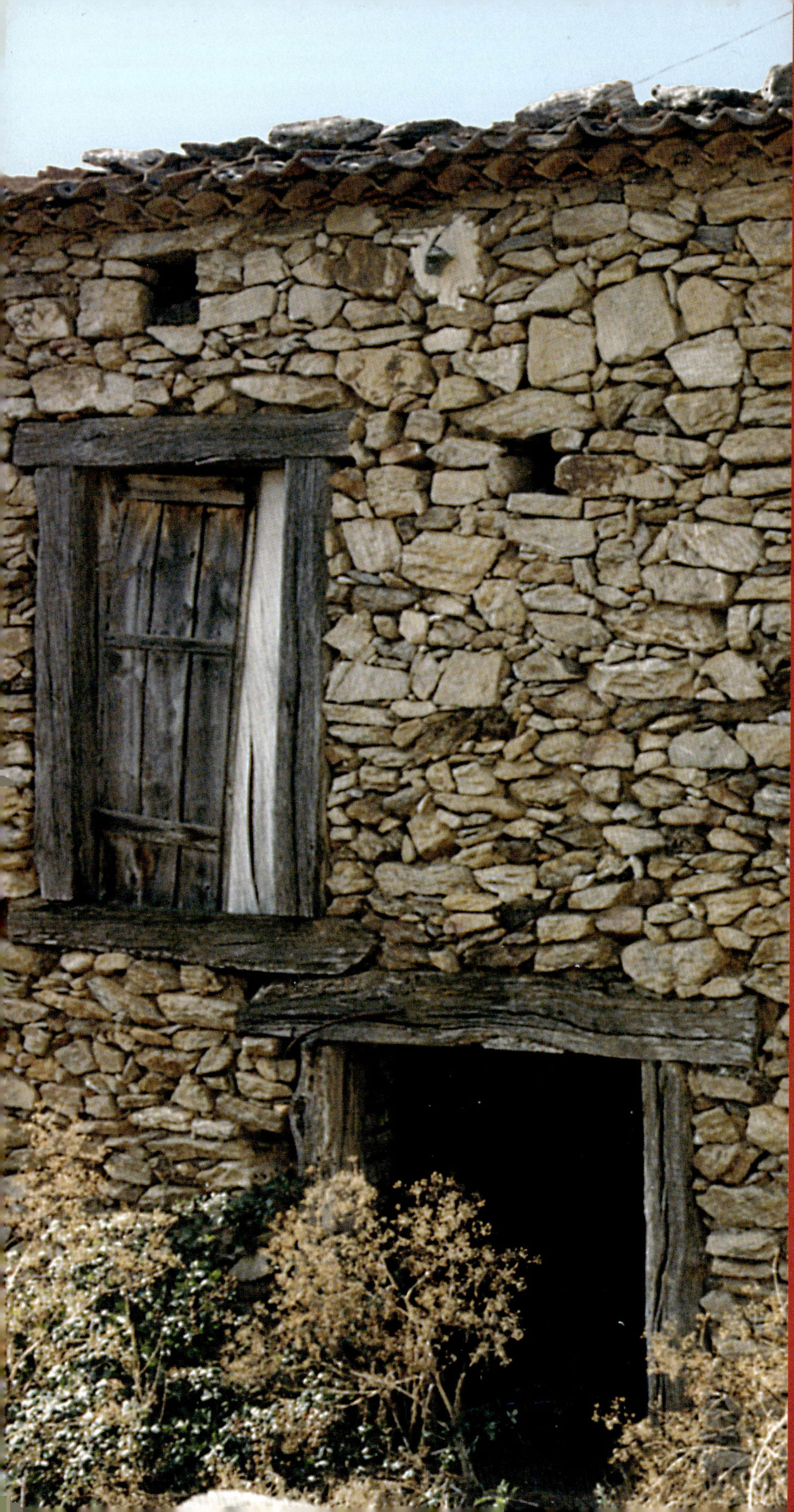

Introduction	8
Restoration of a Farm in Ramsau	10
Old Barn in Val Tidone	20
Barn in Mortagua	32
House in Vilada	44
Tower in Piamonte	54
House in Brito-Guimarães	64
House in Semmerzake	74
Family Hotel in Garraf	84
Restoration of Wolzak Farm	96
Extension of Sattler-Smith House	106
Studio House in Montseny	116
House in Lombardia	126
Farm in the Austrian Alps	136
Can Pujoleta	146
Holiday Home on the Costa Verde	156
House in Schio	166
Ca la Paua	176
Moereels Tower	186
House in Cerdanya	196
House in Taíde	206
Stables in Bavaria	214
Monte dos Mosqueiros	224
House in Horcajuelo de la Sierra	232
Party Barn and Guesthouse	240
Podere 43	248

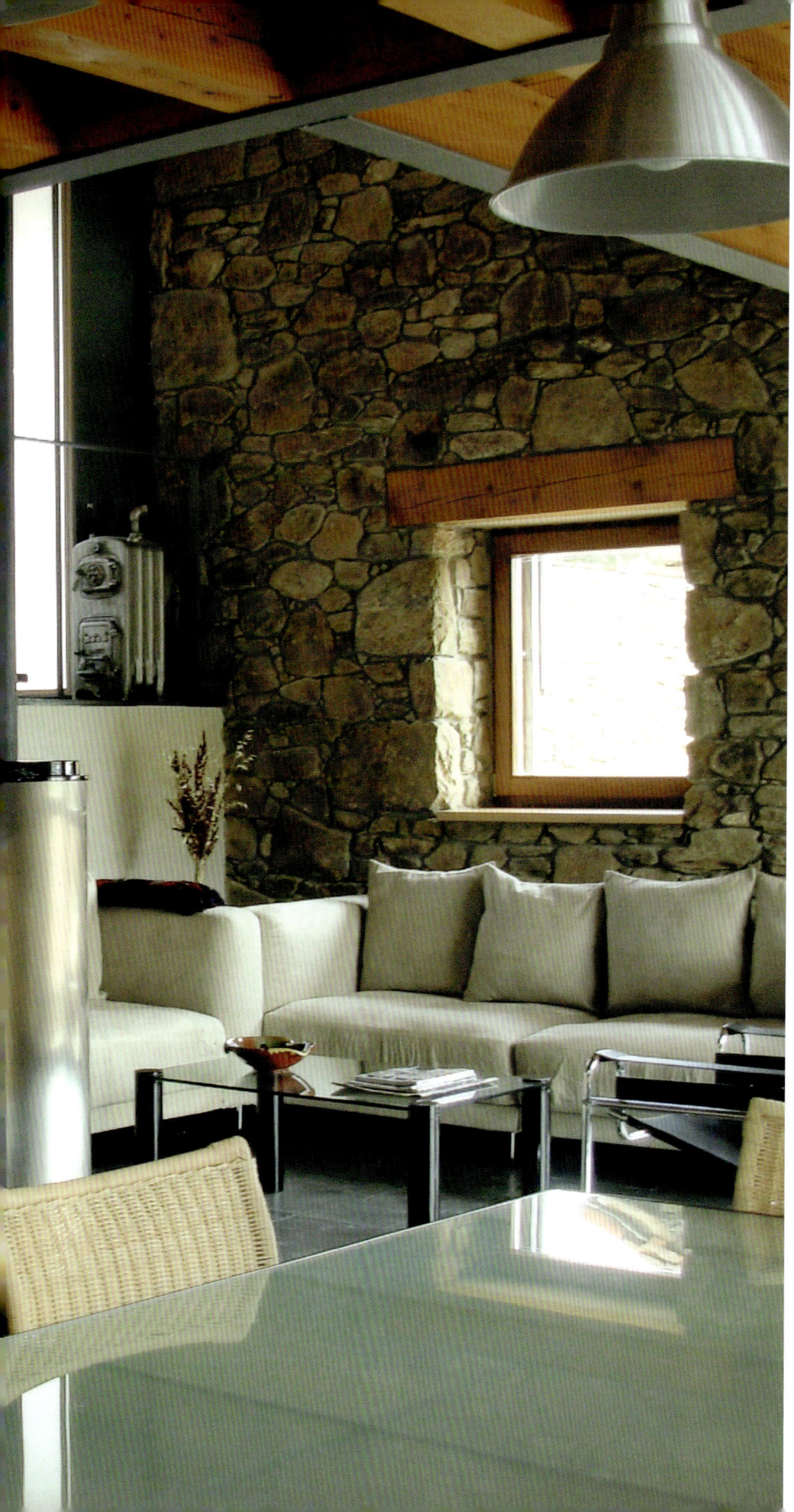

Introduction

The need to be in close contact with nature should be the main reason for looking for a residence outside of the city, and in most cases this is probably the case. The frantic pace of daily life is difficult to cope with and more and more people are starting to search for a tranquil place where they can rest and spend time with their family and friends. This book is an example of how in just a few years many old constructions that have been restored as recreational spaces have now become first homes. The possibility of working from home, the house prices in cities and promise of a higher quality of life make this an increasingly attractive option.

So, why restore a house, which in many cases has become a ruin when it would be much simpler and more economical to demolish the existing building and start from scratch? Regulations may not allow demolition in many cases, but it is also true that, by building on top of bases from the past, the new construction will form part of this past. Perhaps this new construction will later become another page from the place's history.

This book presents diverse projects, which in some cases radically tackle the concept of building restoration. Whilst unafraid of completely transforming what already exists, the architects heed and learn from those who built and lived in the constructions beforehand, applying techniques and materials which are appropriate to the physical and atmospheric conditions.

The uses have changed completely; it is impossible to compare the subsistence economy in which many of these houses originated with the life styles of today's residents.

The challenge for the architect is to fuse techniques and materials from the past with contemporary needs. The use of technology not only increases comfort, but in many cases also helps to simplify structures, lower costs and offer ways of saving energy. This transforms what maybe a privilege for the few into a way of life that respects the surroundings and is in keeping with the constructive requirements of a fast approaching future.

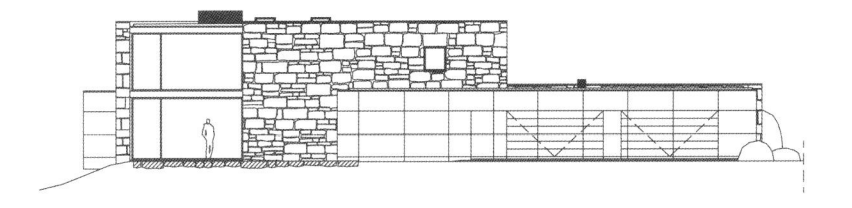

The restoration project was intended to preserve the relationship between the main house, with its complex structure, and the new building, whose homogeneity reflects the volumes of the previous construction.

Restoration of a Farm in Ramsau

Architect: Martin Feiersinger
Photographer © Werner Feiersinger
Location: Ramsau im Zillertal, Austria
Completion date: 2004

Ramsau is a small alpine village in the Ziller Valley, which is characterized by a mix of modest, traditional farmhouses and new and more ostentatious constructions. This farm, which has been handed down through the generations, had been abandoned for some time and was in considerably bad shape. Demolition was considered as an option, but in the end the owners opted for a minimal intervention in the main residence to adapt it to the client's needs. It was then decided to carry out a complete overhaul on the adjacent stables, which had already been through several earlier interventions. The idea throughout the project was to respect the farm's quality as an essential part of the historic fabric of the local population. The restoration of the main house included the destruction of the plasterboard found throughout the upper floor, in order to install interior insulation and leave the woodwork exposed. All the door and window frames were replaced. The entire building was propped up and new foundations were laid. The original staircase was replaced by birch stairs of a more moderate inclination. The attic was transformed into a large loft-style living room.

The stable was converted into a three-story annexed apartment. The planks of wood from the old stable have been reused to clad the new house. The shutters on the façade are reminiscent of the sliding doors of the old stable and like the exterior walls, are surfaced with wooden panels salvaged from the old building.

12 Restoration of a Farm in Ramsau

First floor

Second floor

Attic

0 2 4

Restoration of a Farm in Ramsau 13

North elevation

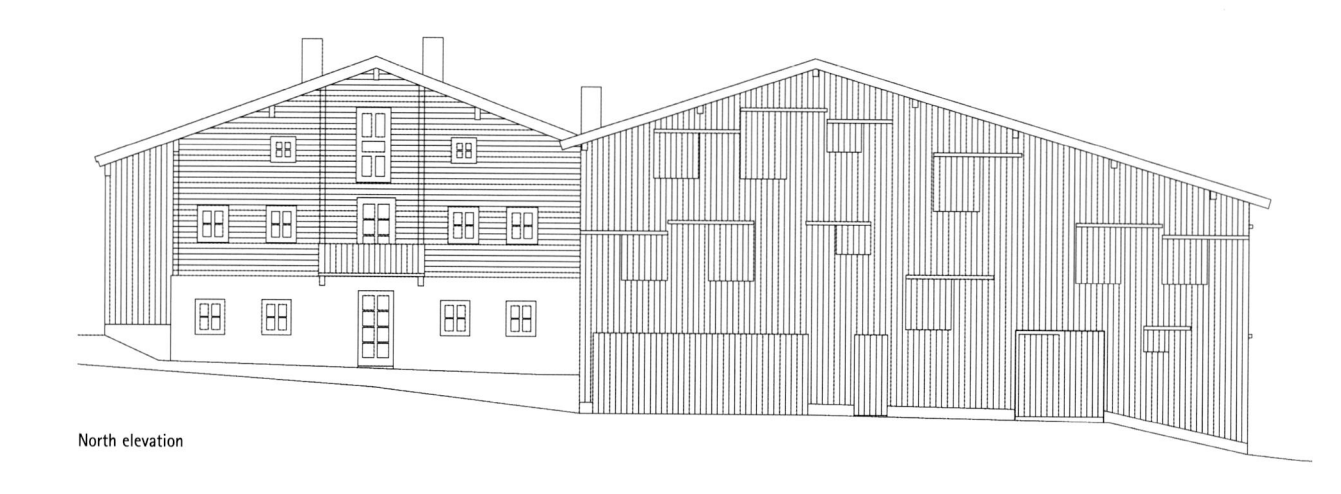

South elevation

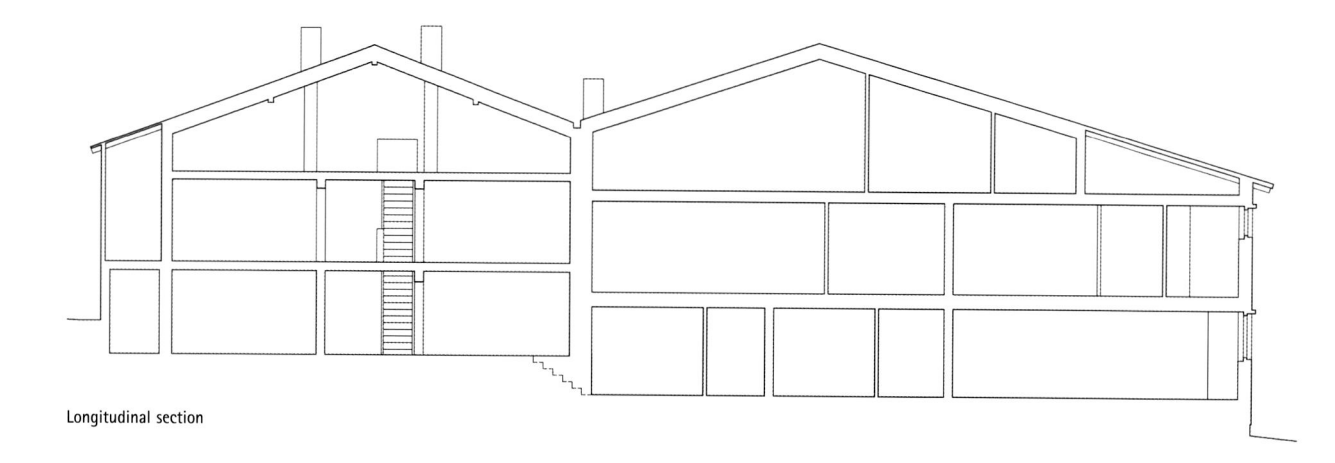

Longitudinal section

14 Restoration of a Farm in Ramsau

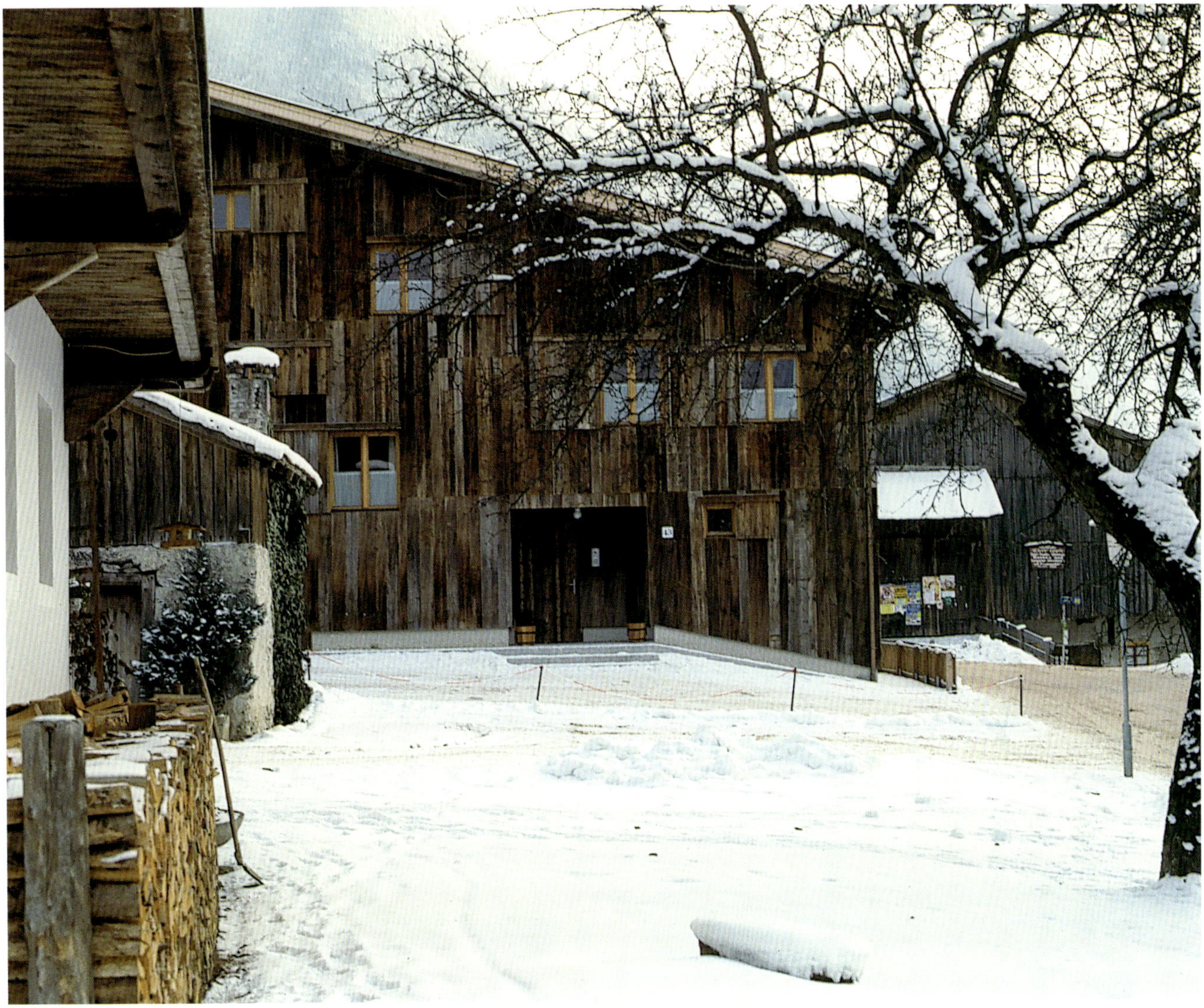

16 Restoration of a Farm in Ramsau

The interior preserves the austere character of the farm, but with an increased sense of comfort, thanks to the new insulation and the use of wood for the surfaces.

18 Restoration of a Farm in Ramsau

Restoration of a Farm in Ramsau 19

The restoration of this barn from the early 20th century, situated in the Val Tidone region on the northeast coast of Italy, has resulted in a major transformation, which unites technology with the area's traditional finishes.

Old Barn in Val Tidone

Architects: Park Associati
Photographer © Andrea Martiradonna
Location: Agazzano, Italy
Completion date: 2005

This project consisted of transforming a construction used for agricultural purposes into a private home with clearly contemporary influences. The aim was to establish highly simple lines and formulas to effectively respond to the demands of a space fit for a large family. The vertical and horizontal planes of the new house act as its main connecting axis, and offer the rooms continuity. The different stairways act as elements that join, articulate and organize the rooms. They have been carried out with a variety of different materials, such as untreated wood, stone or terracotta.

Emphasis has been given to the use and recovery of traditional materials in combination with more technologically accurate choices, in particularly regarding insulation techniques, and the integration of natural ventilation systems. The heating system restores a complex heating network of heaters and fireplaces. These interventions have provided simple and effective solutions to the different parts of a home adapted to all seasons of the year. A shed for storing wood in winter is the only new construction separated from the main house. Also conceived as a shelter, this is entirely clad in wood and has a corten steel roof.

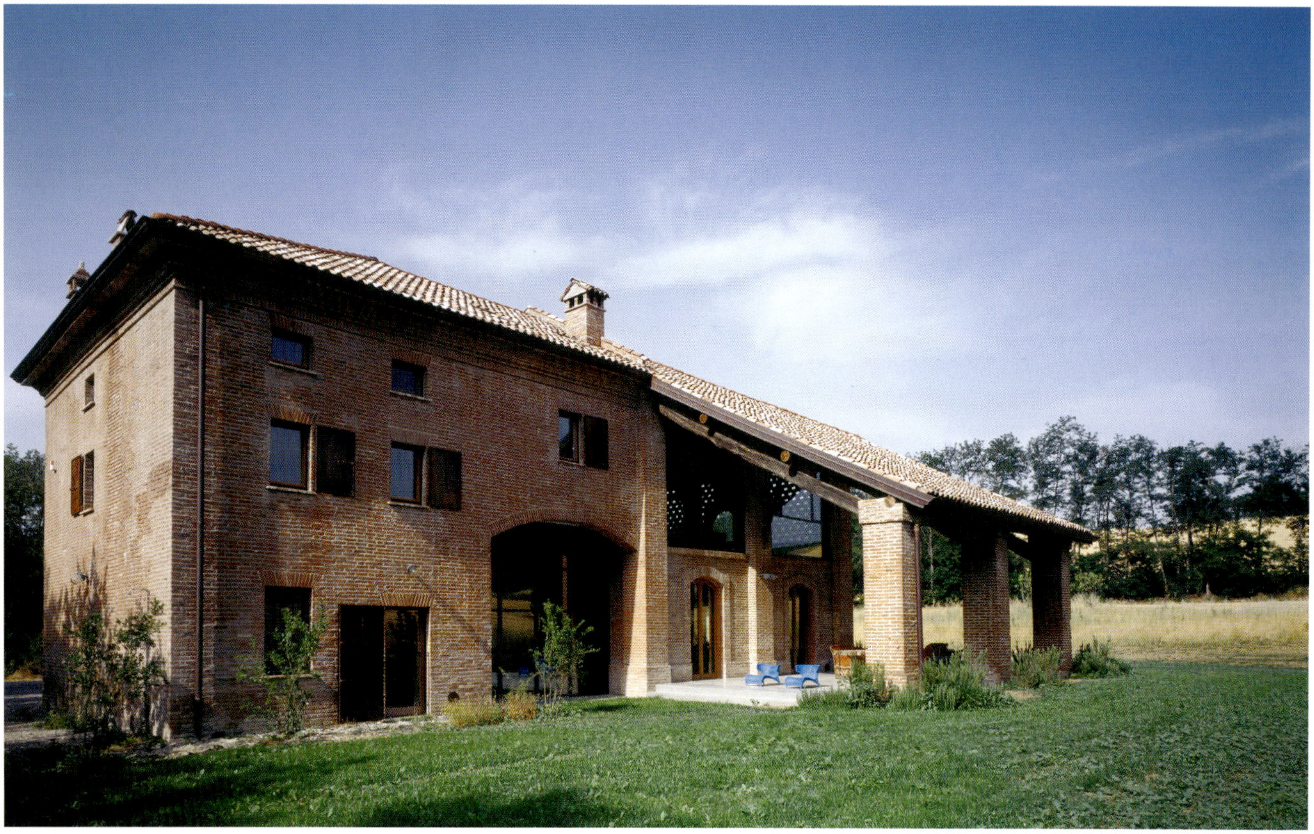

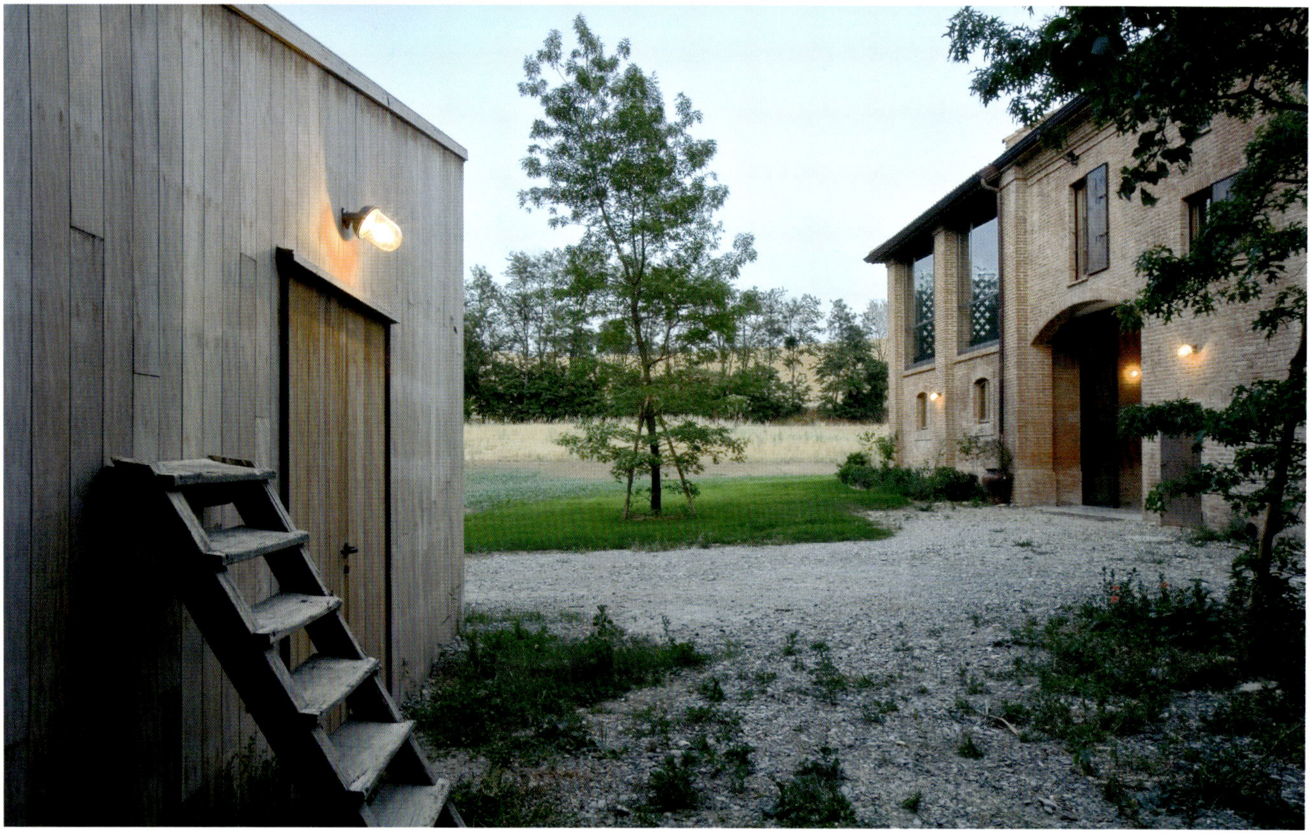

Previous plan

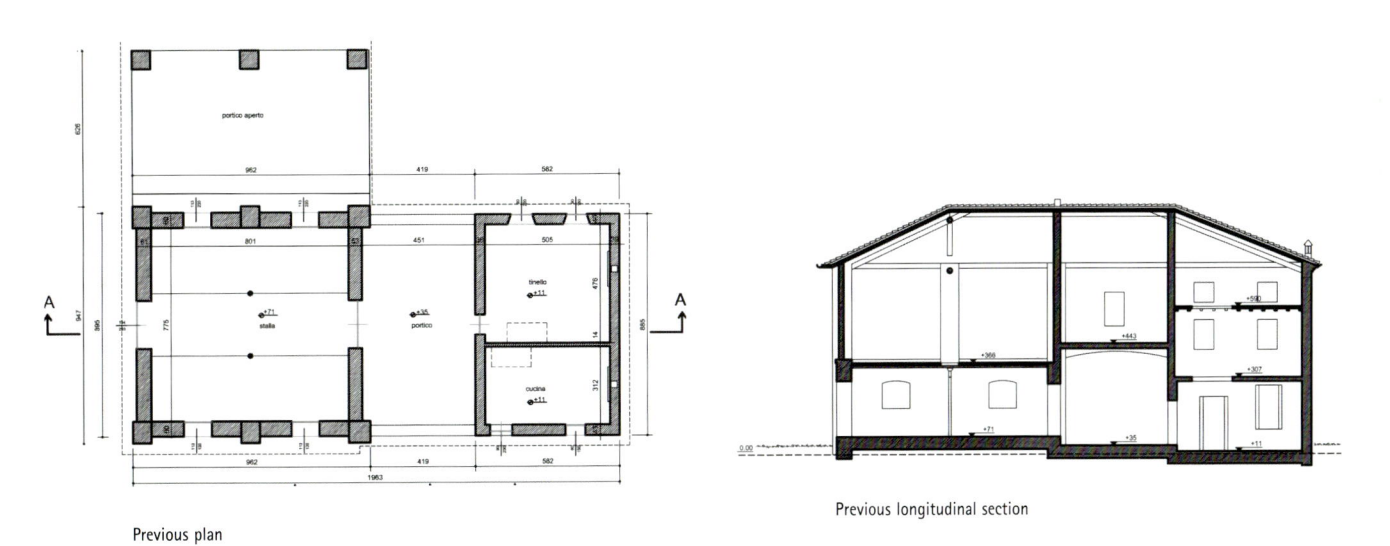

Previous longitudinal section

Old Barn in Val Tidone 23

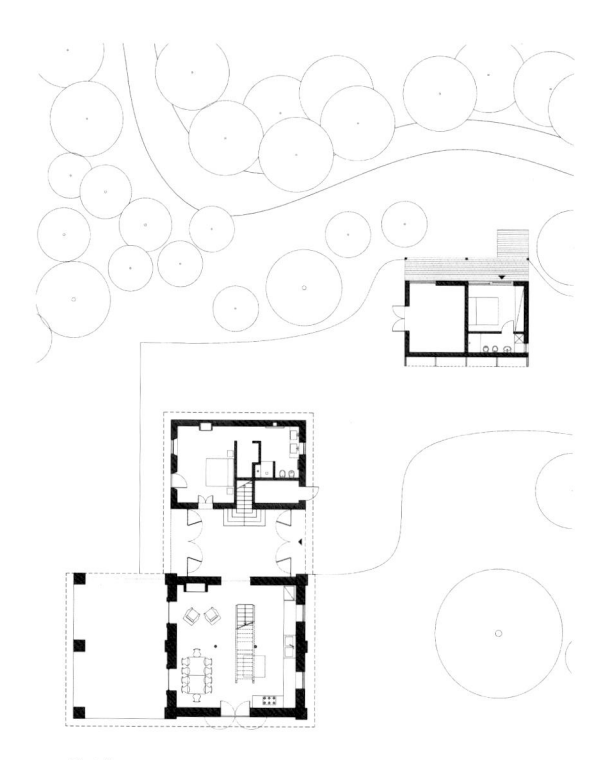

First floor

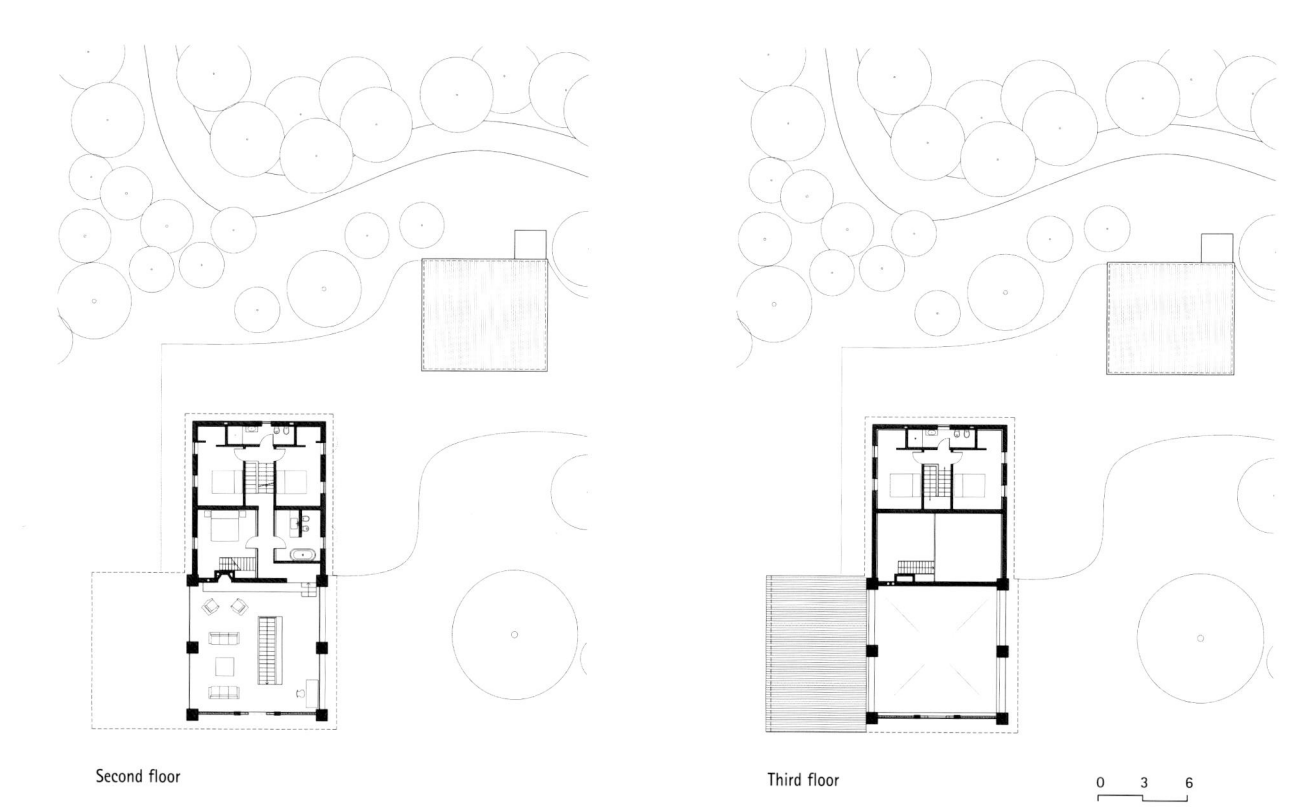

Second floor

Third floor

0 3 6

24 Old Barn in Val Tidone

Old Barn in Val Tidone 25

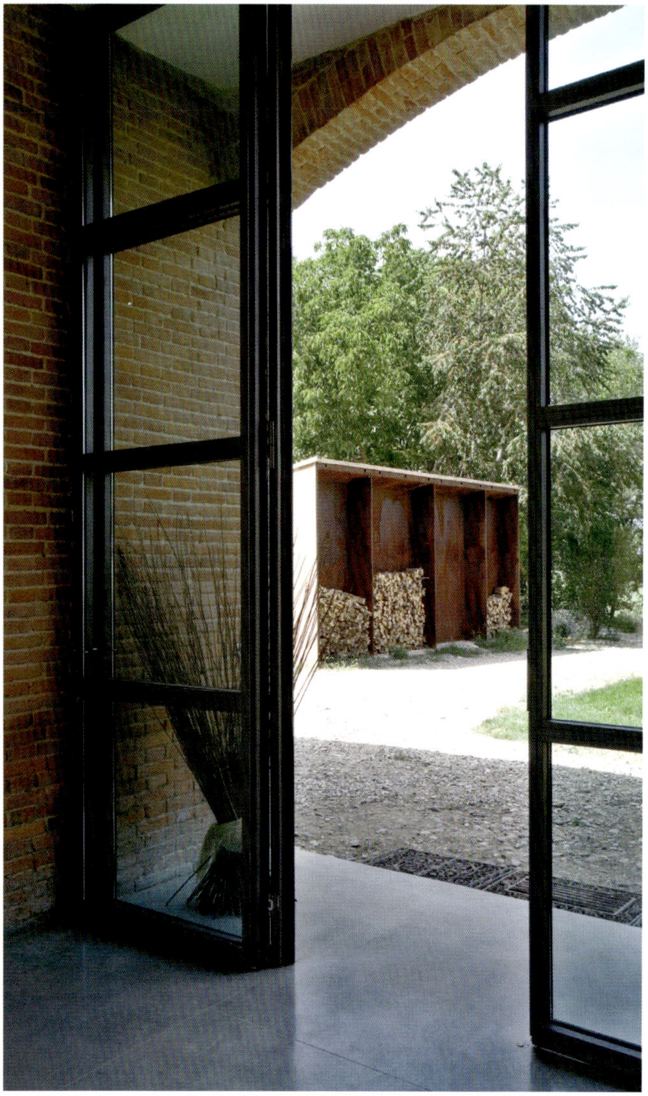

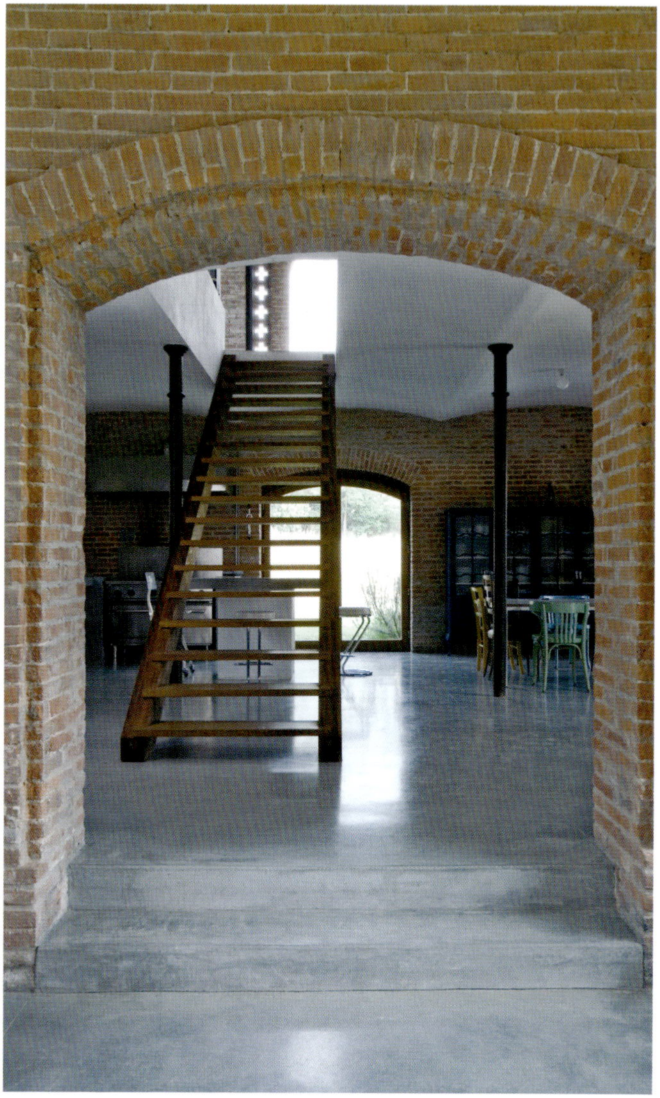

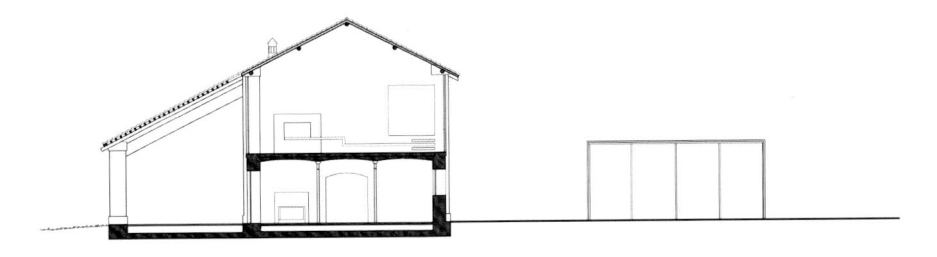

Transversal section

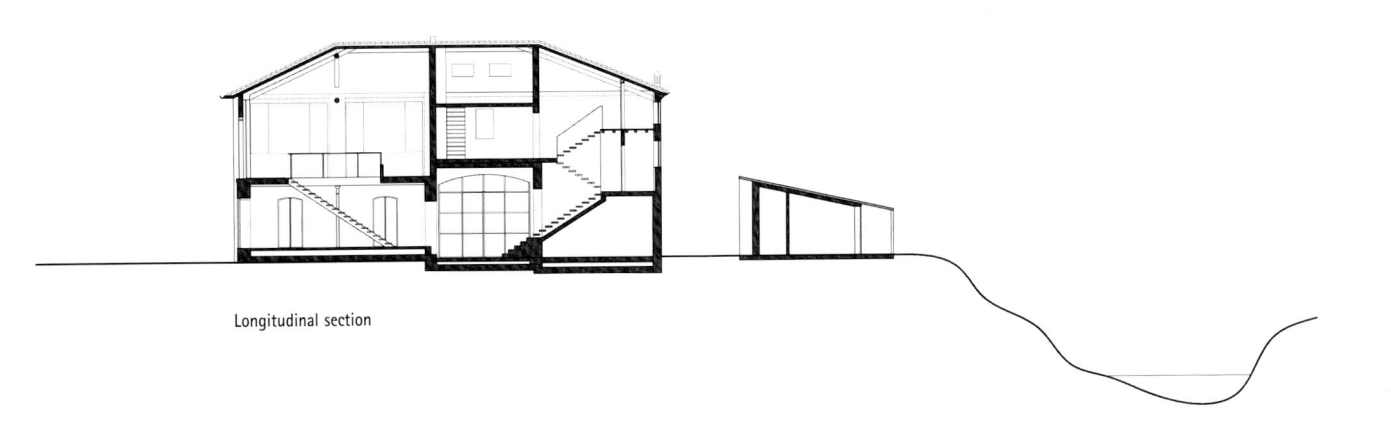

Longitudinal section

North elevation

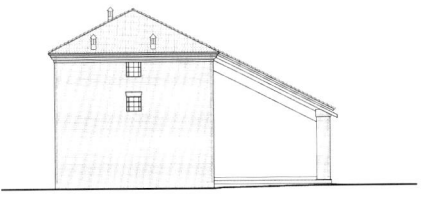

West elevation

South elevation

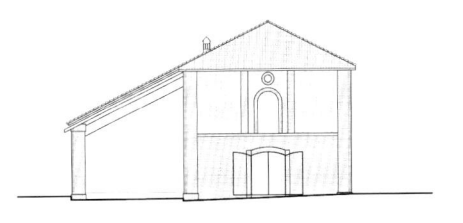

East elevation

Old Barn in Val Tidone 27

The original external structure of the house with its brickwork façade included an elevation, which, in the top part, presented small cross-shaped orifices. The restoration work highlighted the light quality that these orifices contributed to the interior of the house.

Old Barn in Val Tidone 29

30 Old Barn in Val Tidone

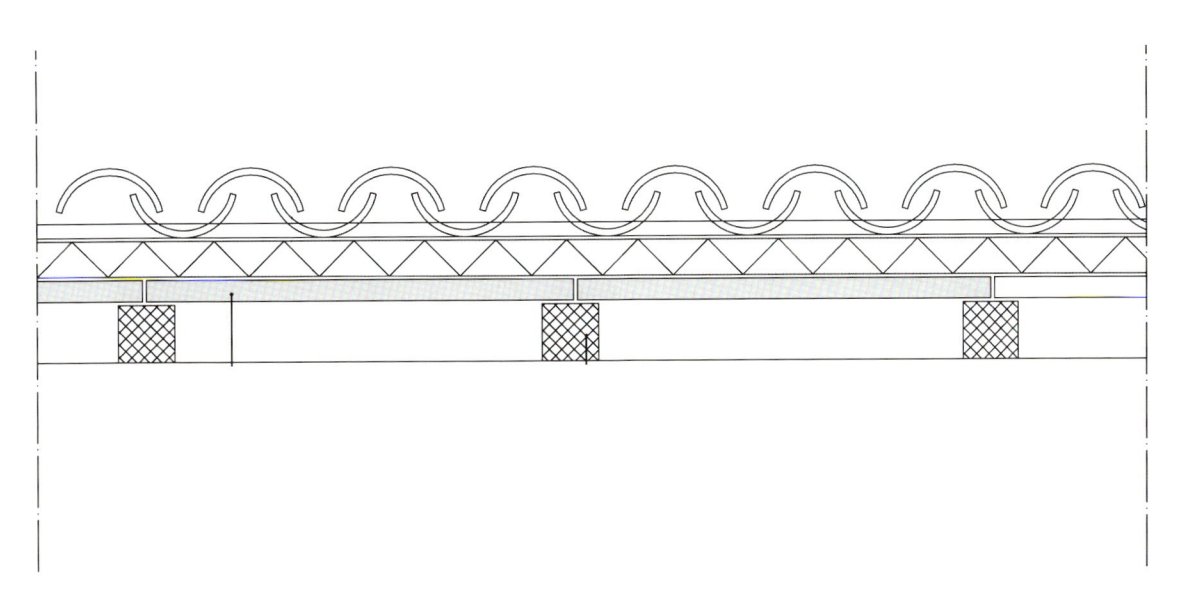

Constructive detail of the roof

Old Barn in Val Tidone 31

This historic agricultural construction composed of a house and a cellar with a barn rests in an enclave whose first traces of inhabitants date back to Roman times. It has now been restored and converted into a contemporary residence.

Barn in Mortagua

Architect: Joao Méndes Ribeiro
Photographer © Fernando Guerra
Location: Cortegaça, Portugal
Completion date: 2005

The project consisted in the transformation of the barn, belonging to the group of farm buildings, into a small single-family home. The program developed from its essential structure, with its clean volumetry and harmonious dimensions. The restoration evokes the spaces of this rural area's typical constructions. The interior spaced has been determined by the decision to maintain the slate façade in tact. The layout has been reduced to the most basic spaces: the kitchen, dining and living area on the ground floor and bedroom with bathroom on the upper floor. The nucleus of the house is the double height living room. In the upper section a sheet of wood serves as a desk and is joined to the stairs, whose strategic location creates the ideal layout and circulation of the spaces. The large window protected from the sun by treated wooden laminates opens the house to the garden and its surroundings. The pre-existing elements, which have been preserved, are differentiated from the new applications thanks to the colors and textures of the materials: wood and stone for the vertical finishes and tiles on the roof. White dominates inside accentuating these contrasts.
The straw loft and the main house are connected via a gallery that separates the farm from the street. The access to the straw loft has been modified and is now through the connecting section between the two blocks.

34 Barn in Mortagua

The restorative program revolves around the elemental structure of the straw loft, whose pure and simple volumes evoke traditional rural constructions.

First floor

0　1　2

Front transversal section

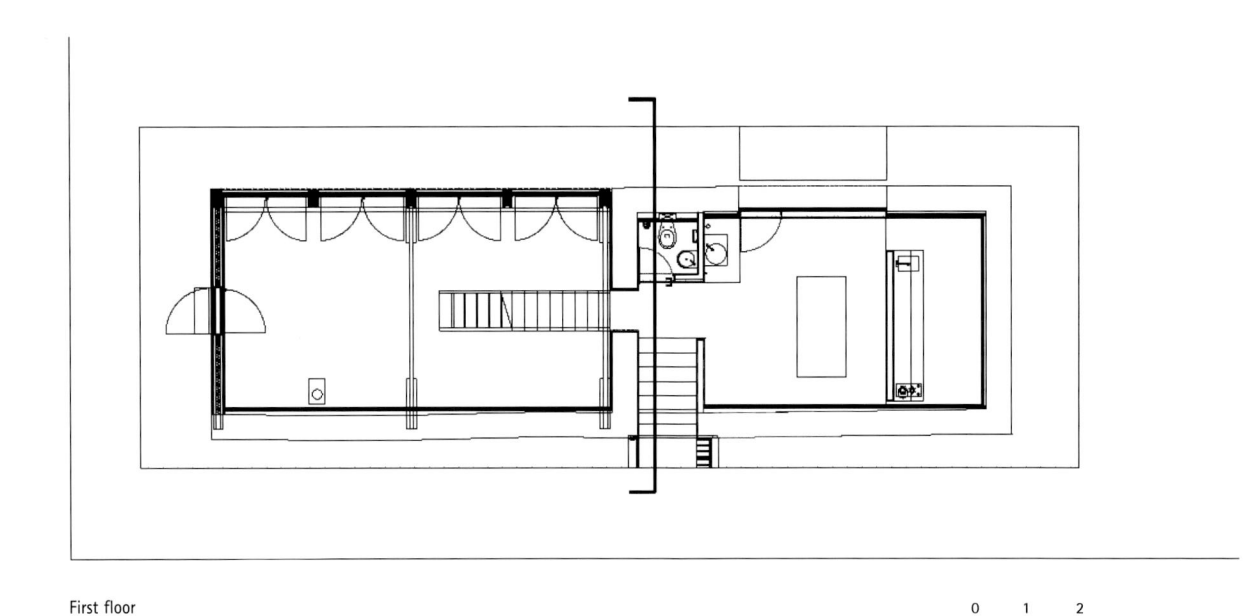

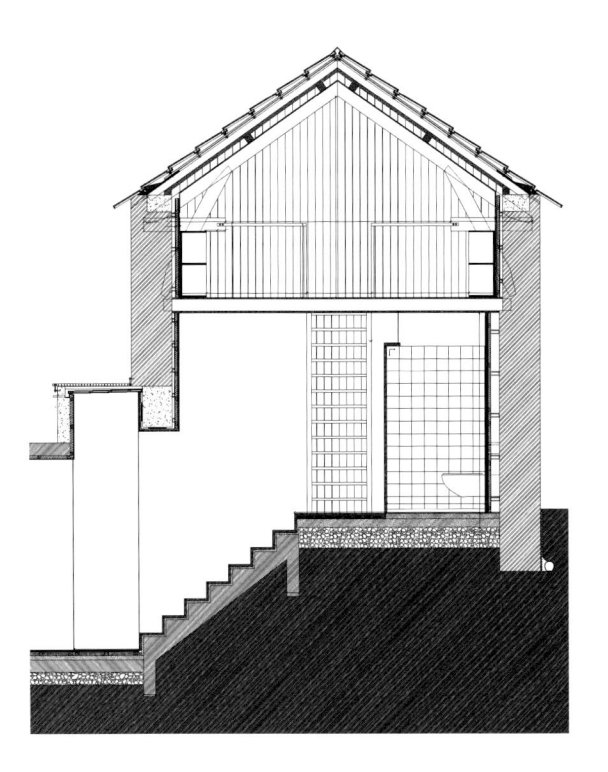

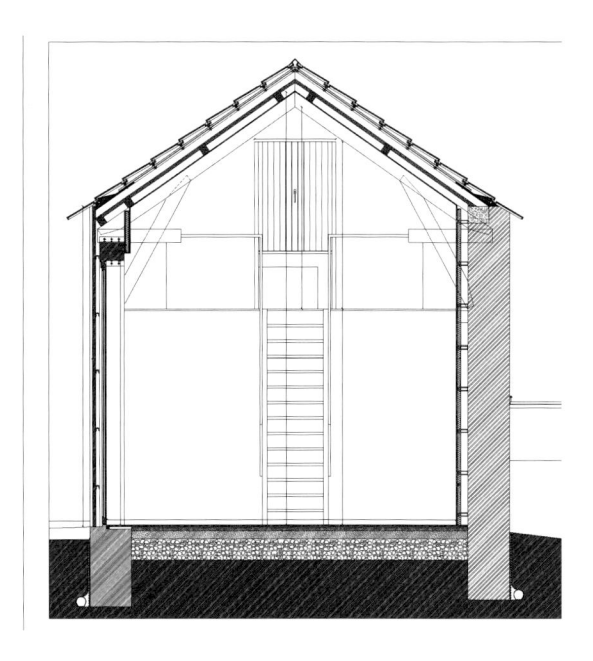

Rear transversal section

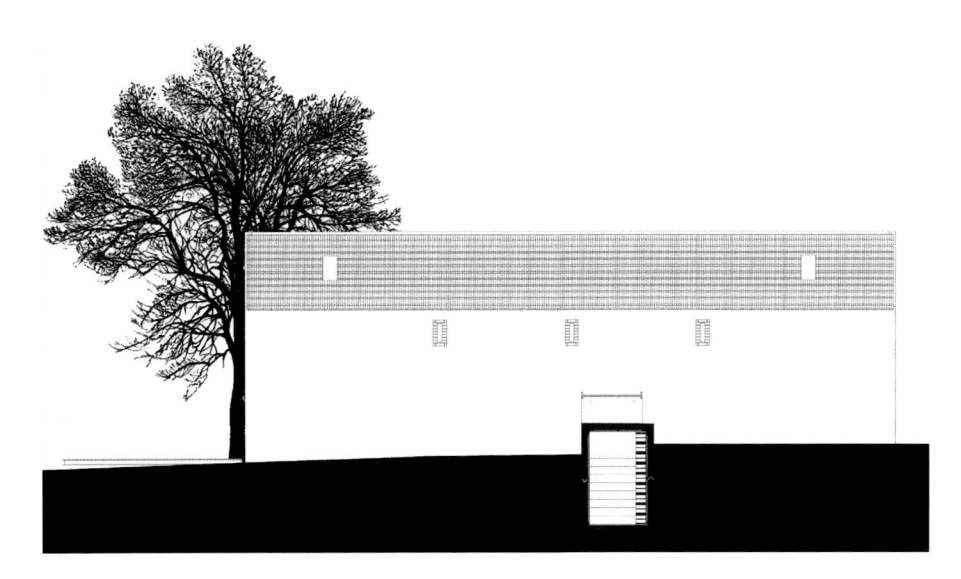

North-south elevation

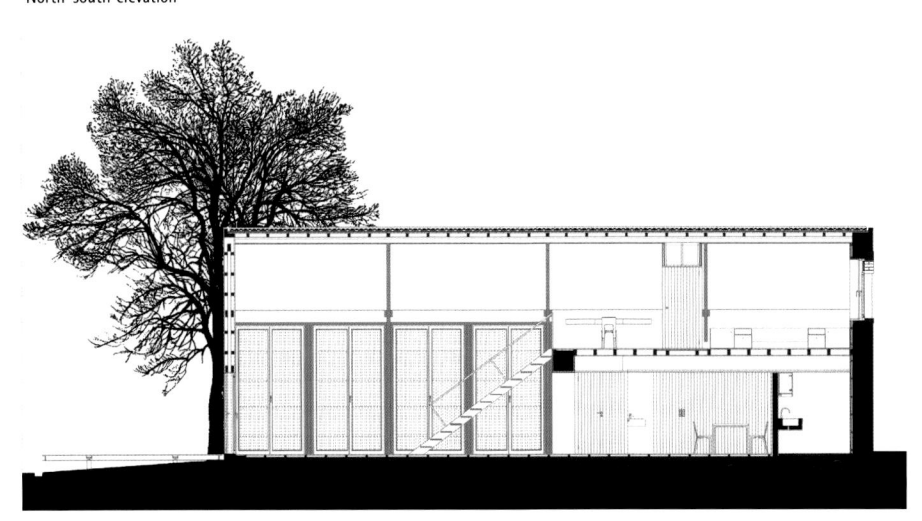

Right side longitudinal section

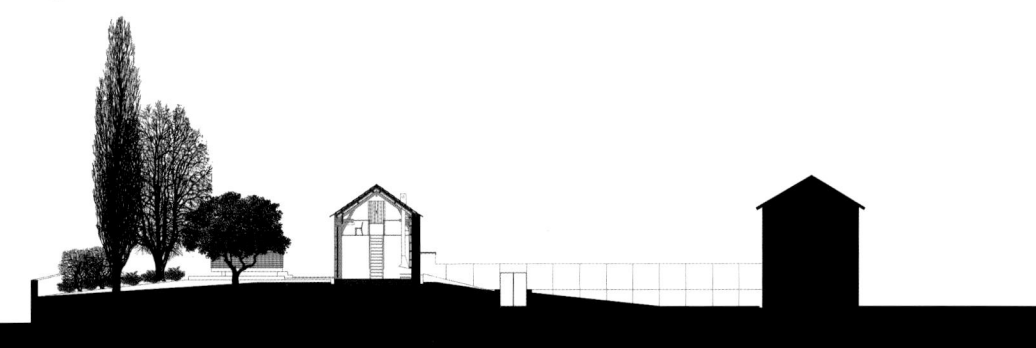

Transversal section

Barn in Mortagua 37

38 Barn in Mortagua

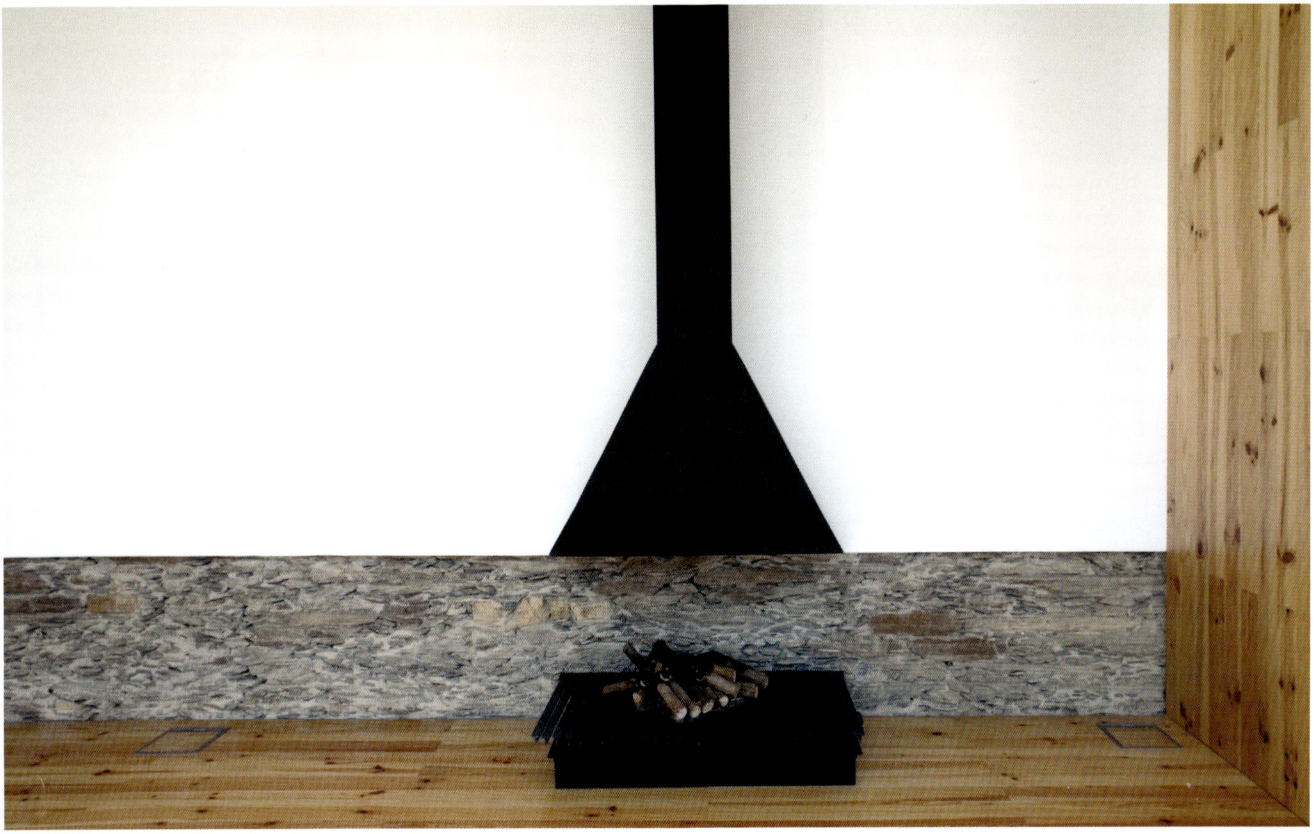

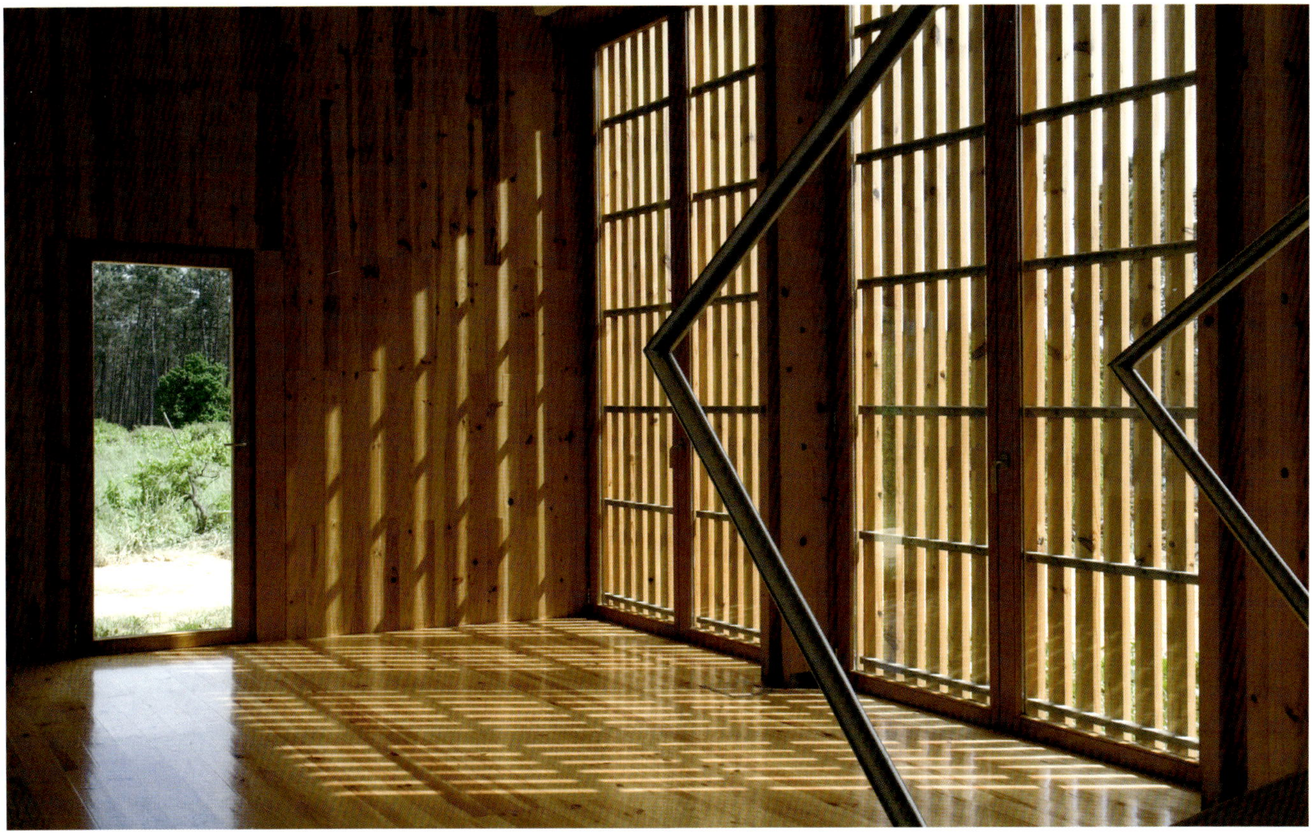

40 Barn in Mortagua

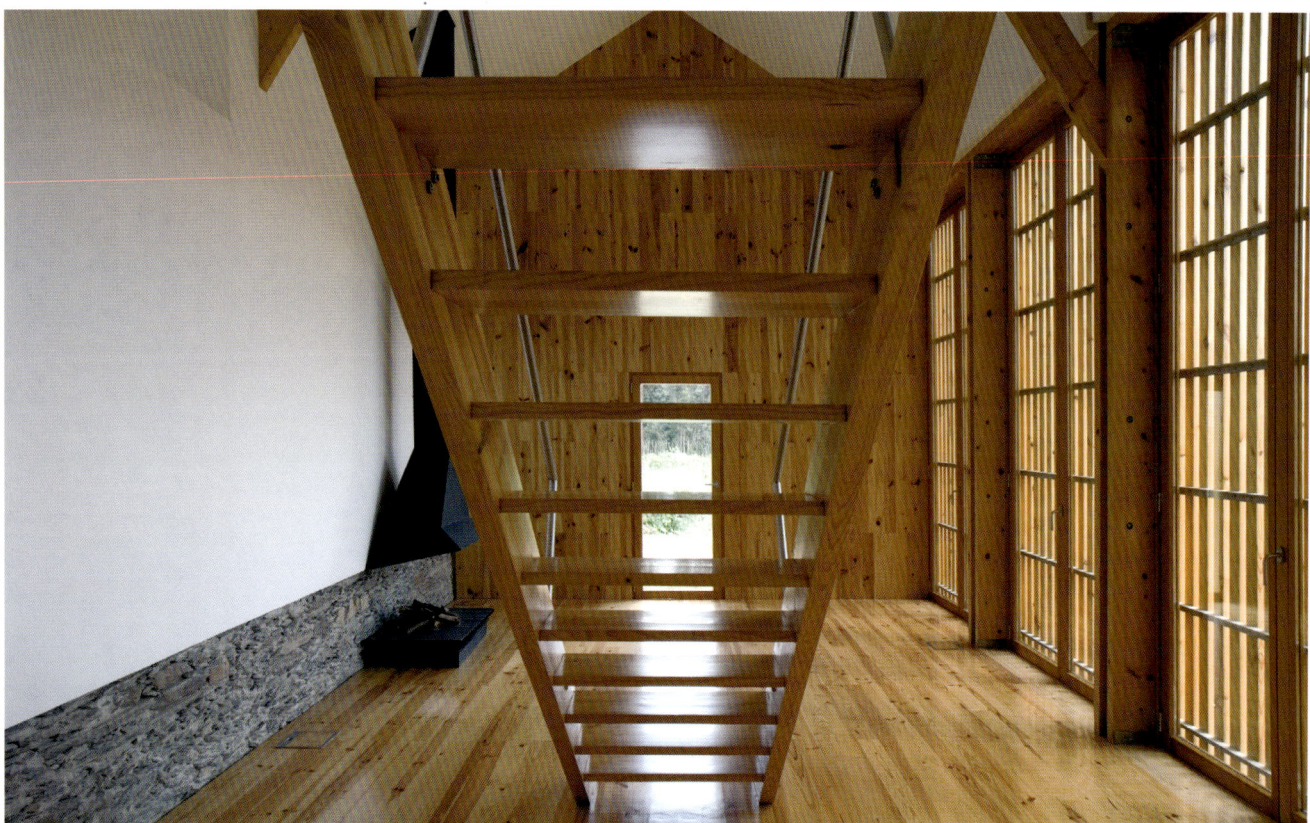

Axonometry

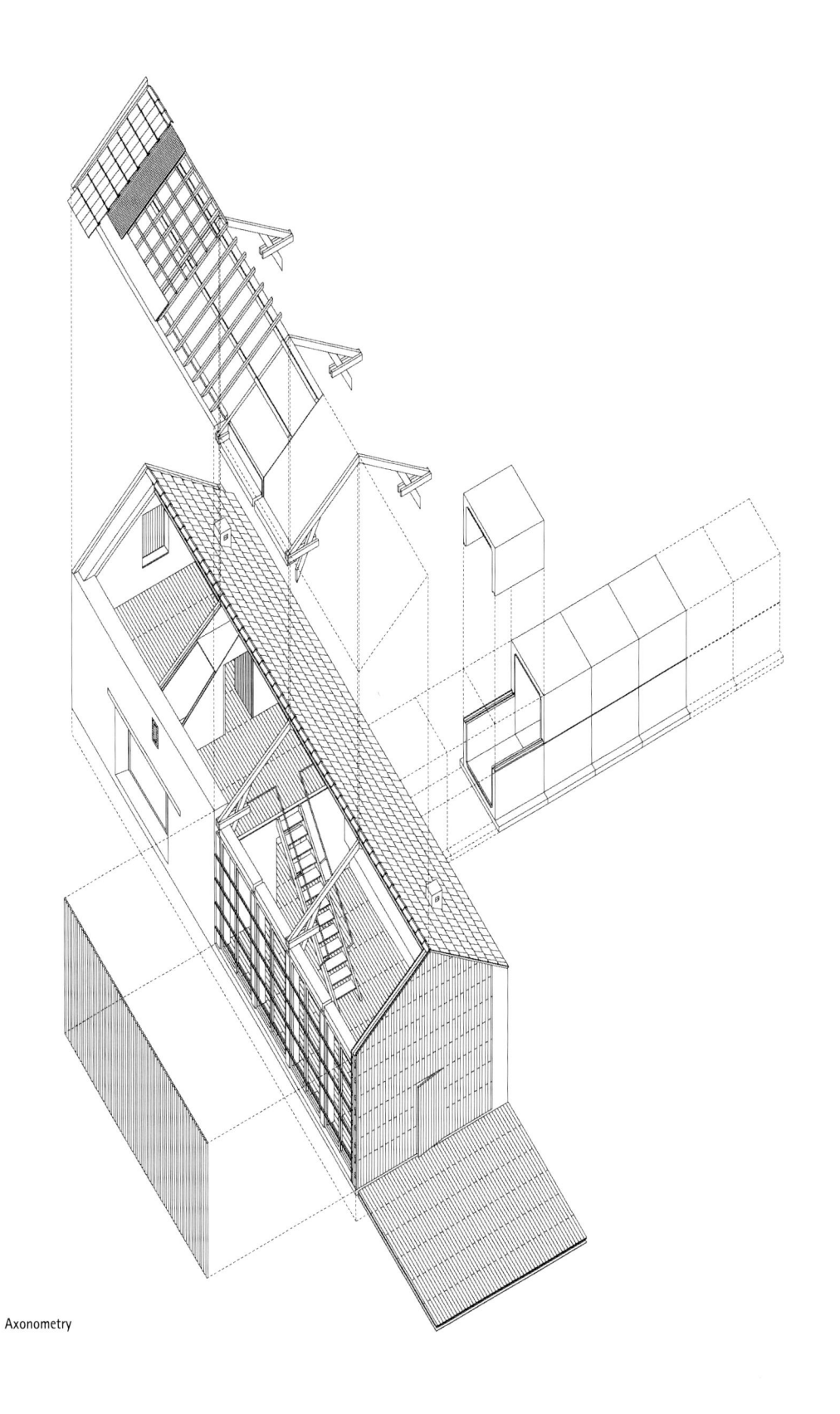

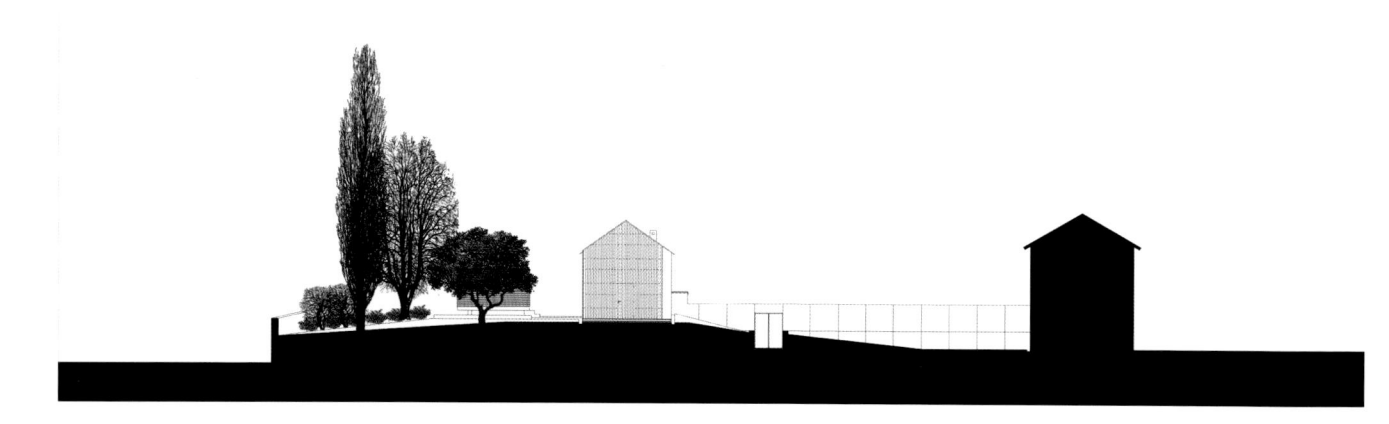

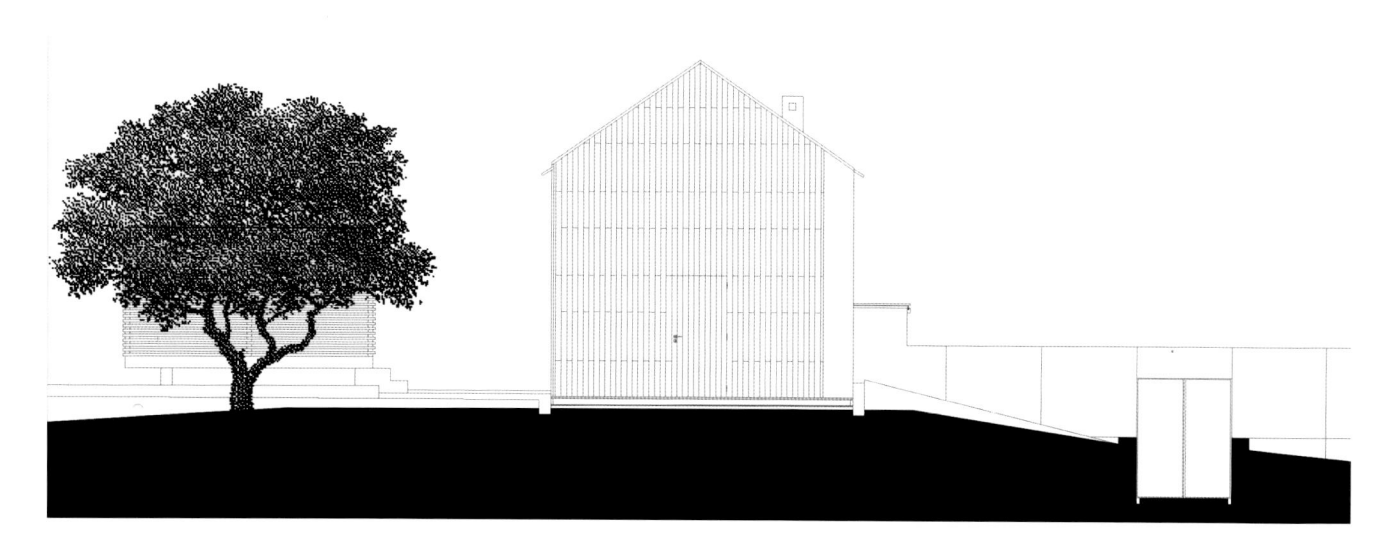

Elevations

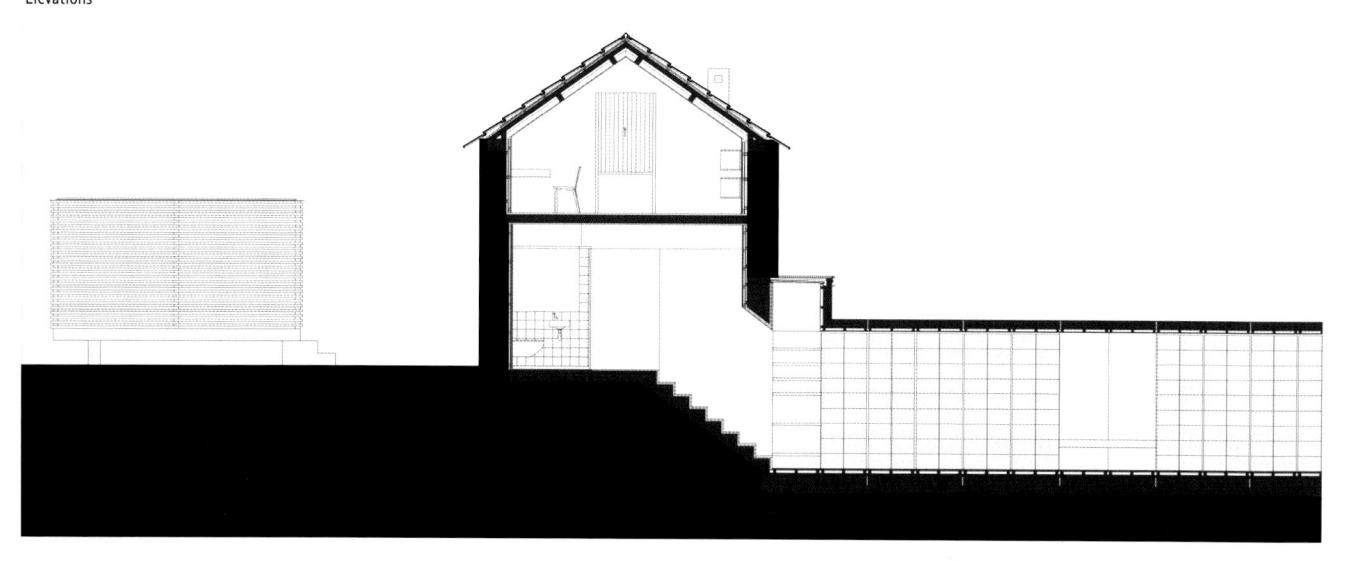

Transversal section

42 Barn in Mortagua

Barn in Mortagua 43

This single-family house, situated in a village in the pre-Pyrenees, is the last construction of a small group of single-family houses. The owners acquired the house when the structure was still in the construction process and decided to renovate it.

House in Vilada

Architects: Agustí Costa Arquitectes
Photographer © David Cardelús
Location: Vilada, Spain
Completion date: 2006

The intervention was mostly carried out in the interior and the garden, given that the characteristics of the neighborhood had to be maintained. Despite this, certain parts of the external structure were modified, such as the windows for example, which were enlarged to allow more light to enter. A true advantage in an area where temperatures in winter can be very low. The treatment of materials, however, was carried out according the regulations.

The project mainly consisted in removing the partition walls and vertical divisions, creating an open structure throughout the house. The intention was to connect the interior with the exterior by using similar materials on both, such as concrete or the polished cement surfaces in the bathroom.

The house includes a ground floor, a semi-basement and an attic. The main lounge, as well as a bathroom and a library, are located on this top floor, where the best views can be appreciated. The semi-basement consists of the garage and a study that stretches to the outside through an airy pavilion that reaches the garden. The pavilion acts as a lath house, since it filters the sun's rays that enter the study. Being connected with the garden, the study has been designed as a fresh place for summer use. The normal program for the house develops on the ground floor. The garden, which, depending on the area, acquires the necessary finish for its use, is divided by a natural change in level. Trees and bushes have been added to the native vegetation, such as a box, hawthorn or juniper bush, which integrate the garden with the house's wild surroundings.

Garden plan

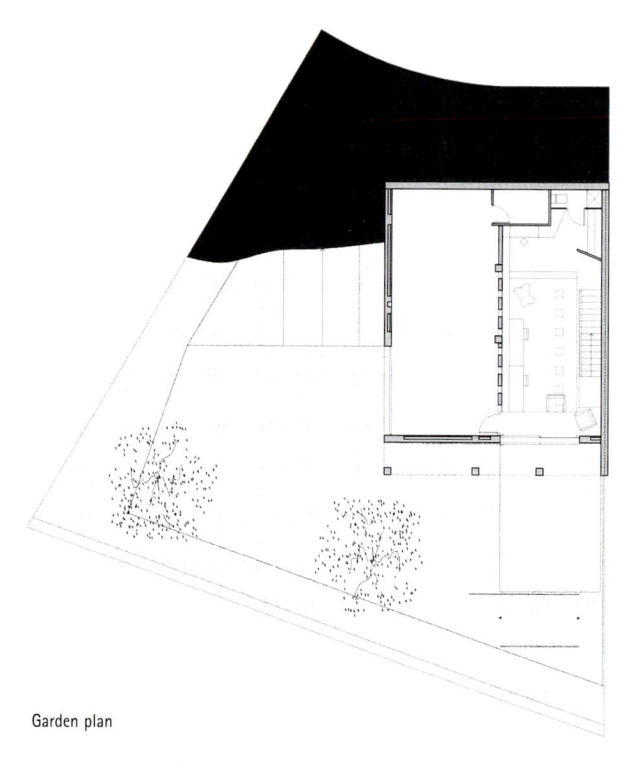

First floor   0 2 4

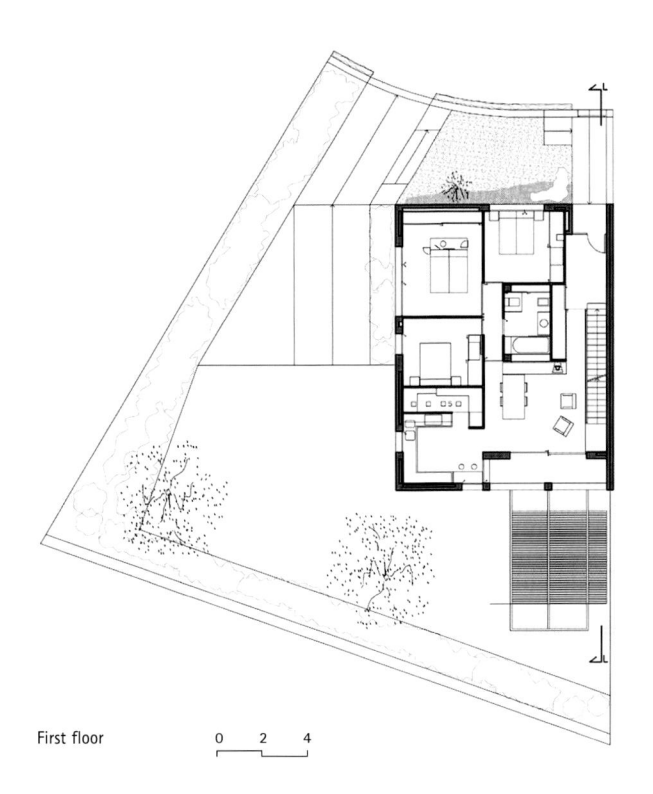

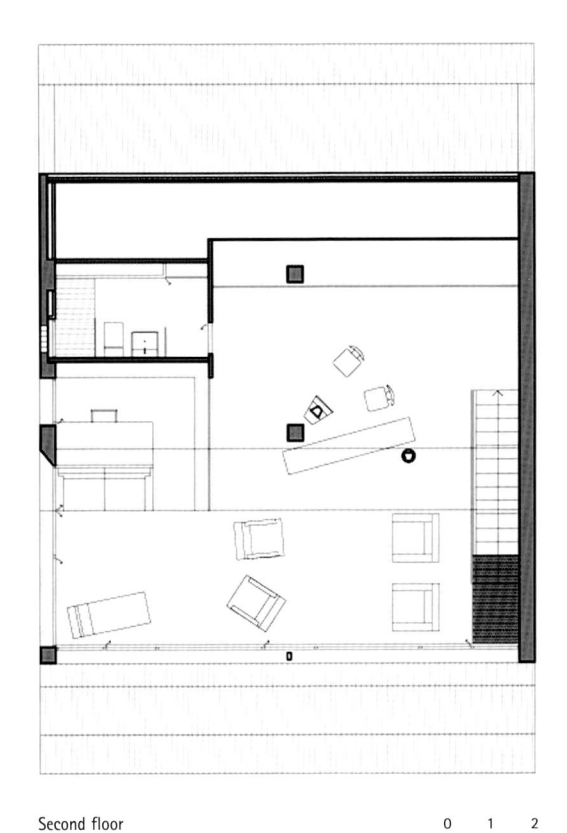

Second floor   0 1 2

House in Vilada   47

48 House in Vilada

The photos on the opposite page show the façade's transformation, which has been opened in several places. The land's natural unevenness has been integrated into the house to gain space.

50 House in Vilada

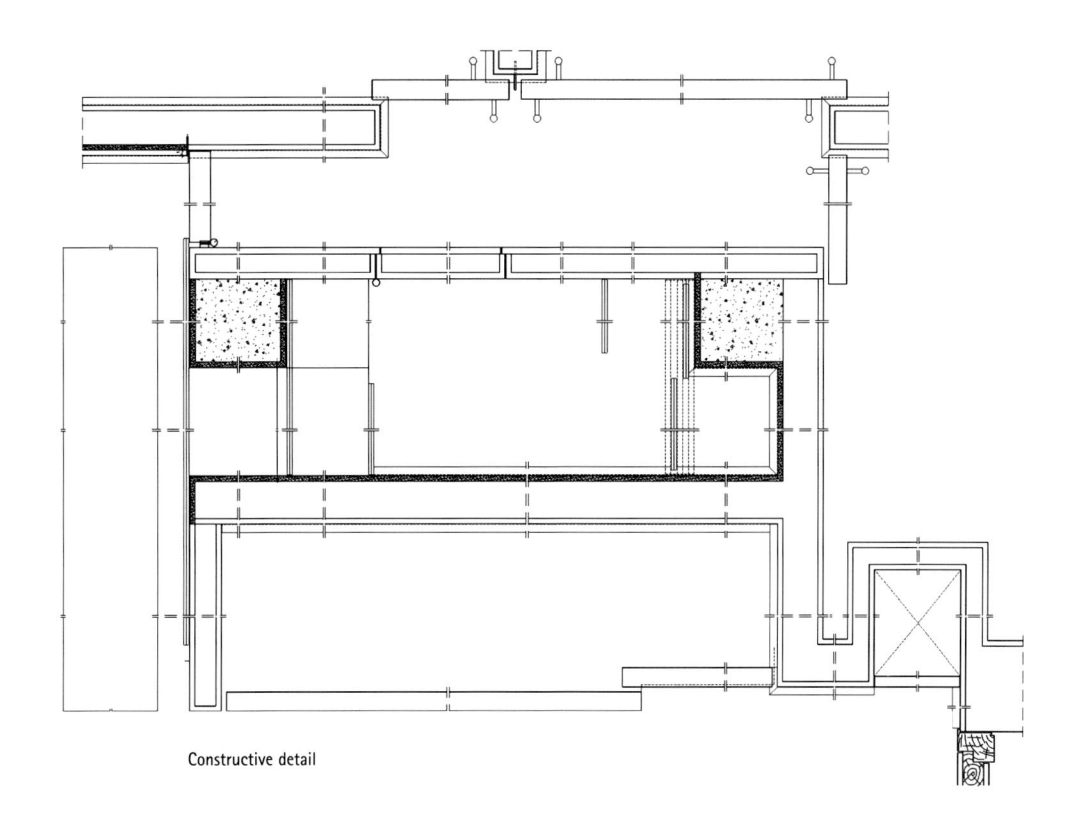

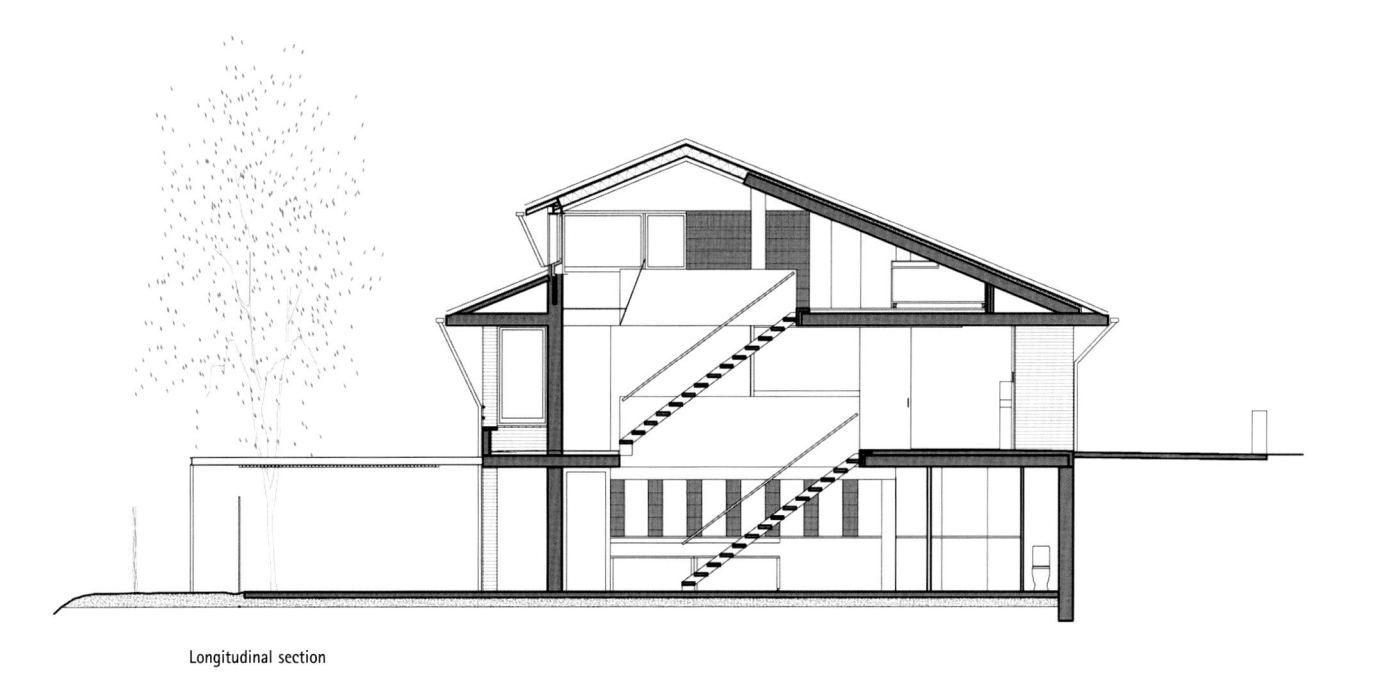

Constructive detail

Longitudinal section

52 House in Vilada

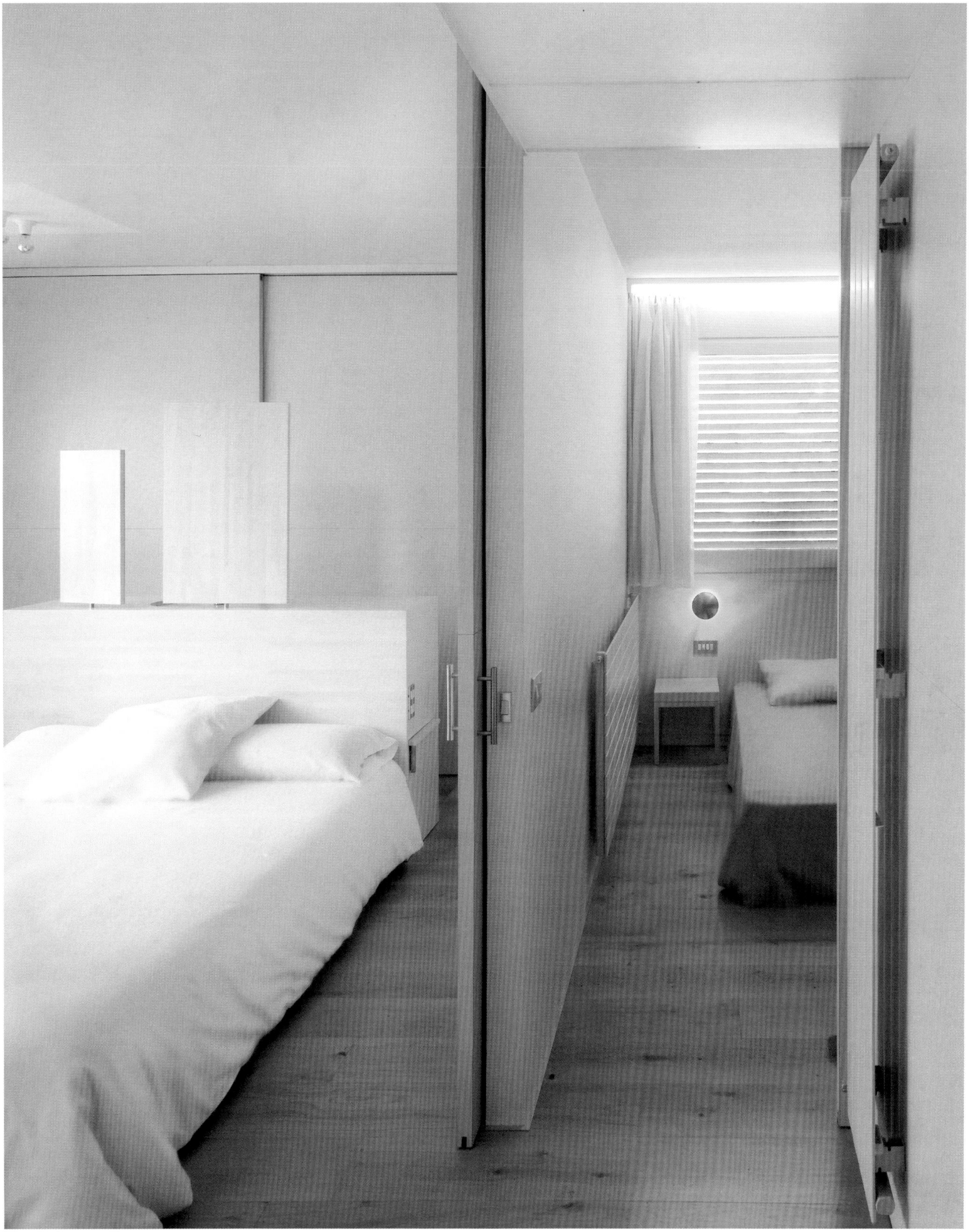

This small and exquisite tower, built at the end of the 19th century, is located on the historical site of a small village at the foot of the Piamonte hills, which descend down to Lake Maggiore.

Tower in Piamonte

Architects: Luca Rolla, Piero Camoletto
Photographer © Andrea Martiradonna
Location: Bee, Italy
Completion date: 2006

The building includes three bedrooms on three different levels, which constitute a total of 550 ft². The construction was in an extreme state of deterioration and the building had to be completely restructured. The roof was pulled down and another was built using techniques from the region. The plaster was removed exposing the original stone, which was subjected to a drying process and sealed to protect it from damp rising from the floor. The wooden beams were replaced by steel to lighten the structure and the floors alternated the application of wood with that of metal grating, thereby achieving a transparent flooring and a feeling of continuity. Space was also gained by covering the stairwell on the top floor and installing sleeping areas there thanks to the metal grating. The attic was removed and, having been totally renovated, it is now possible to appreciate the new structure from the ground floor. The opening of a skylight allows sunlight to reach the lower level, where the lounge is located. Thanks to the translucent glass panels, the light liberally bathes the entire space. The metal stairway is a fine corten steel laminate folded and toughened using struts, whose texture accompanies the strength of the bare stone. Problems from damp are solved thanks to the use of thick stone for the ground floor, while on the upper stories the flooring is covered by whitewashed birch laminates.

Previous plans

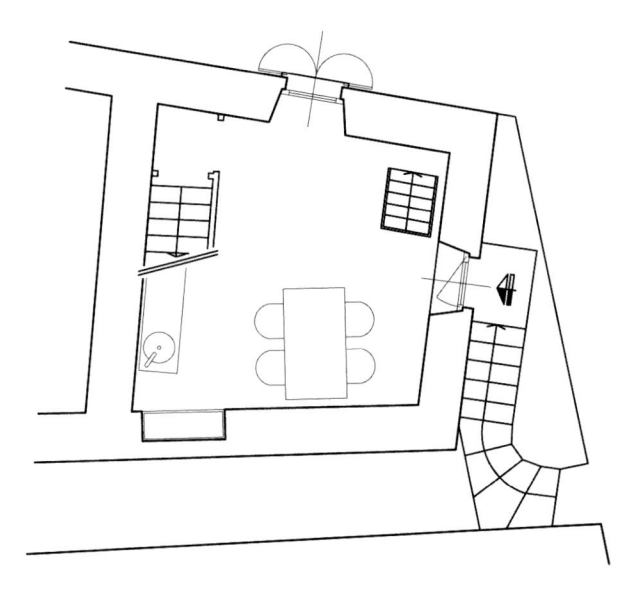

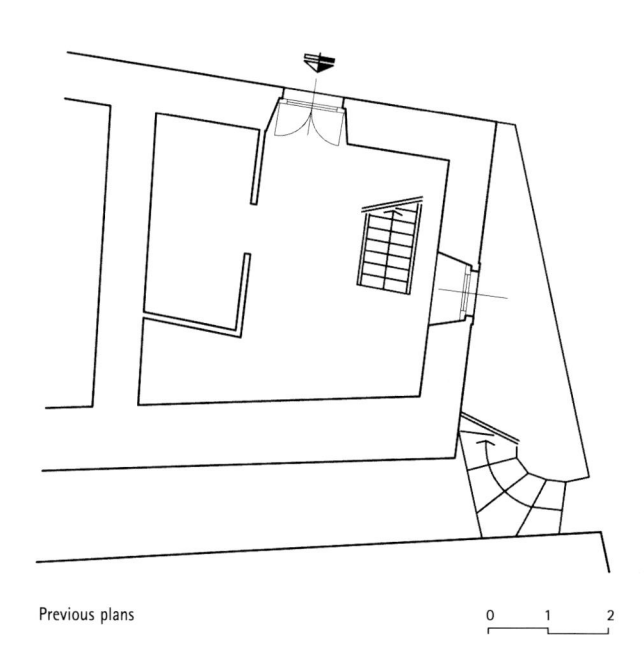

56 Tower in Piamonte

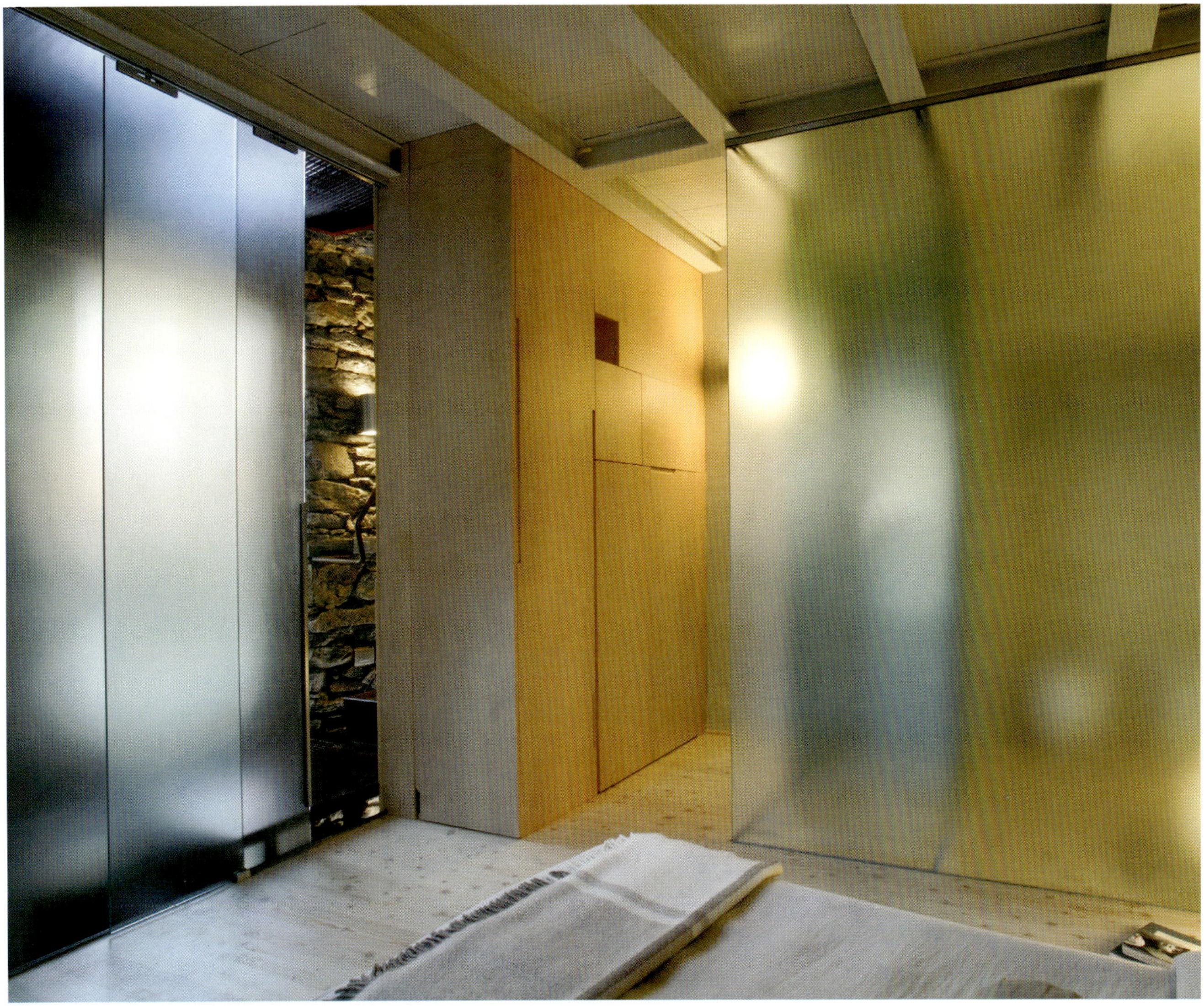

New plans

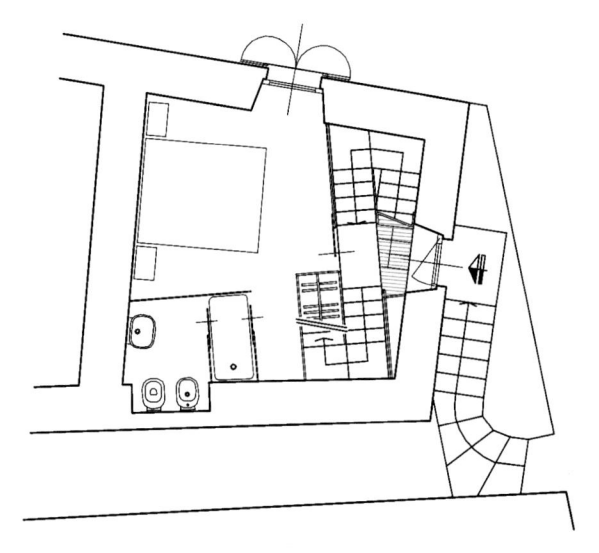

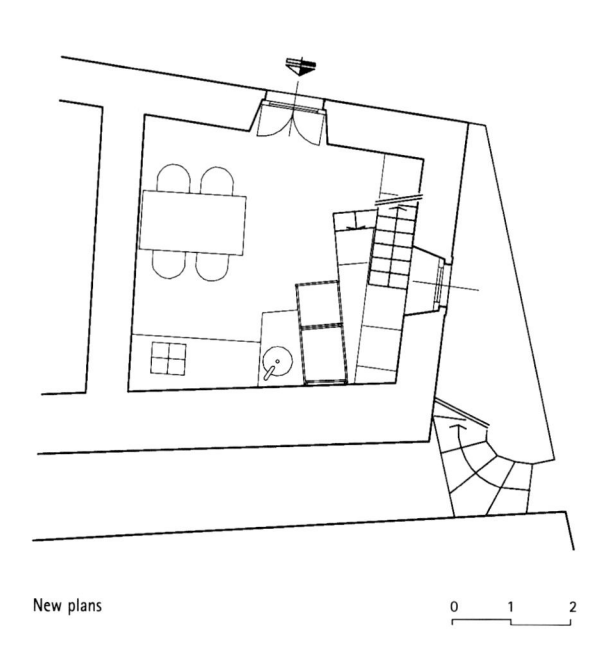

0 1 2

The restorative concept for this vertical house highlights the roof structure as a formal element and increases the fluidity between the spaces thanks, for example, to the use of metal grating.

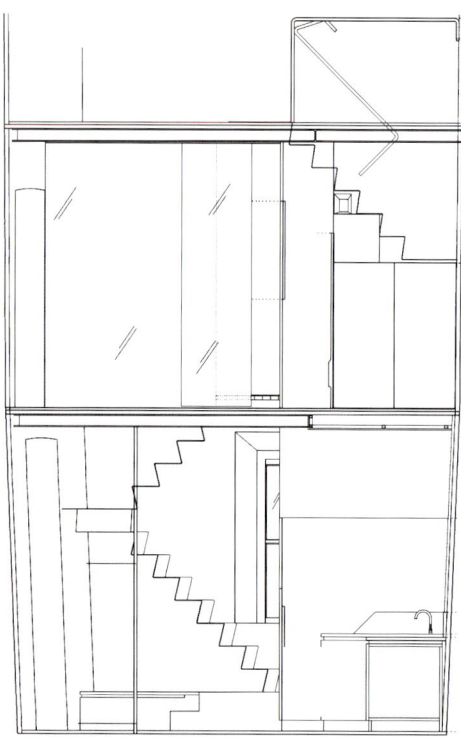

Transversal section

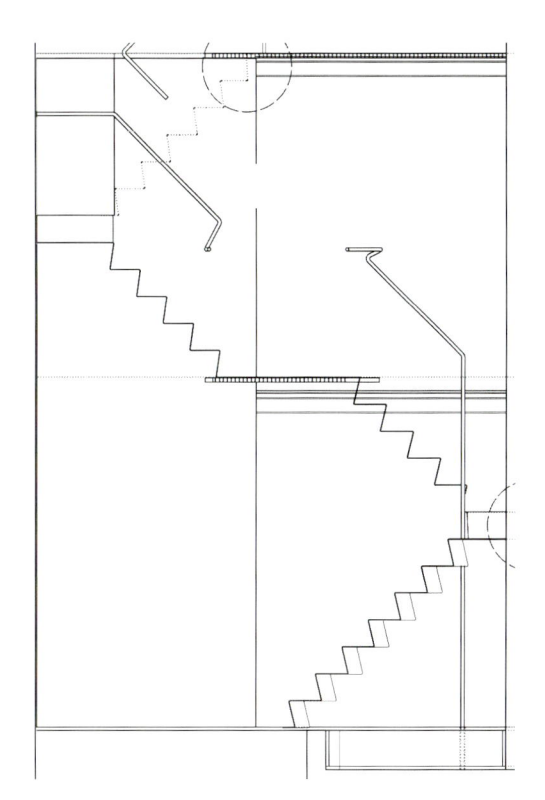

Detail of the stairs

Tower in Piamonte 61

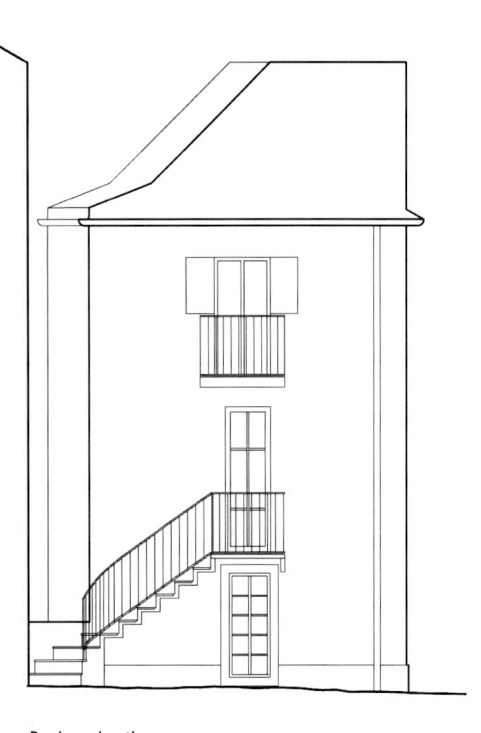

Previous elevations

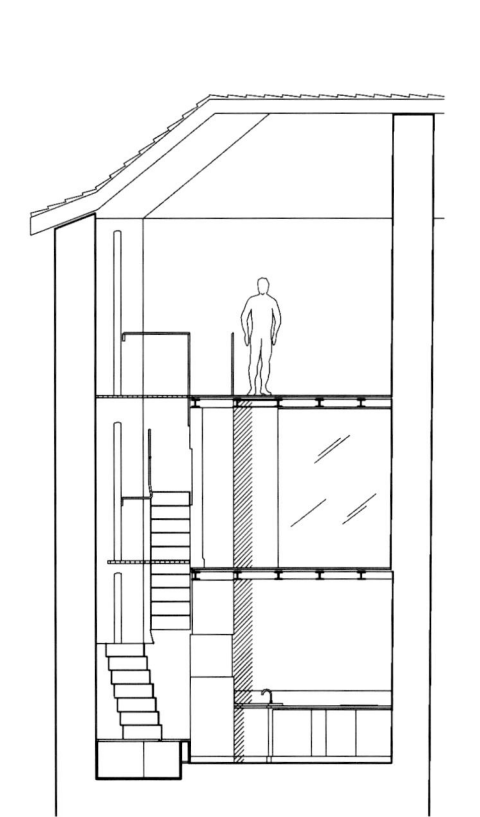

Front section

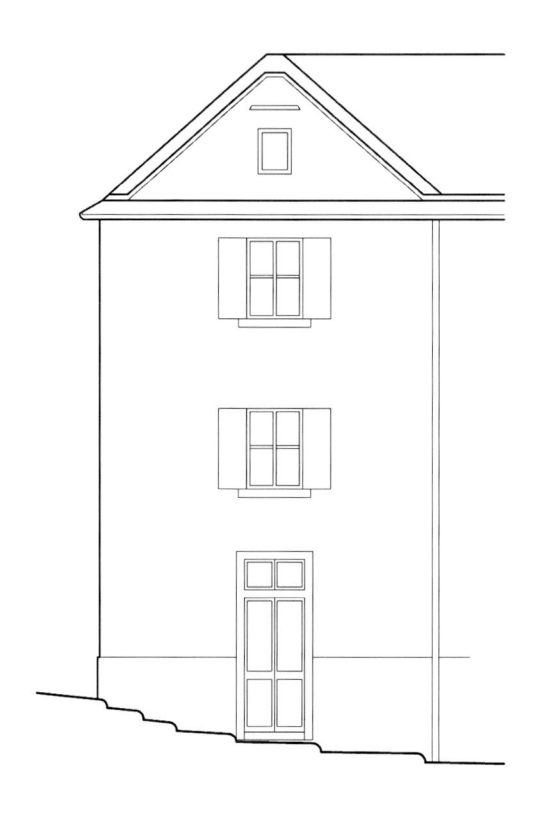

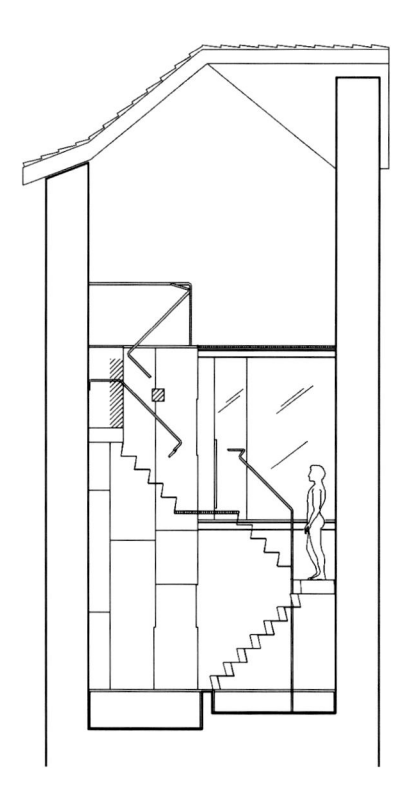

Left side section

62 Tower in Piamonte

Tower in Piamonte 63

This holiday home has been restored as a two-story home with various annexes. Despite its privileged position at the foot of a tree-covered hillside, surrounded by fields and next to a river, it had been left to ruin.

House in Brito-Guimarães

Architects: Topos Atelier de Arquitectura
Photographer © Xavier Antunes
Location: Brito-Guimarães, Portugal
Completion date: 2005

The stones from the ruins were used to reconstruct the central courtyard around which the spaces of the house are arranged. The volumes were set out to create two stories in the part of the house that accommodates the bedrooms. One of the façades was shut by way of a glazed wall that seems to be suspended in mid-air, and under which a stream runs from the nearby river. The house has been rebuilt on the land's natural slope. This unevenness has been balanced both inside and out, by way of small flights of stairs and stepped slabs. The inside of the house connects visually and through the materials used with the surroundings by using local stone to cover a large part of the floors of the communal areas like the bathrooms. The rest of the interiors, such as some of the partitions, have been clad in polished Ipe, which is very tough and resistant. The large glass surfaces bring the landscape into the home, while in the interior courtyard a garden has been designed which reflects, in miniature, the house's surroundings. The façades have been rebuilt respecting the original materials and techniques. The exterior walls, like the fireplace in the lounge use corten steel, which establishes a new connection between both areas. In the exterior garden, slabs of natural granite and washed concrete have been used to construct the flagstones and steps that balance out the level changes.

66 House in Brito-Guimarães

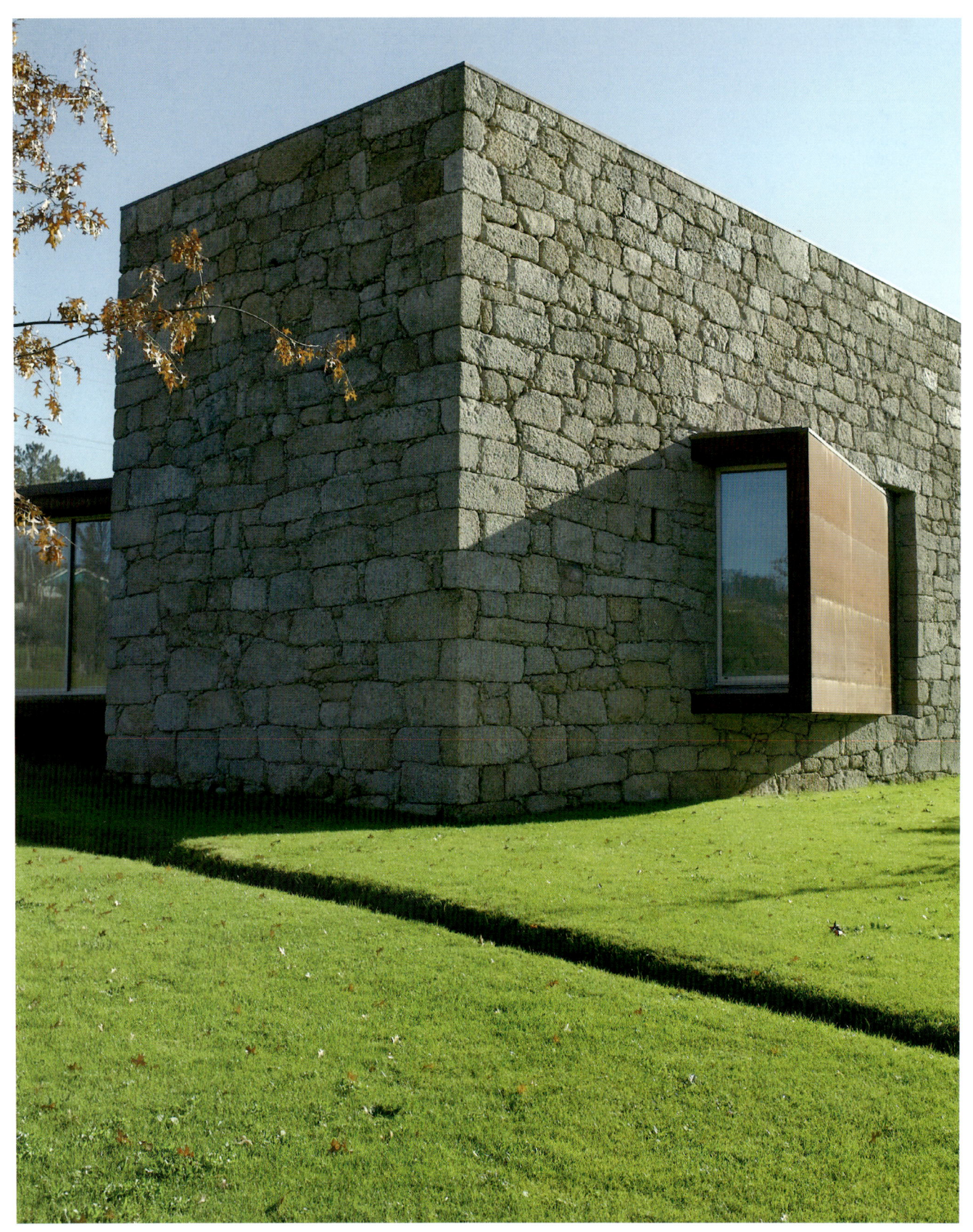

Despite the preservation of the original stone façades, the work of restoring and extending this holiday home has transformed a humble farmhouse into a sumptuous space, open to its surroundings.

68 House in Brito-Guimarães

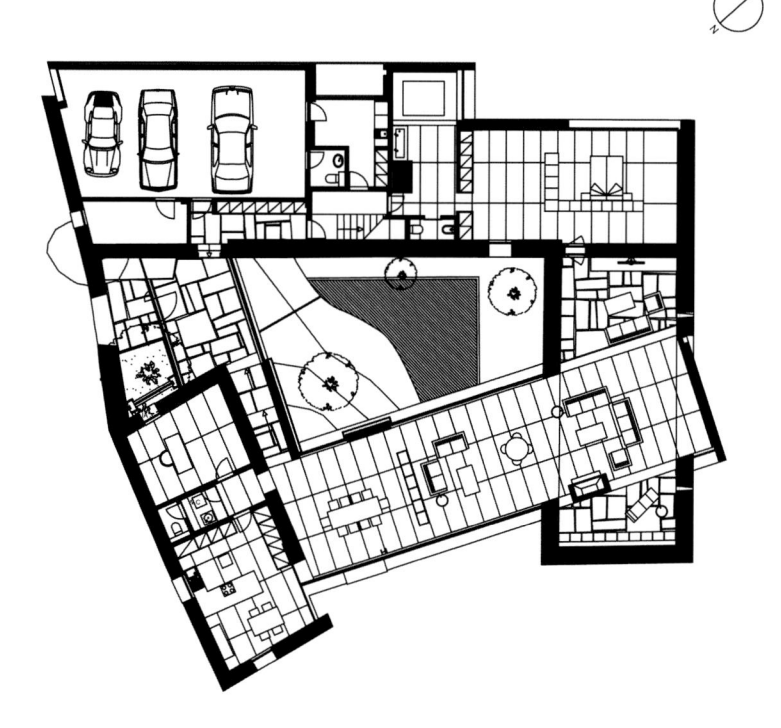

First floor

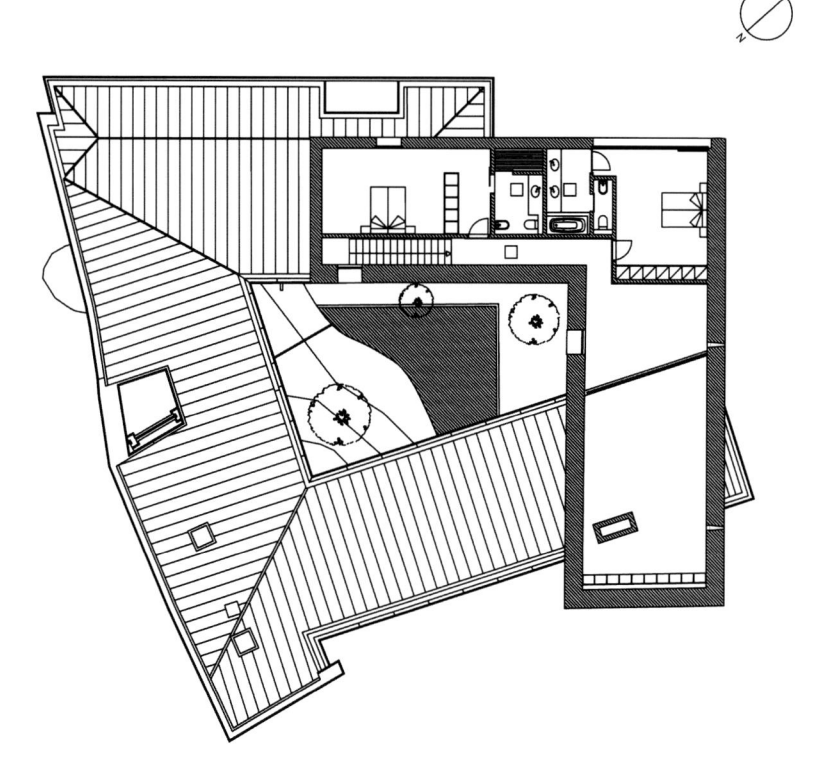

Second floor

House in Brito-Guimarães 69

Transversal section

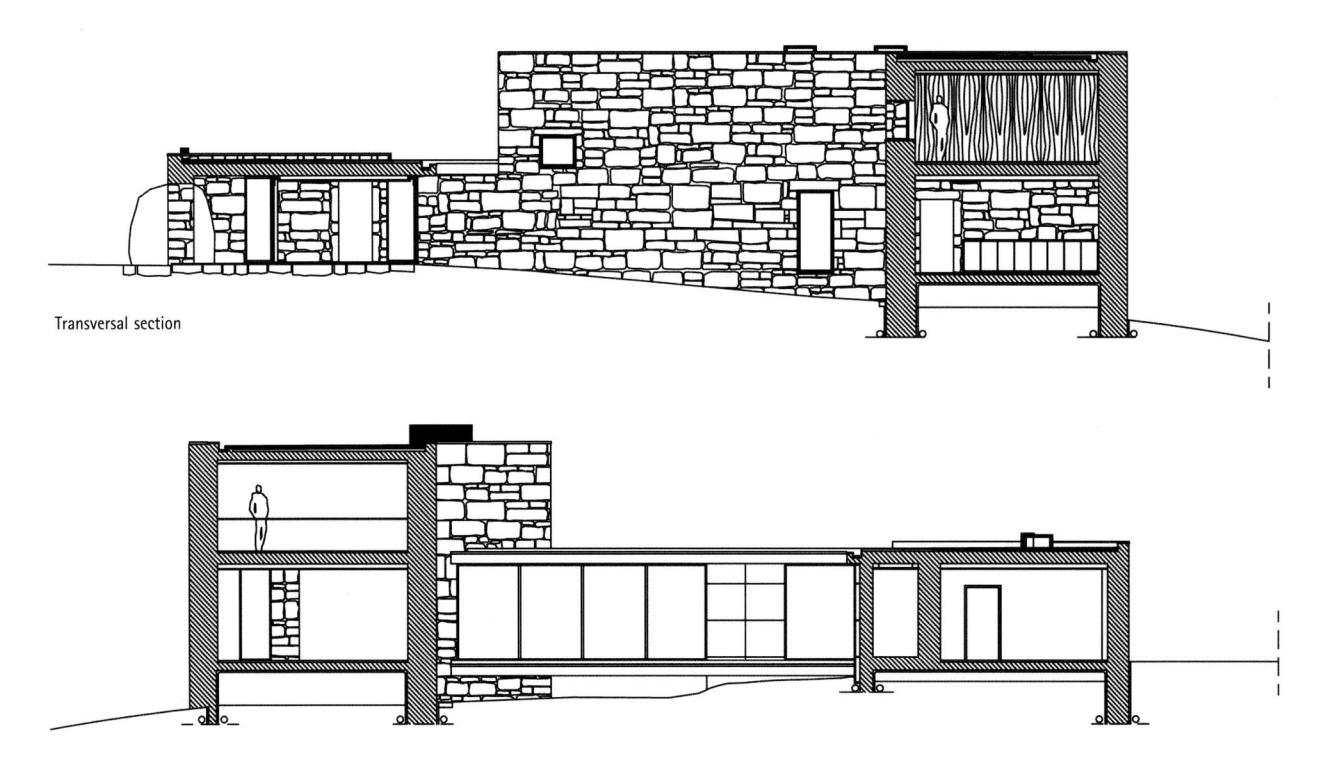

Transversal section

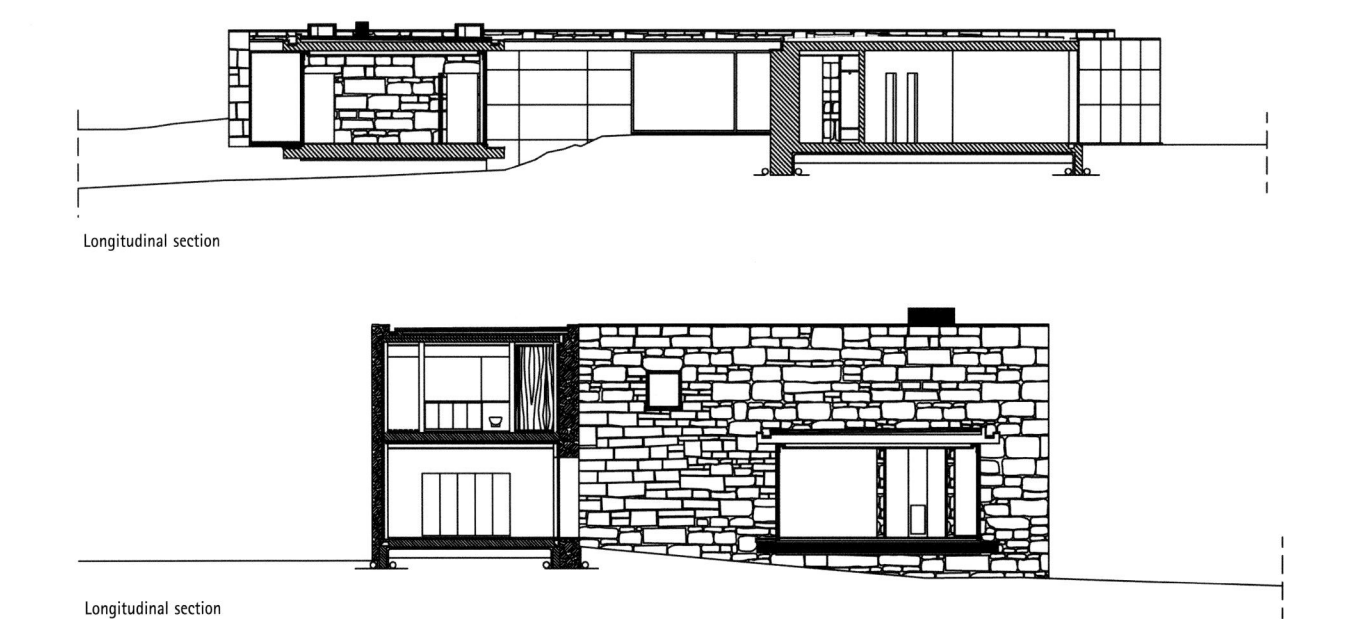

Longitudinal section

Longitudinal section

House in Brito-Guimarães 71

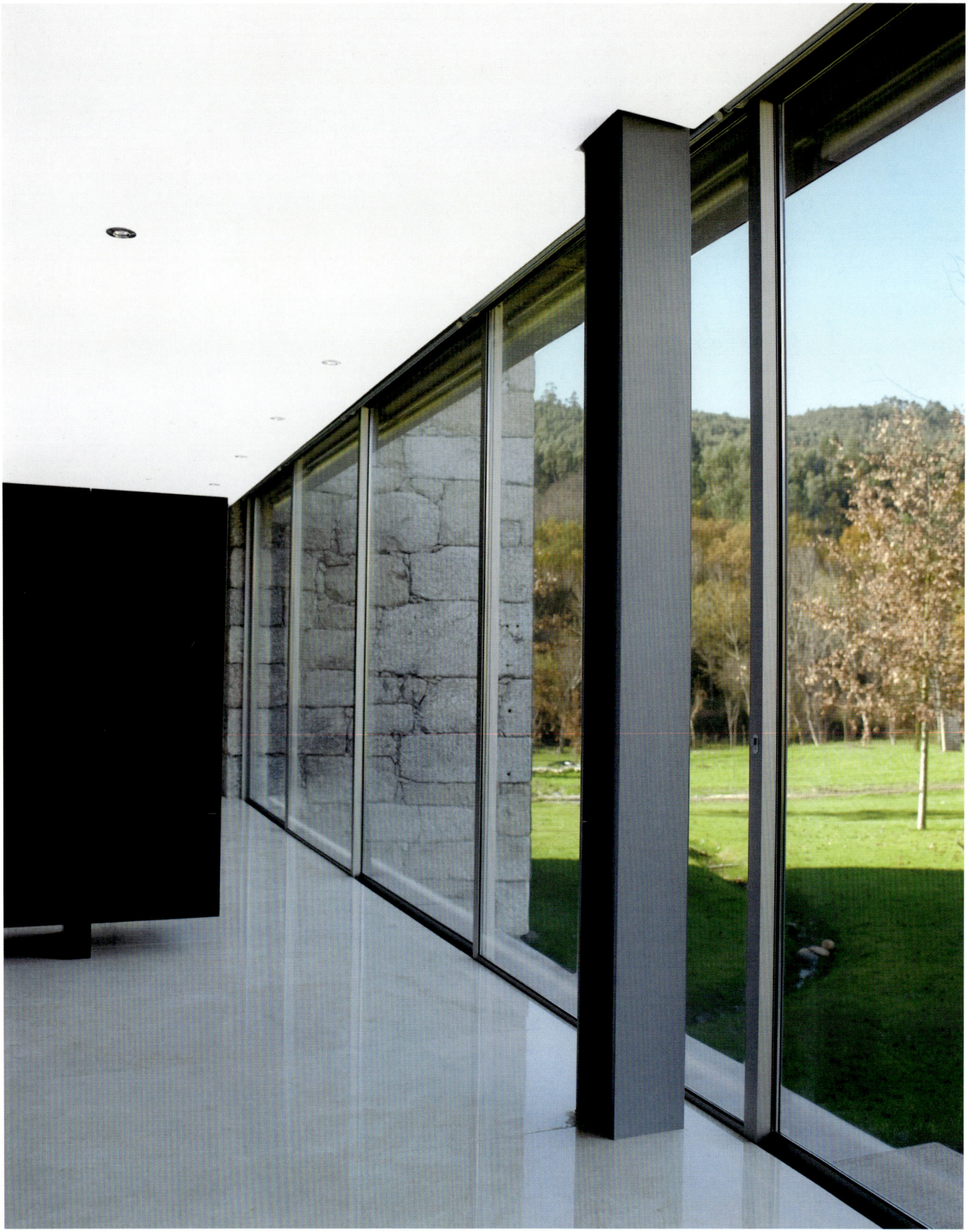

North elevation

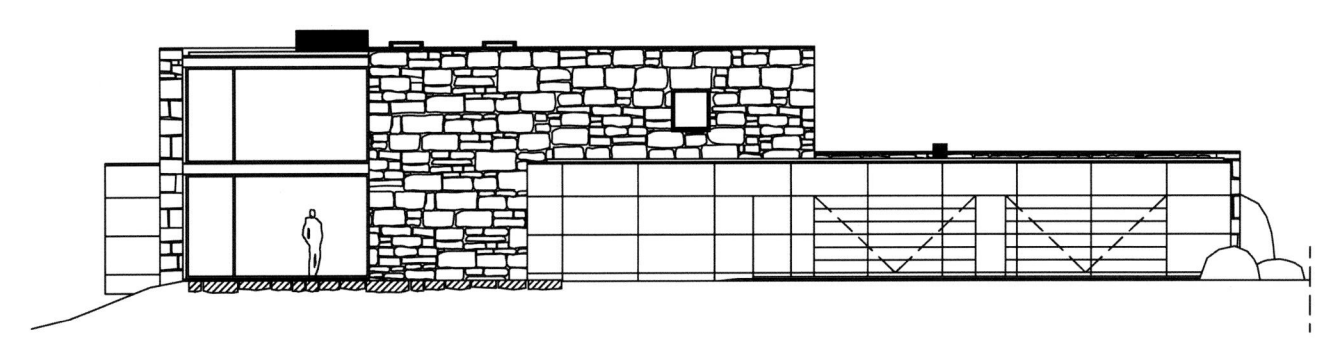

East elevation

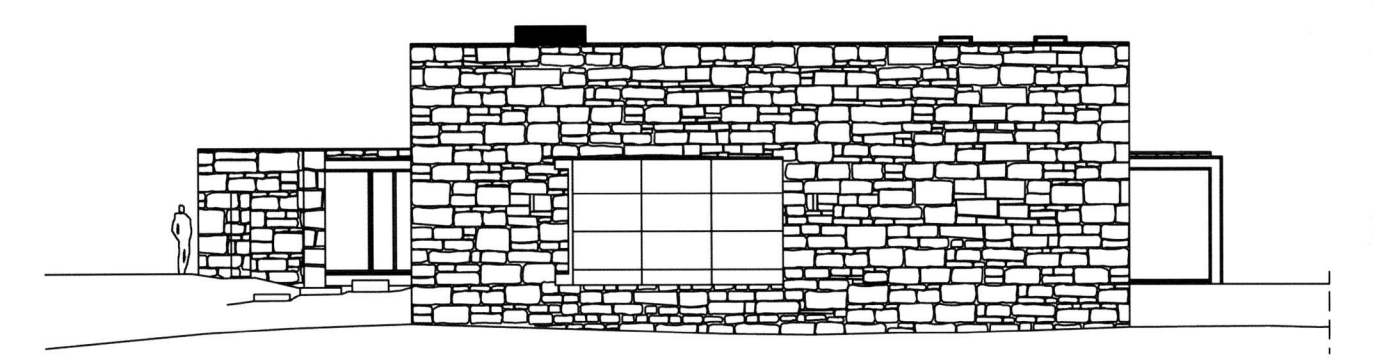

South elevation

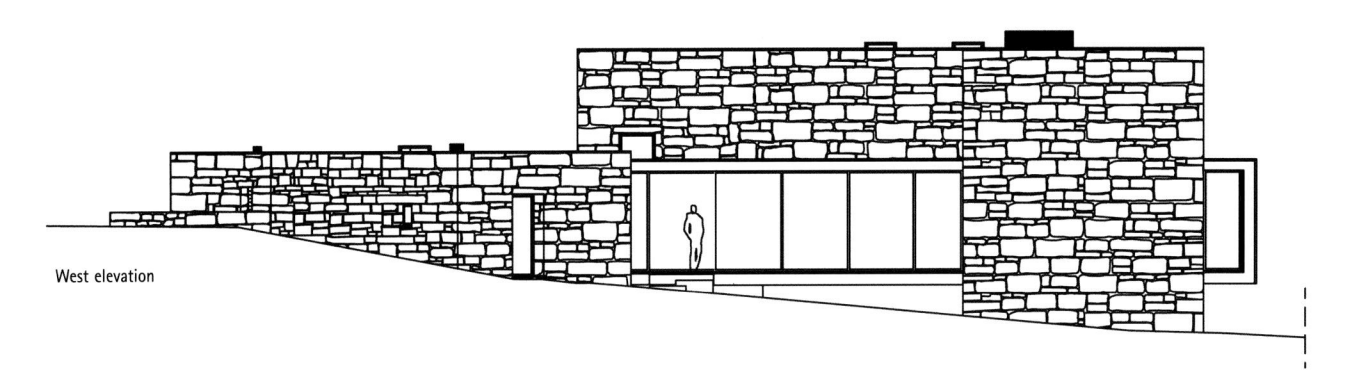

West elevation

House in Brito-Guimarães

Semmerzake is a picturesque village close to Gante with a protected historic center. This farm, although not in the center, still forms part of the urban framework. The conservation of the materials and exterior structure therefore became a fundamental premise and determined the intervention.

House in Semmerzake

Architect: Jo Taillieu
Photographer © Jeroen Musch
Location: Semmerzake, Belgium
Completion date: 2005

The original building was composed of a main house, an annex and a shed. The architect decided to empty the interior of these buildings preserving the walls as protection for the central building, but putting up new glass walls, which highlight the texture of the existing construction. The floor plan of the main house is square and the reform meant a reduction in circulation space. This meant the passageway between the bedrooms was converted into a dressing room. Given the depth of the plan, mirrors have been located, which cover the wall from the floor to the ceiling. The lights, positioned high up, offer a greater degree of clarity.

The budget played an important part in this renovation. The steel, which was originally proposed, was replaced by African wood from controlled felling and strategies were used to enlarge the structures, such as creating built-in furniture. Numerous prefabricated elements were introduced, which provide the rooms with more flexibility. This allows the studio, for example, to be divided in two by way of a thin wall. The sustainable consumption of energy is favored via the installation of heating that operates through a water pump, and the system of ventilation beneath the floor, which automatically regulates the temperature.

76 House in Semmerzake

Previous plan

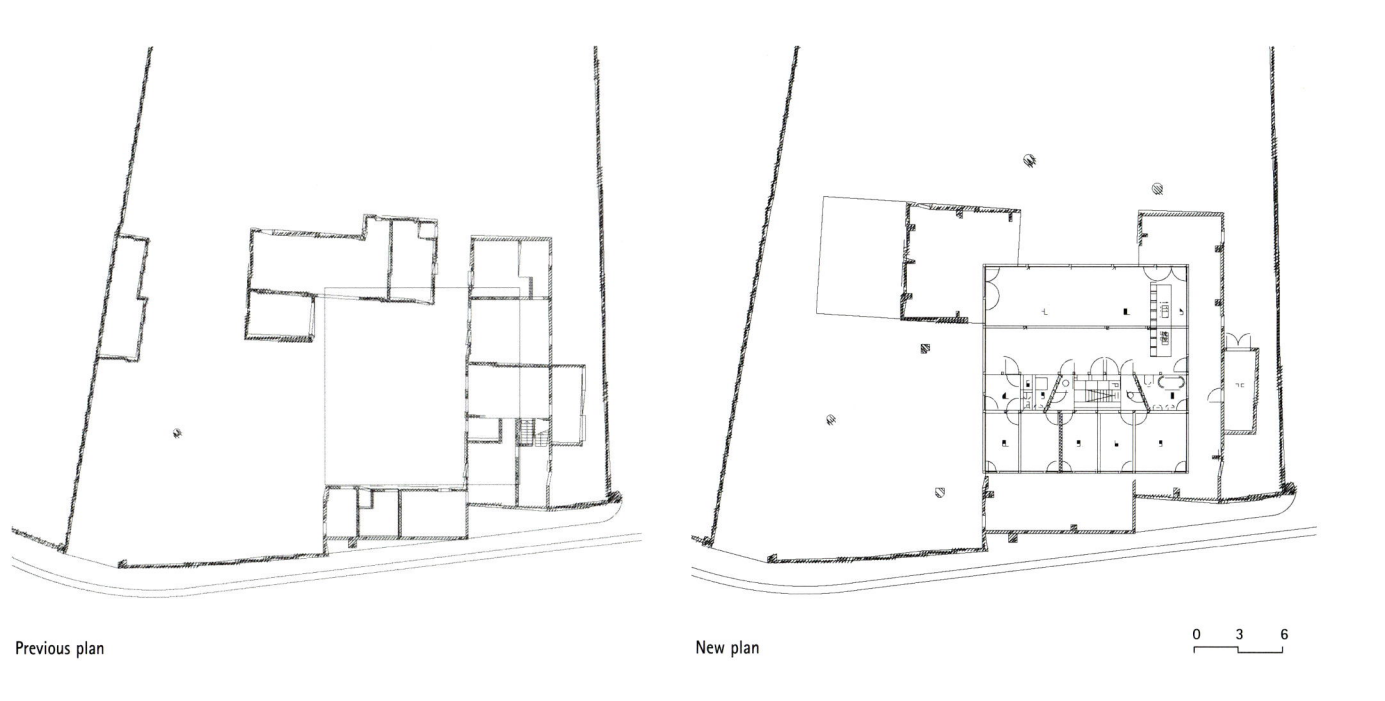

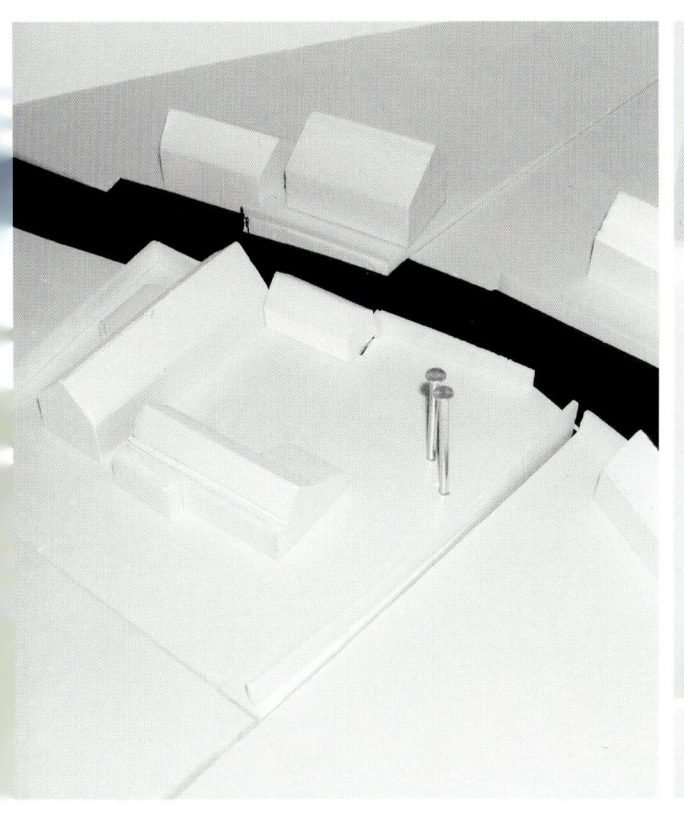

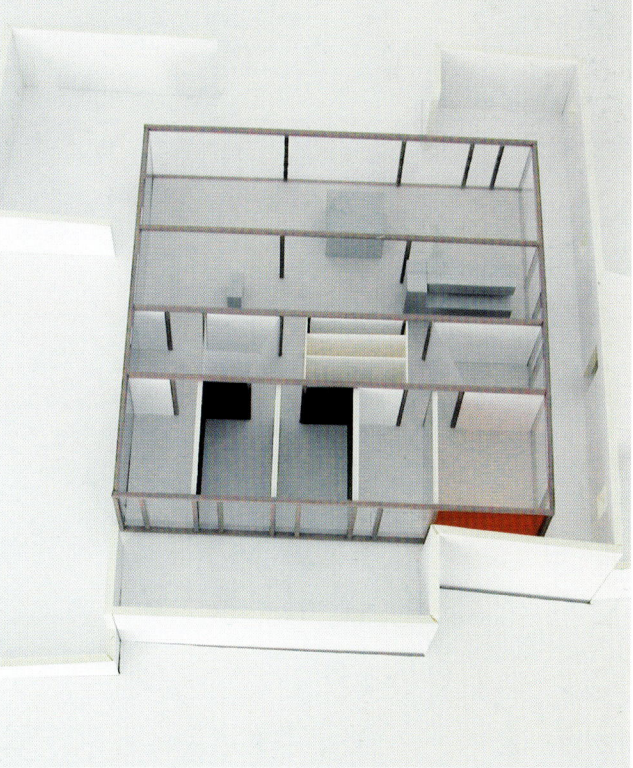

New plan

0 3 6

The photos on the left show the opening of the house to the exterior and the restructuring work of the garden, in close contact with the house.

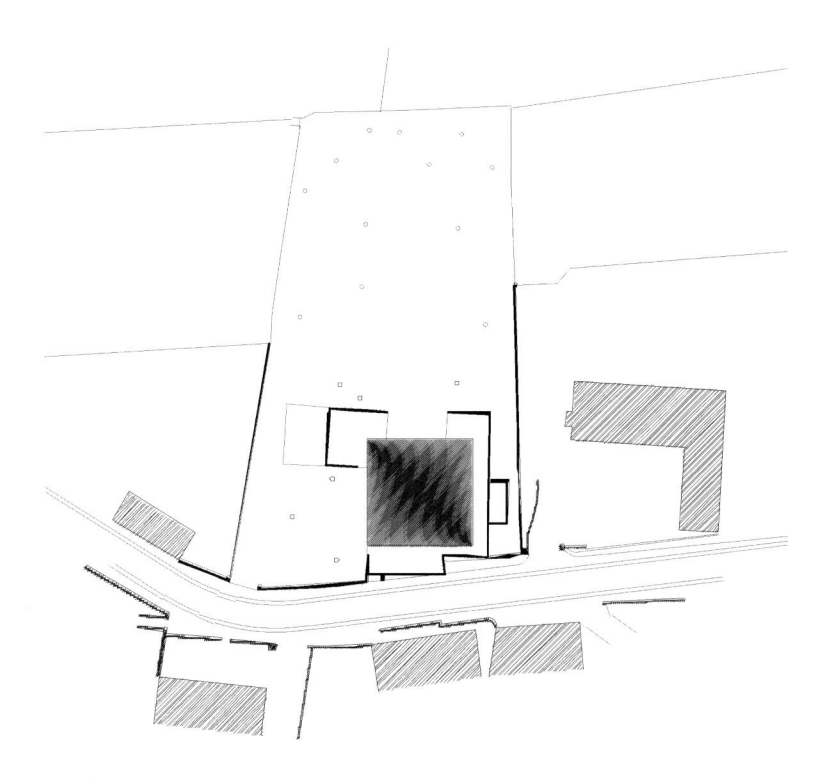

Plan of previous situation

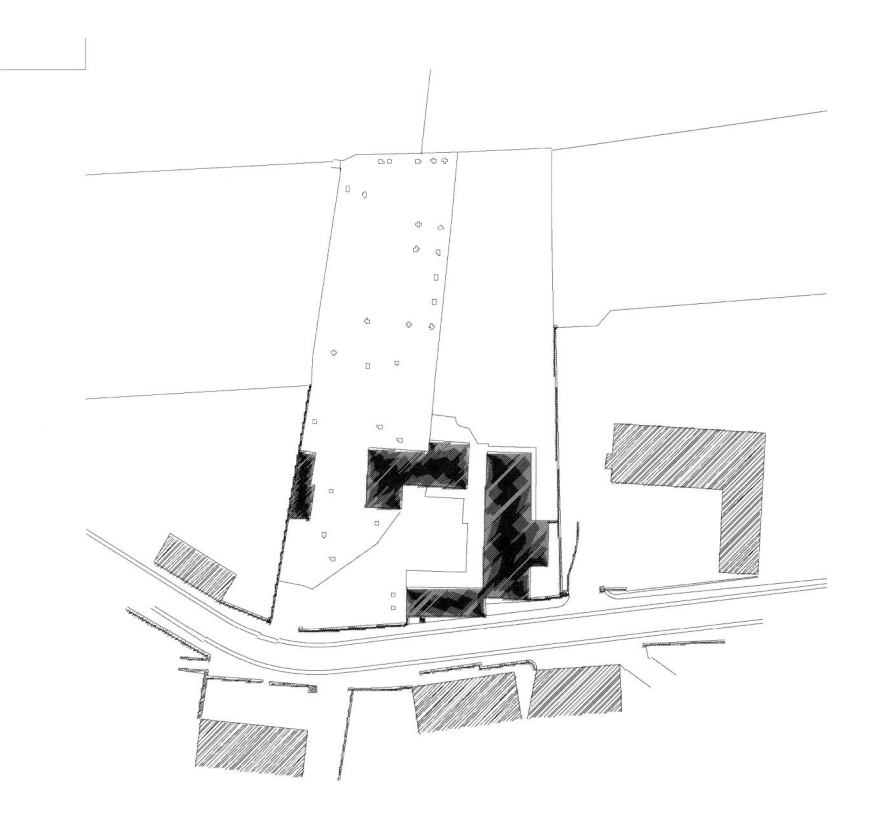

Plan of new situation

78 House in Semmerzake

House in Semmerzake 79

80 House in Semmerzake

Northwest elevation

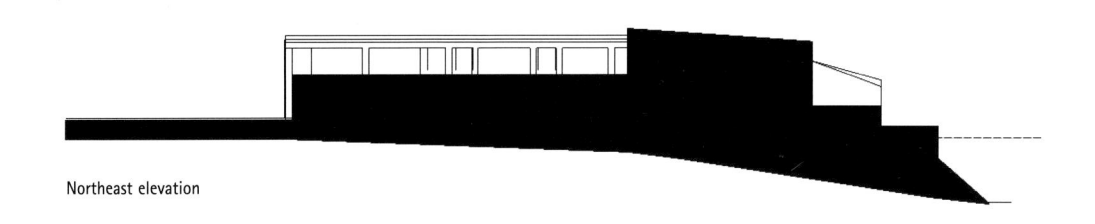

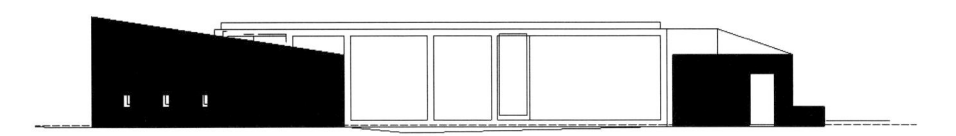

Northeast elevation

Southeast elevation

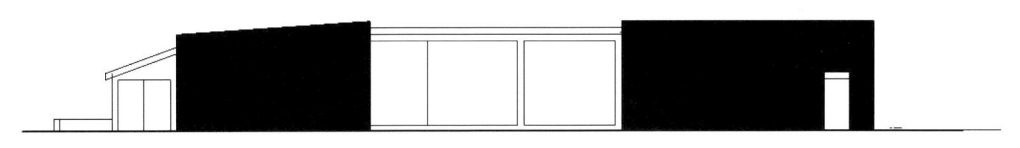

Southwest elevation

House in Semmerzake 81

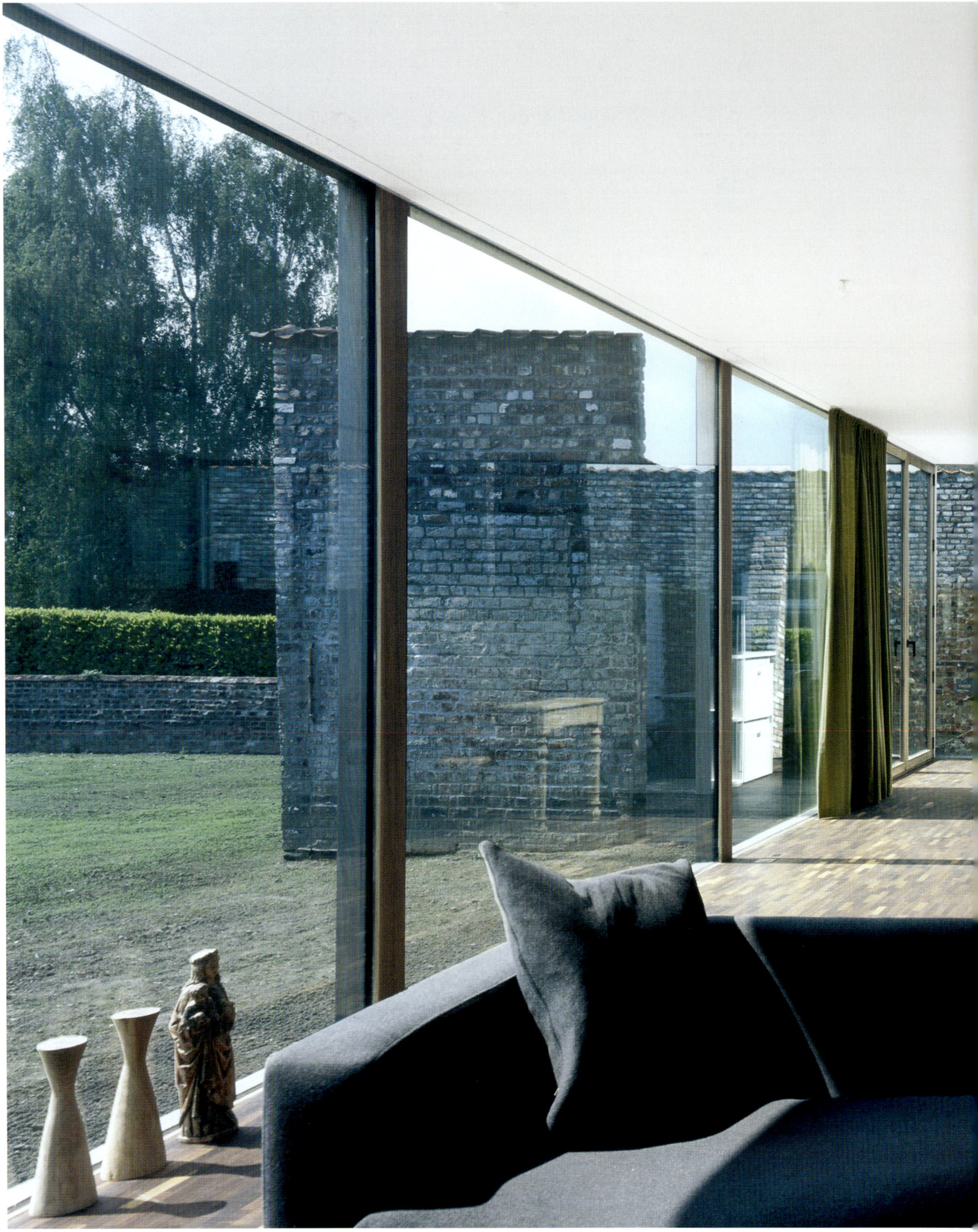

House in Semmerzake 83

There are still some idyllic and calm spots to be found a few miles from Barcelona, where the beauty of the wild landscape invites serenity. This country house, whose origins date back to 1780, was reformed with the idea of converting it into a relaxing place for all the family.

Family Hotel in Garraf

Architect: Francesc Rifé
Photographer © Eugeni Pons
Location: Olivella, Spain
Completion date: 2006

The restoration project was organized from the house's basic structure. The beams and façades were recovered, and the plaster that covered the original stone was removed. The openings for the windows were restructured and others were opened to optimize the entry of light. Outdoor matt black paint was applied to one of the rear façades, where a balcony of sheet metal was built, also painted black, which creates a counterpoint to the volumes.

Inside, the almost complete reconstruction accentuates elements from the past by way of contemporary materials and structures. The house is accessed through the old kitchen, which has been conserved and whose wood-burning oven has been preserved. From here we can access the dining area and the living and private spaces. Due to the uneven terrain, the rooms have been situated at different heights, linked via short flights of steps. The central staircase, a glass and black sheet metal cubic volume, forms the backbone of the ground floor spaces and also houses a small, intimate reading area. New interior windows connect rooms and extend the views to the exterior from various points in the house. The most spacious room has been reserved for the dining area, presided by a fireplace and flanked by large windows on the wall of the façade and by a long wooden bench on the interior wall, which is reminiscent of kitchens of the past. On the upper floor, the bedrooms and the bathrooms are interspersed with open spaces used as dressing rooms, making the most of both the layout of the existing floor plan and the entry of natural light.

The natural stone façade, which conceals the plaster beneath it, recovers the close contact with the floors of the village streets and with the surrounding houses.

Family Hotel in Garraf 87

First floor

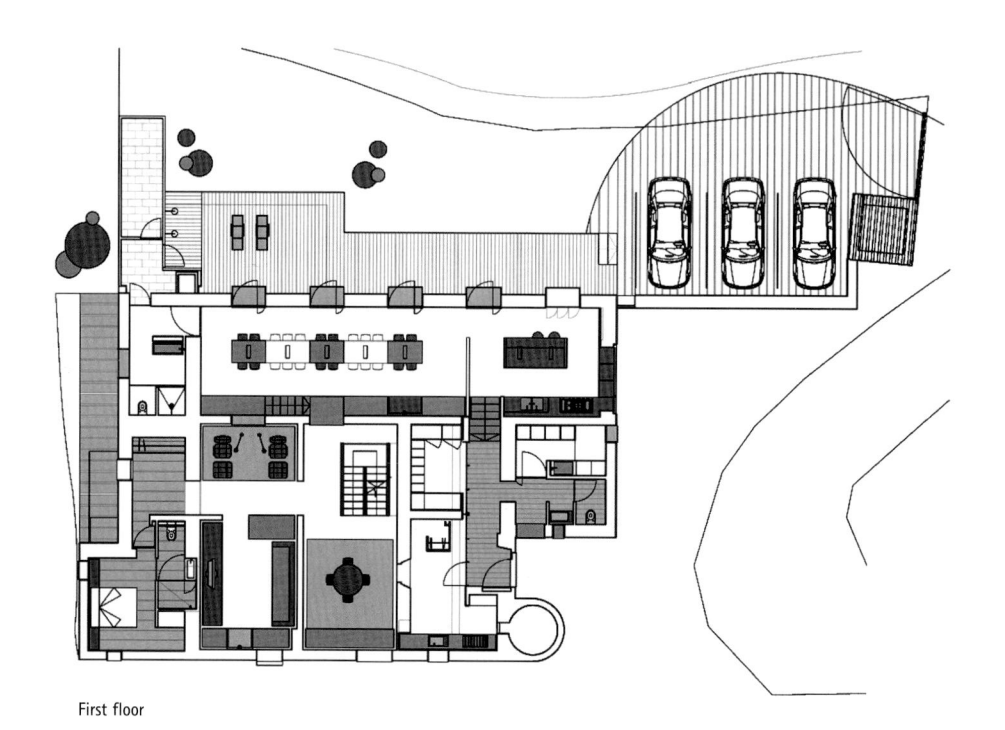

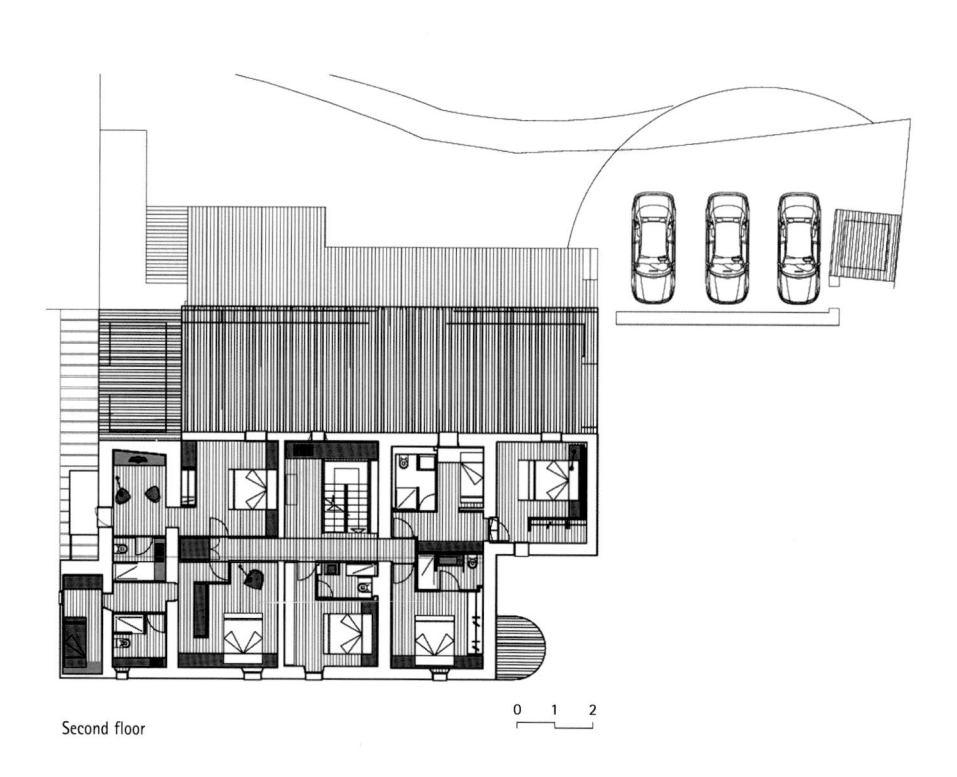

Second floor

0 1 2

Family Hotel in Garraf **89**

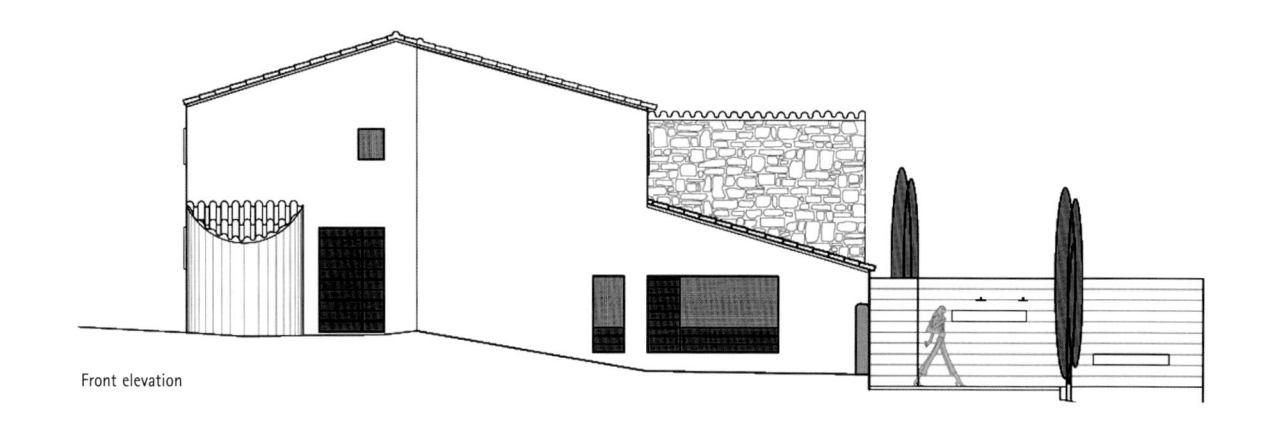

Front elevation

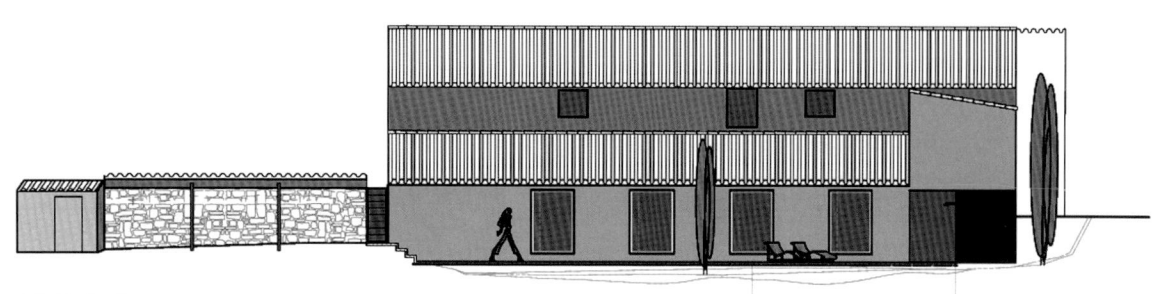

Left side elevation

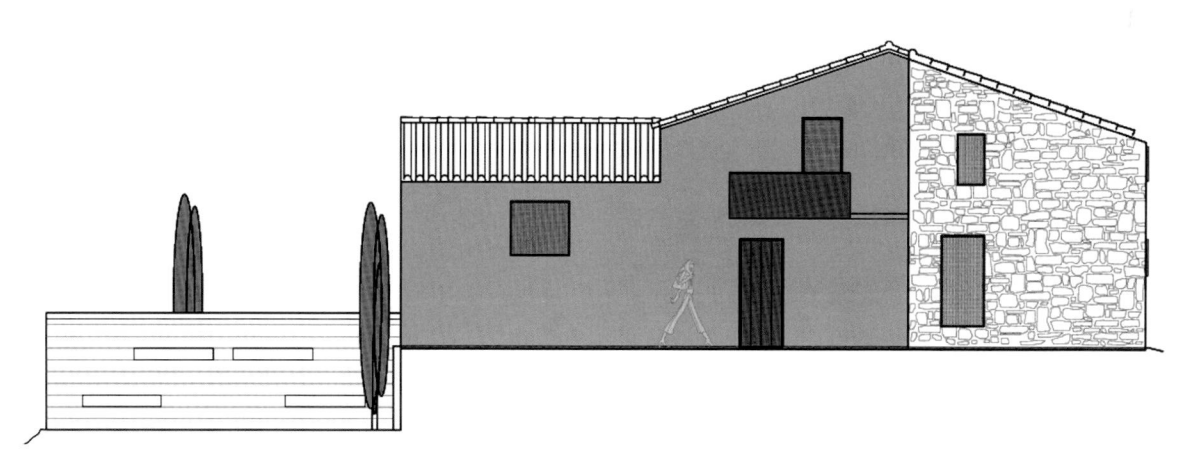

Rear elevation

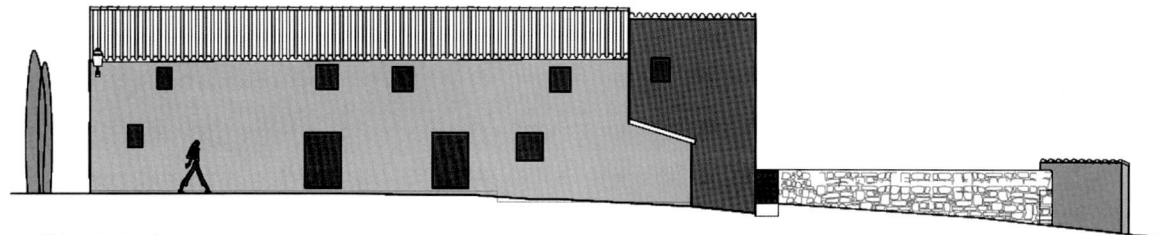

Right side elevation

90 Family Hotel in Garraf

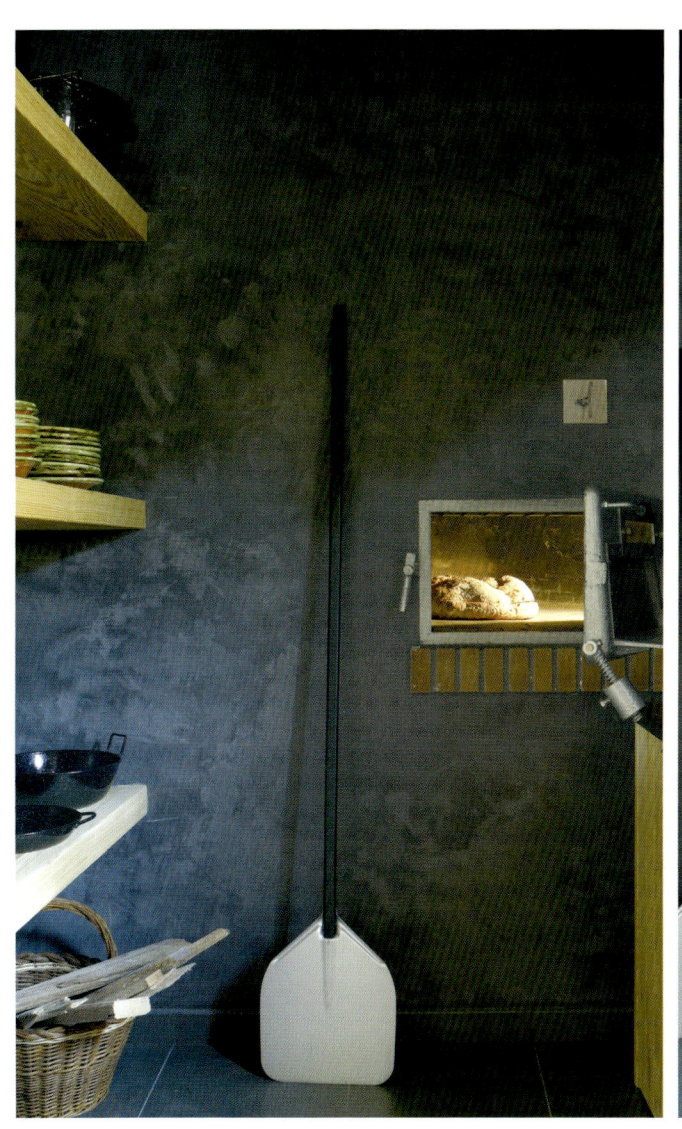

Family Hotel in Garraf 91

Right side longitudinal section

Left side longitudinal section

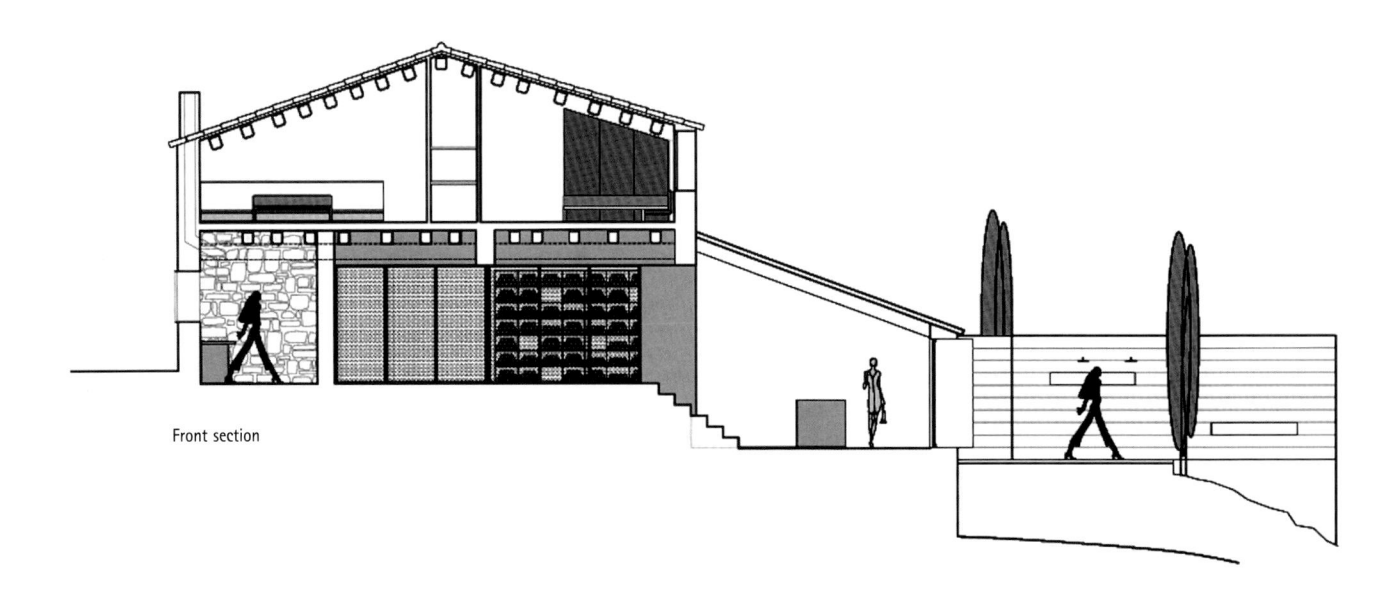

Front section

92 Family Hotel in Garraf

Family Hotel in Garraf 93

94 Family Hotel in Garraf

Family Hotel in Garraf 95

The great challenge for the architects working on this project was to preserve as much as possible the character and spatial qualities of a big old farm and at the same time adapt it to meet the needs of a contemporary family.

Restoration of Wolzak Farm

Architects: Search Architecten
Photographer © Christian Richters, Jeroen Musch
Location: Zutphen, Holland
Completion date: 2004

To start with there was an idea of demolishing some of the elements adjacent to the farm and replacing them with a new annex. The space would have been reduced making it more practical for a family. However, the splendid distribution of the farm and its T-shape structure would have been lost. The architects' proposal was to leave the volume of the main house in tact, so it could accommodate all spaces for daily use. The barn would also be conserved, to perhaps later be converted into an indoor swimming pool. This maintained the original geometry of the farm. The stable however was demolished, and in its place a new annex was erected with sloping lines, which make it appear stretched as if it had been dragged to the empty space where the stable once stood.

Regarding the organizational program, the main house was separated from the new volume. The spaces for daily use have been situated in the farm, with an extension of the new annex's ground floor, where a large open kitchen has been installed. The main entrance is located between these two volumes. The studio, the guest area and the garden shed have also been located in the new annex, separated from each other by a greenhouse. The load bearing walls are formed from prefabricated wooden laminates that define the finishes and the general ambiance of the interior. The façades and the roof have been clad in a continuous layer of vertical wooden laminates, which appear open, semi-transparent and closed all at once. The tiled wall of the old stable has been preserved, whose main door frames a beautiful oak tree.

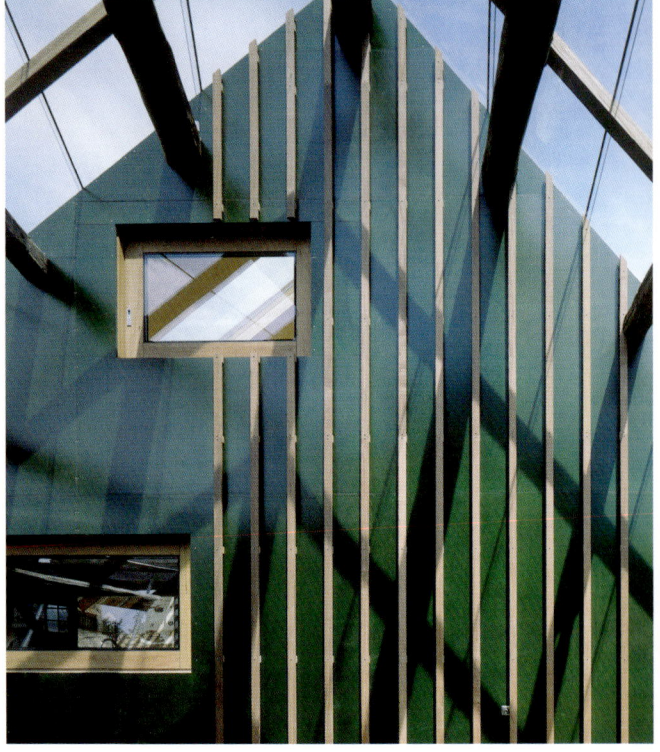

This bold transformation has refined the external elements. This allows the construction's external shell to dominate and at the same time to integrate smoothly with the environment.

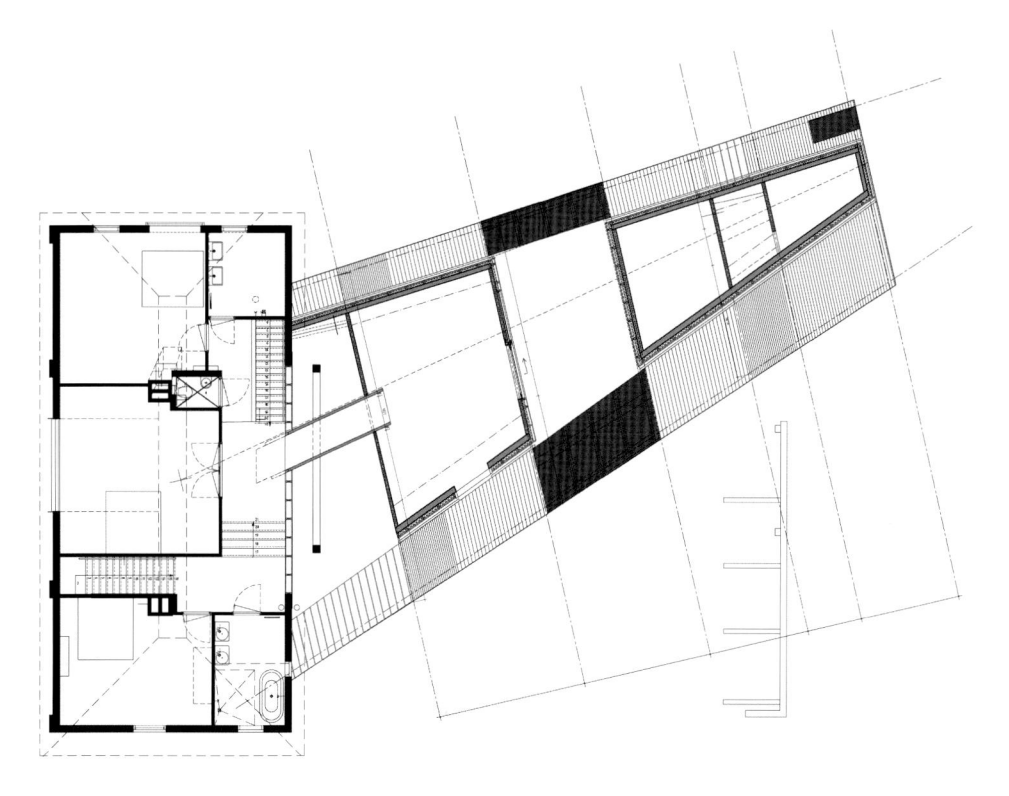

First floor

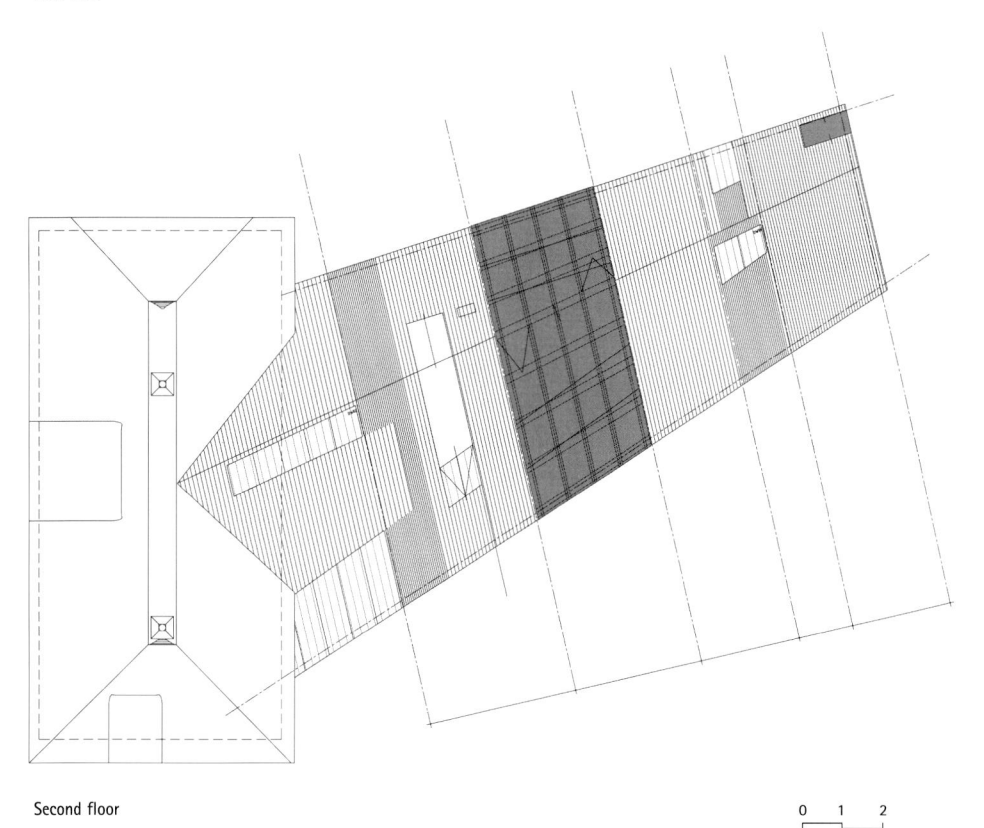

Second floor

Restoration of Wolzak Farm 99

100 Restoration of Wolzak Farm

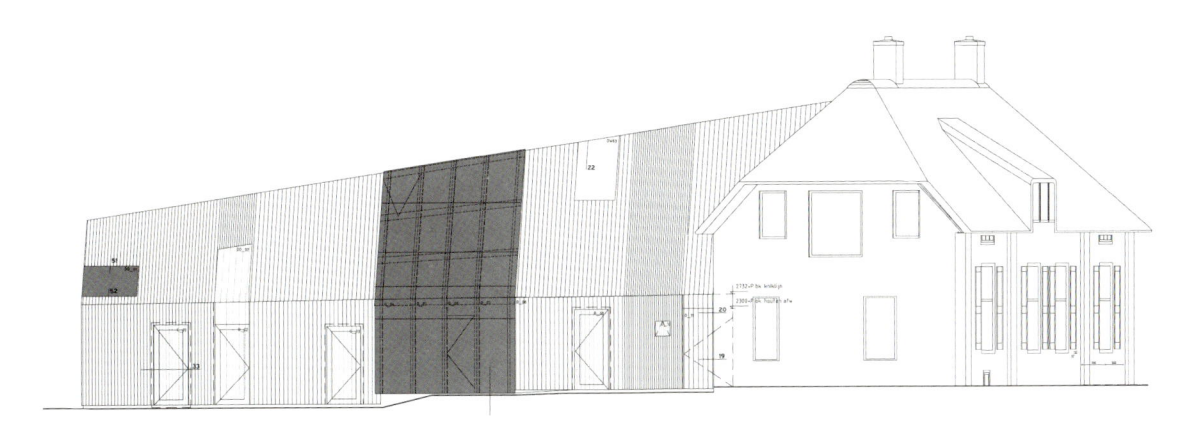

East-west elevation

Restoration of Wolzak Farm 101

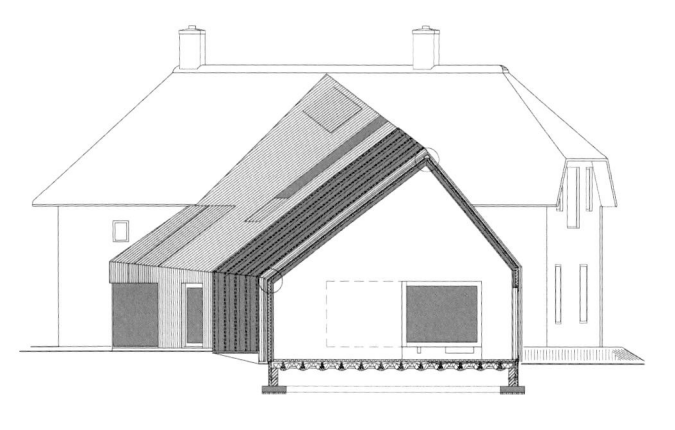

Transversal section of the annex

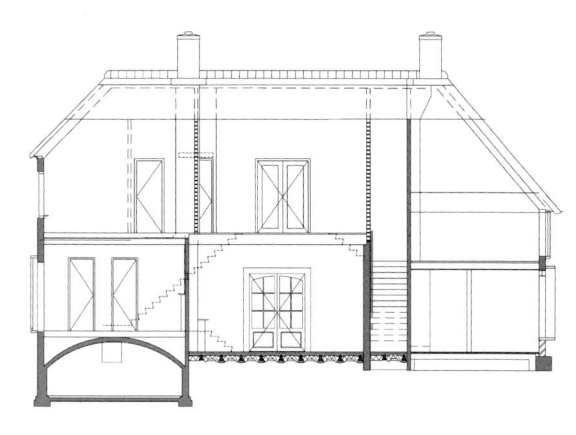

Transversal section

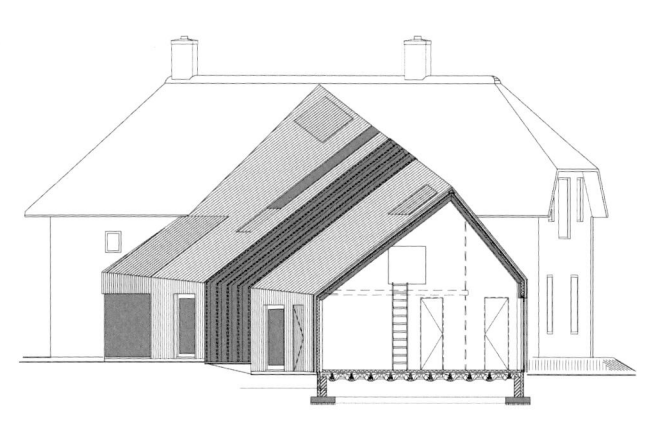

Transversal section of the annex

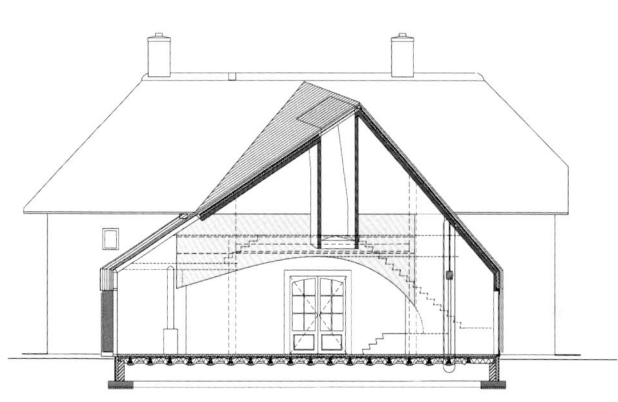

Transversal section of the annex

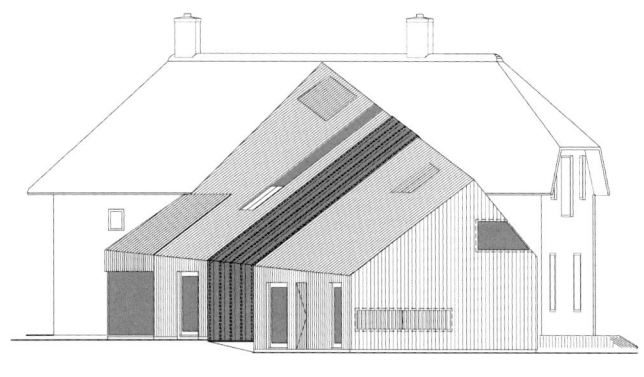

Front elevation of the annex

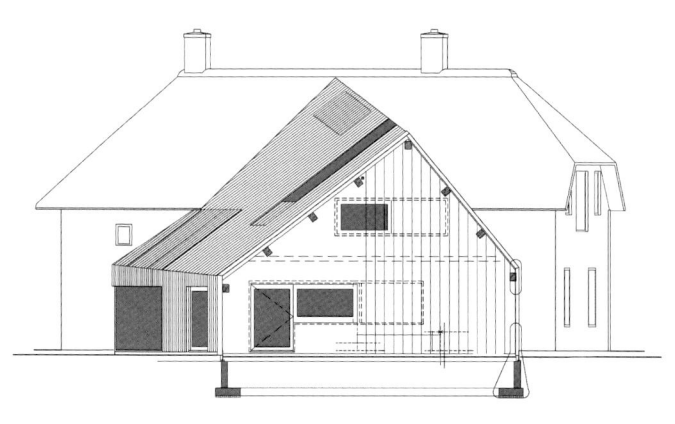

Transversal section of the annex

102 Restoration of Wolzak Farm

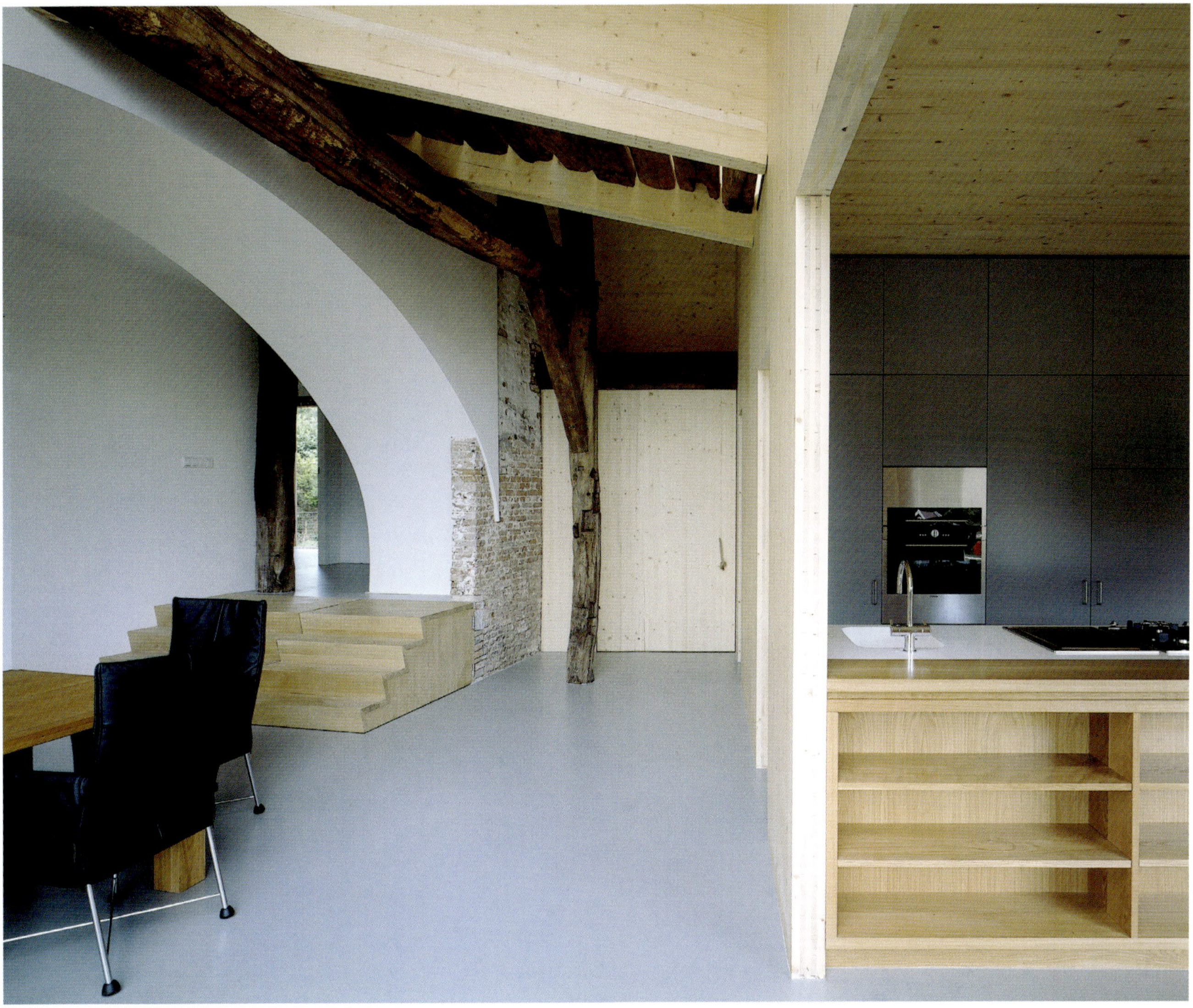

104 Restoration of Wolzak Farm

Restoration of Wolzak Farm 105

The owners bought this old 1950s ranch with the intention of demolishing it and starting from scratch. However on discovering that this wooden cabin was made from planks salvaged from old railway carriages, they opted instead for its restoration and extension.

Extension of Sattler-Smith House

Architects: Mayer & Sattler-Smith Architects
Photographer © Kevin G. Smith
Location: Anchorage, Alaska
Completion date: 2005

Two new steel clad annexes stand next to the existing construction together with a small grove of trees, preserving the unique character of the place. Due to the close proximity of the old trees, the front annex is supported by steel pillars. This ensures its stability, which could be under threat from the movement of the trees' roots. The next annex was built so that each floor has a view of a different part of the landscape, while also offering the interior privacy. The living area is located in the semi-basement and connects with the central courtyard. This joins the three buildings and can therefore not be seen from outside. The three blocks connect via an arctic porch with stairs (very characteristic of Alaska). The combination of exposed concrete blocks and wood both inside and out produces an intermittent effect. The upper part of the annex, a translucent steel and glass cube used as a living room and as a winter garden, projects outwards to make the most of the sunniest part of the plot. Surrounded by trees, it extends into a large terrace and benefits from exposure to the sun throughout the day. Thanks to the translucent glass strips and its raised position above the middle height of the surrounding buildings, its privacy is also protected. Local black stone and dark wood cover the floors except in the kitchen area, situated on the ground floor, which benefits from the natural color of the wooden floor.

The old ranch, whose previous state can be appreciated in the photo above, had been built from wood salvaged from old railway carriages.

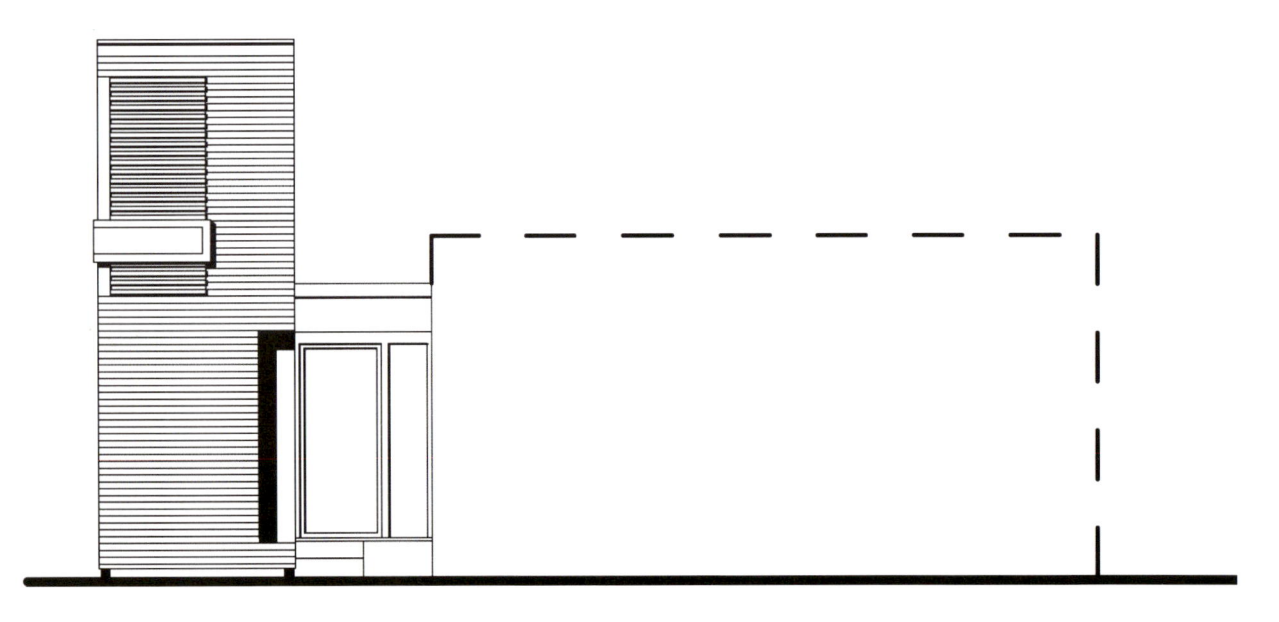

South front elevation

Extension of Sattler-Smith House 109

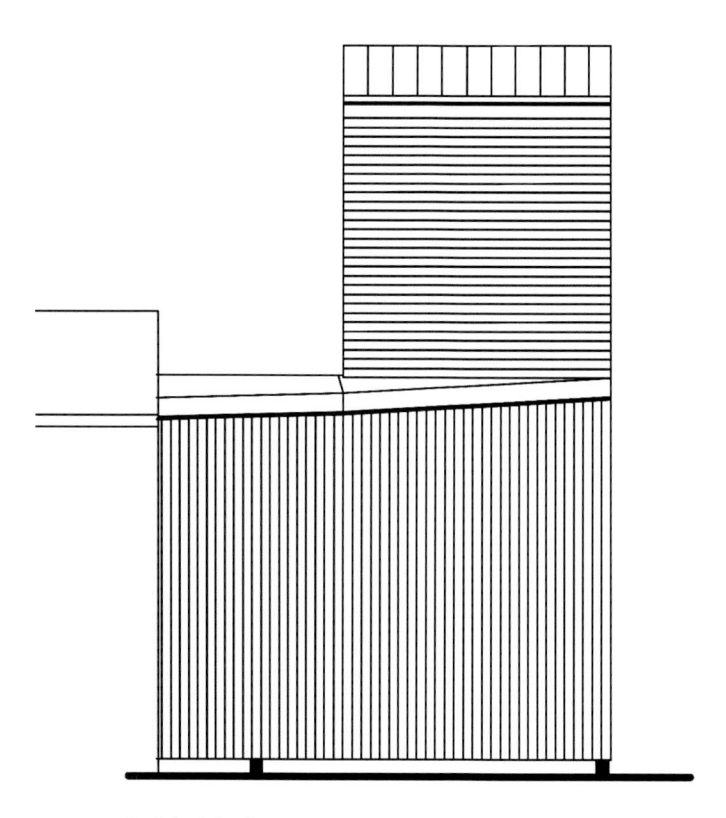

North front elevation

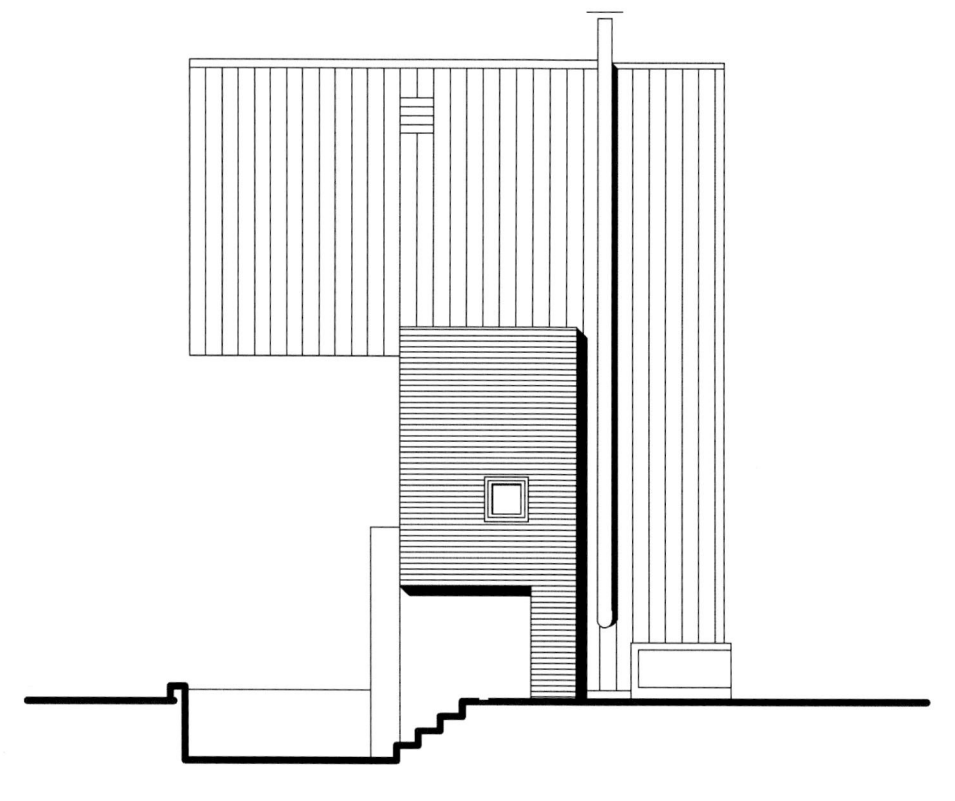

North rear elevation

110 Extension of Sattler-Smith House

Extension of Sattler-Smith House

112 Extension of Sattler-Smith House

Transversal section

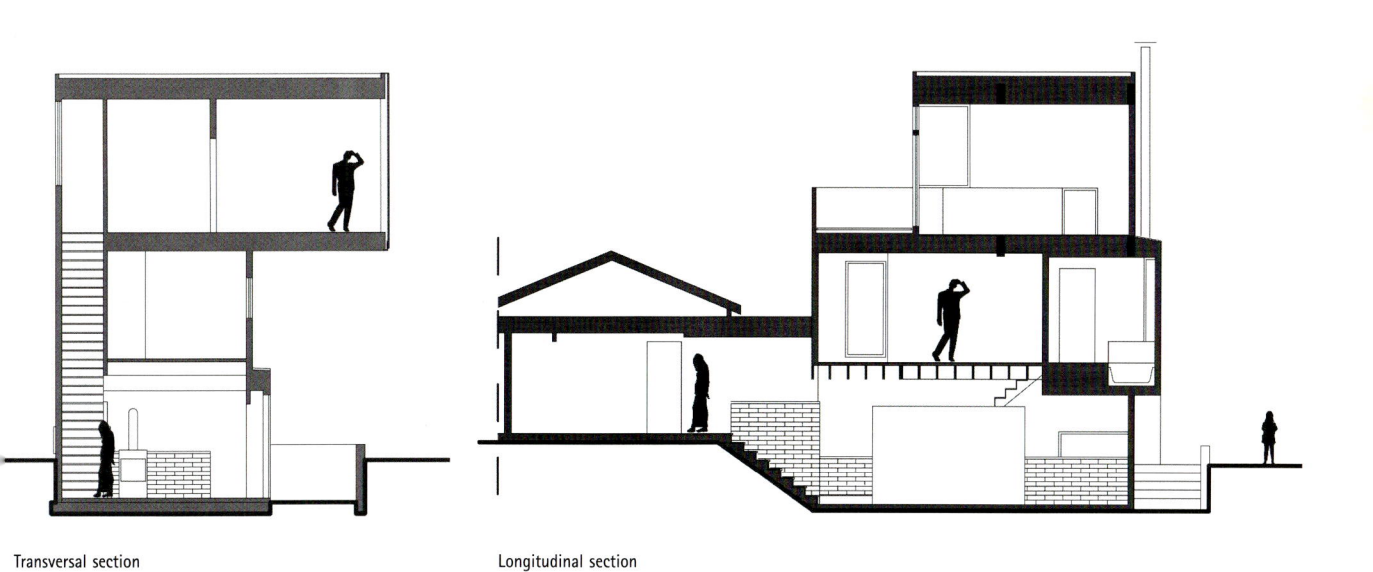

Longitudinal section

Extension of Sattler-Smith House 113

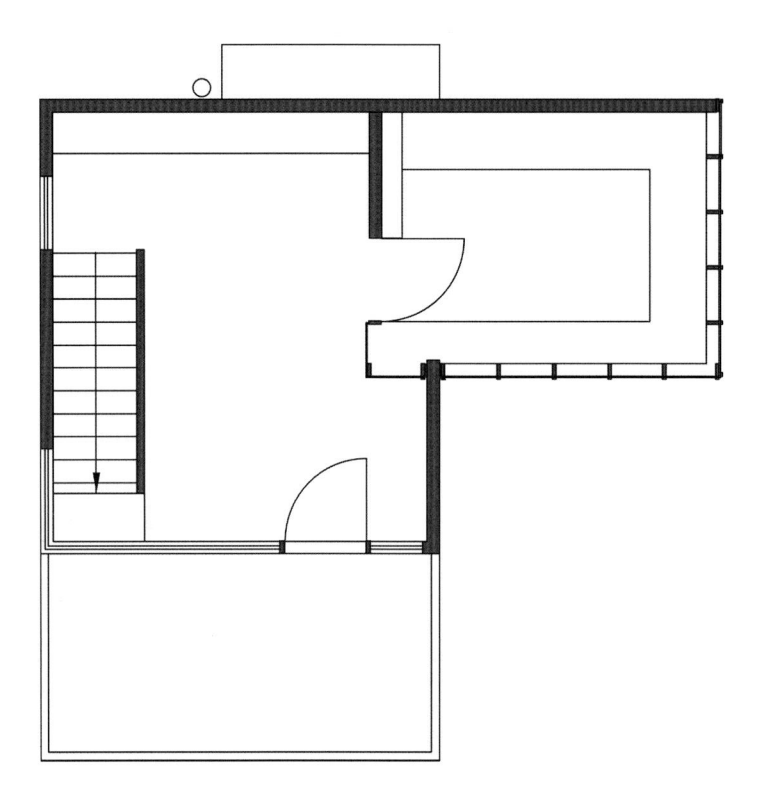

First floor of the annex

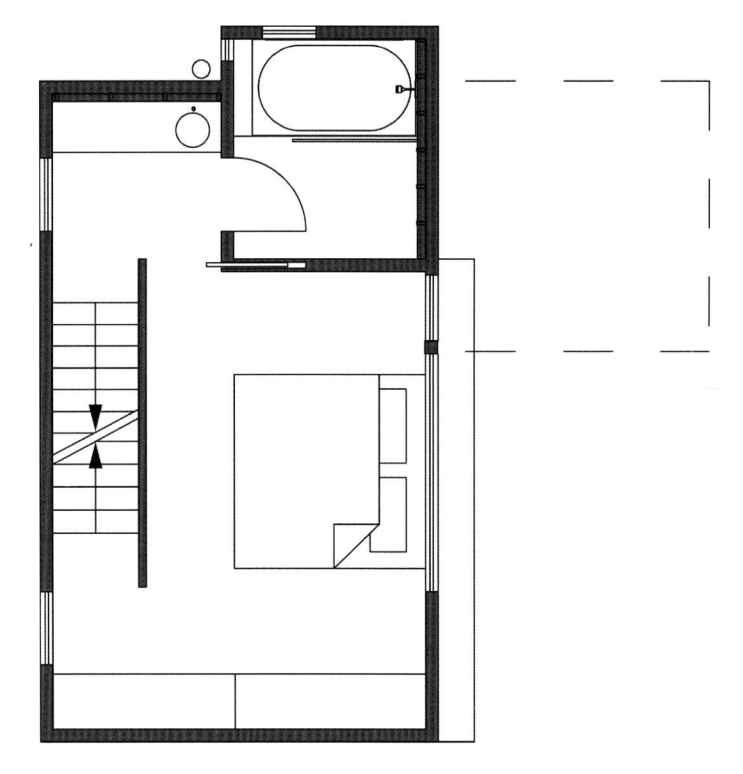

Second floor of the annex

0   1

114 Extension of Sattler-Smith House

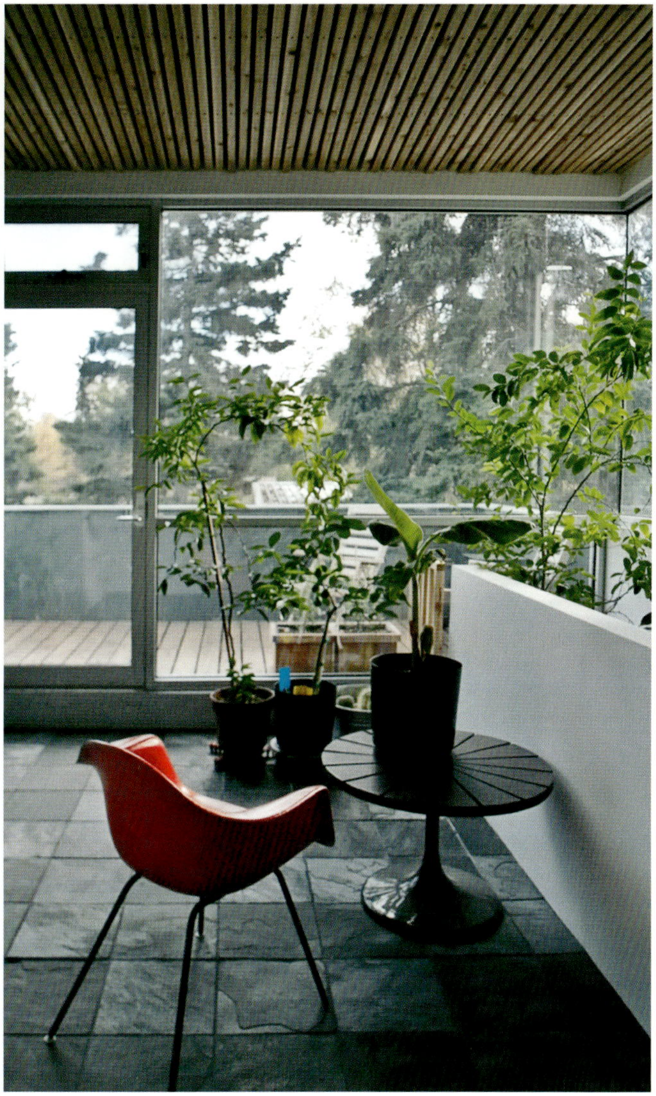

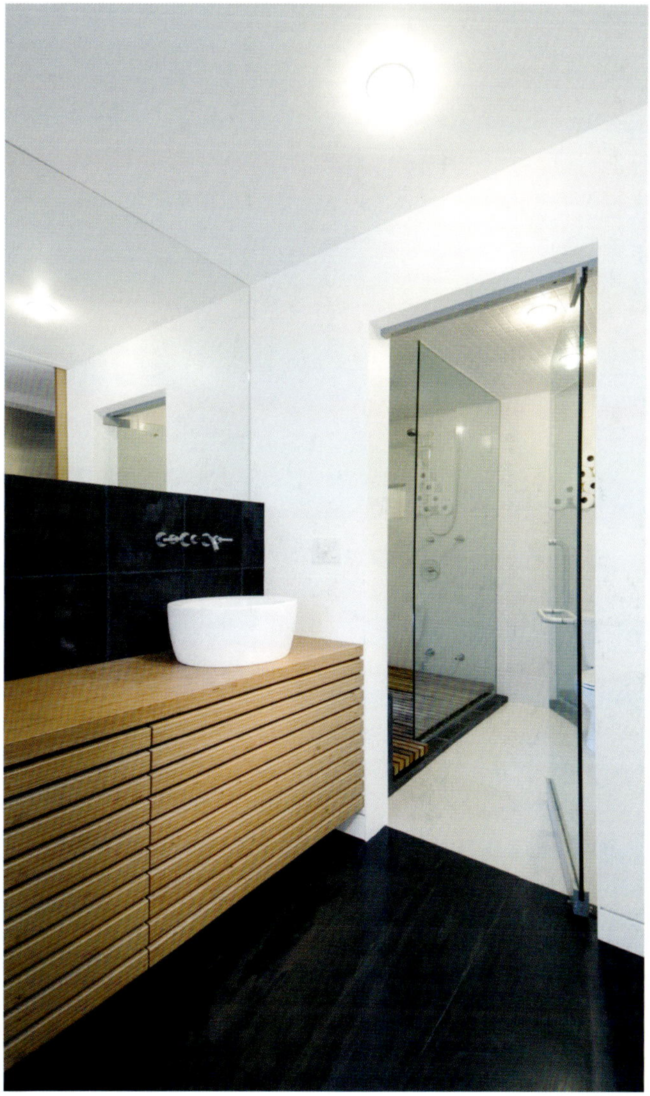

This restoration has been carried out on a construction used for tool storage dating back to 1776, which had been abandoned. Its condition was in a severe state of deterioration. The result of the intervention is a fluid interior with well-defined spaces where the functions of the home, a workplace and even a showroom co-exist.

Studio House in Montseny

Architect: David Gallifa
Photographer © Eugeni Pons
Location: Seva, Spain
Completion date: 2006

The floor plan, almost a perfect square measuring 28 x 30 ft, with a central pillar, was divided up on the two lower levels and open in the attic, which was used as a granary.

The load bearing walls are 20 inches thick and the ceiling framework is formed from beams and copper sheets, with wooden floorboards on the first floor and ceramic tiles on the second. The roof is surfaced in Arabic tiles with a structure of beams and wooden sheets. The essence of the project consisted in reinforcing the structures, preserving the existing elements where possible and intervening decisively using contemporary techniques and materials where necessary. The west-facing roof and façade, which had to be opened with new windows, were reinforced as were the floors and central pillar. Partitions were eliminated to create an open-plan space, allowing light to enter and offering more views of the surroundings. The original volume was returned to the construction, for which a rear annex was demolished. The ground floor of over 1300 ft^2, is a unique space where the kitchen, dining area and living room are all located. The space can be extended towards the porch and separated by three sliding and concealable partitions. On the first floor, movable divisions allow the creation of one or two spaces, depending on what is desired. Beneath the roof is a multifunctional space that can be used for work, meetings, reading or simply contemplation. Each flight of stairs is made from a different material and together they form the backbone of the house.

The open and multifunctional spaces allow structural elements to be left visible.

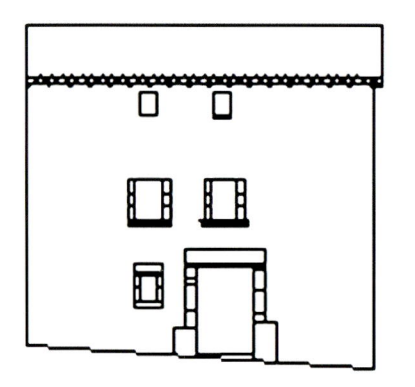

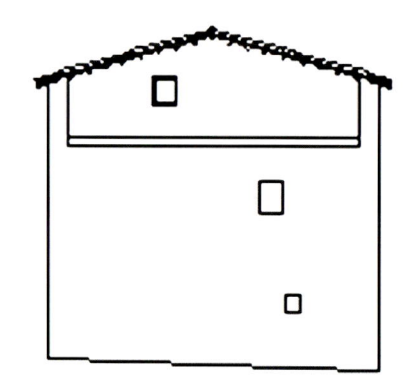

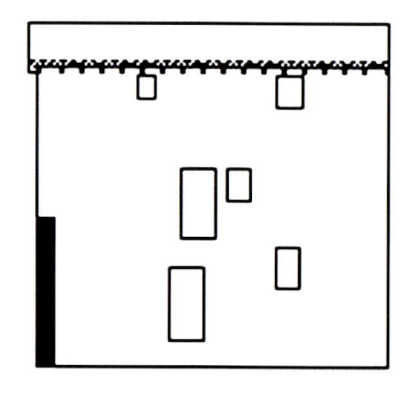

Previous elevations

118 Studio House in Montseny

Studio House in Montseny

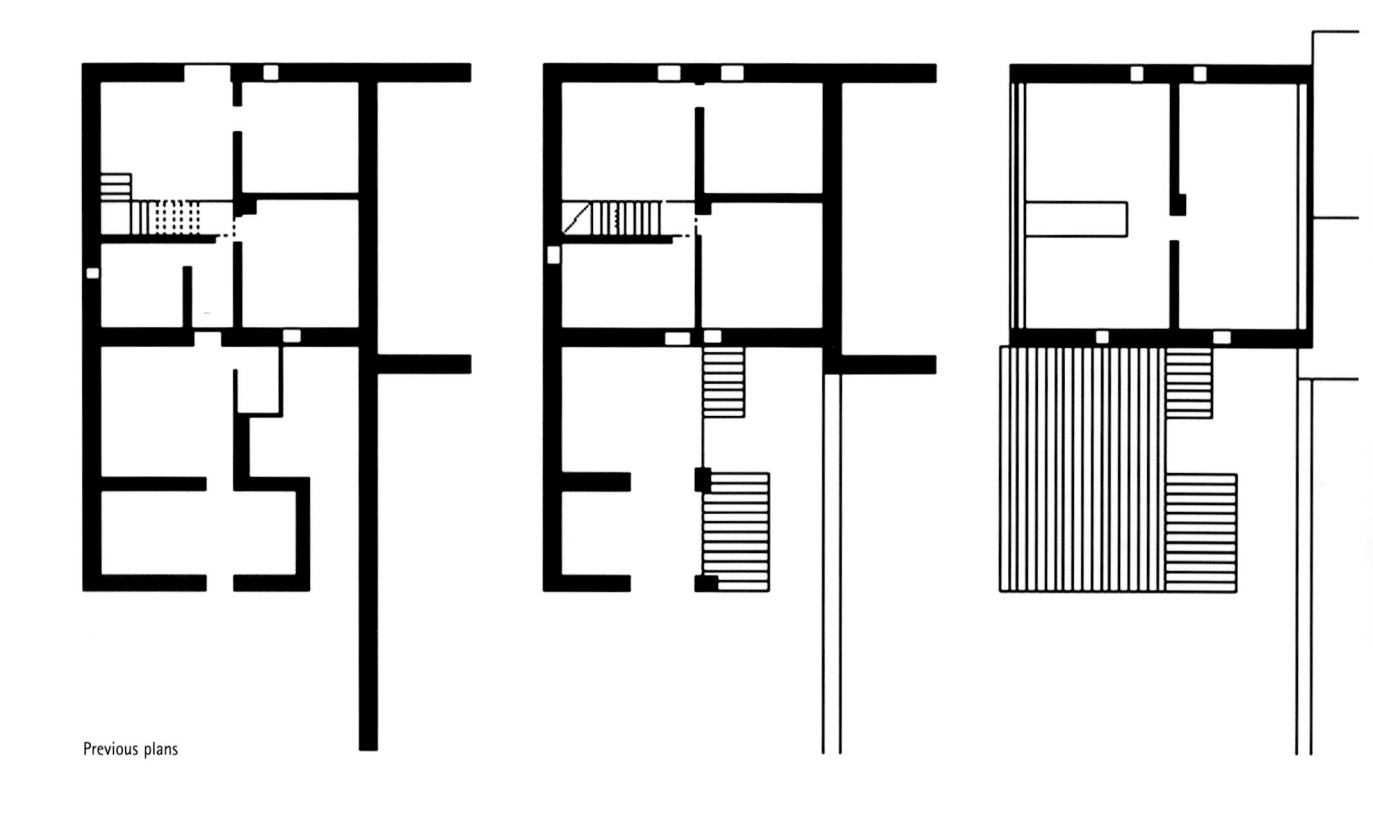

Previous plans

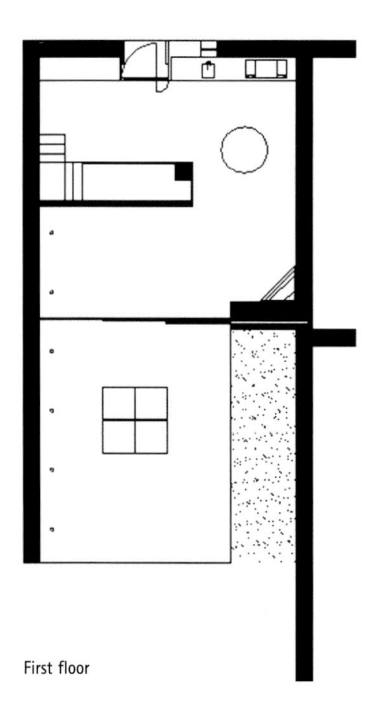

First floor

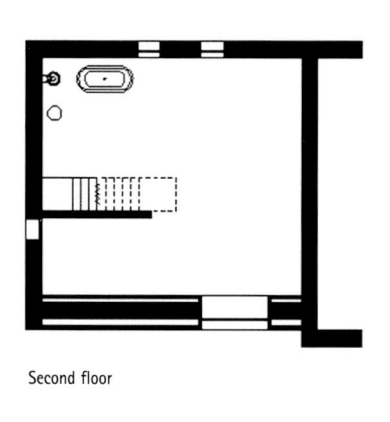

Second floor

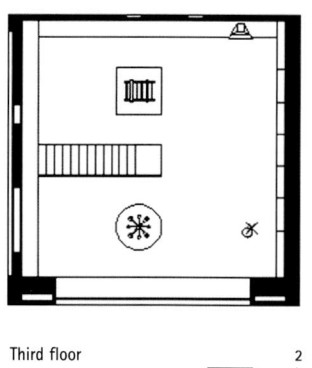

Third floor

120 Studio House in Montseny

Studio House in Montseny

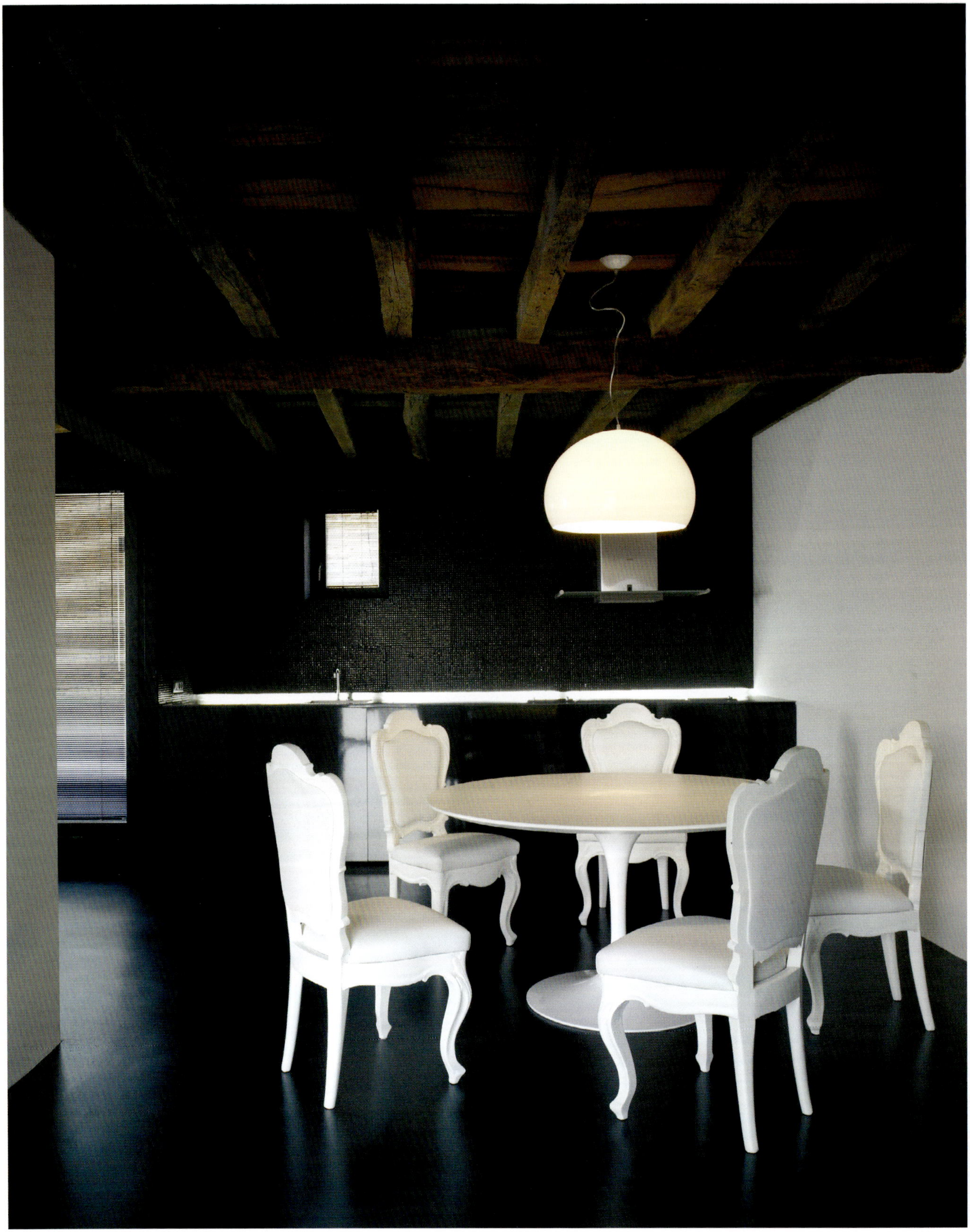

In the open kitchen the old beams or the original sink form a counterpoint to the contemporary elements such as the glazed surfacing of the wall or the stainless steel countertop.

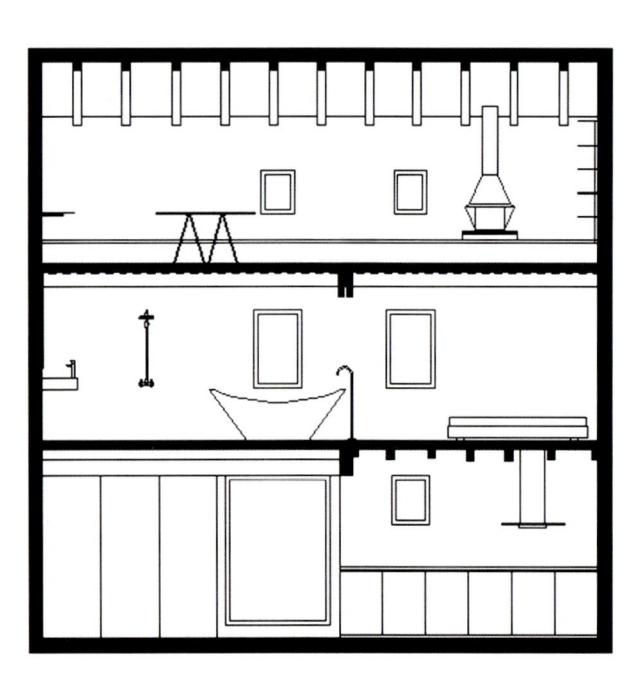

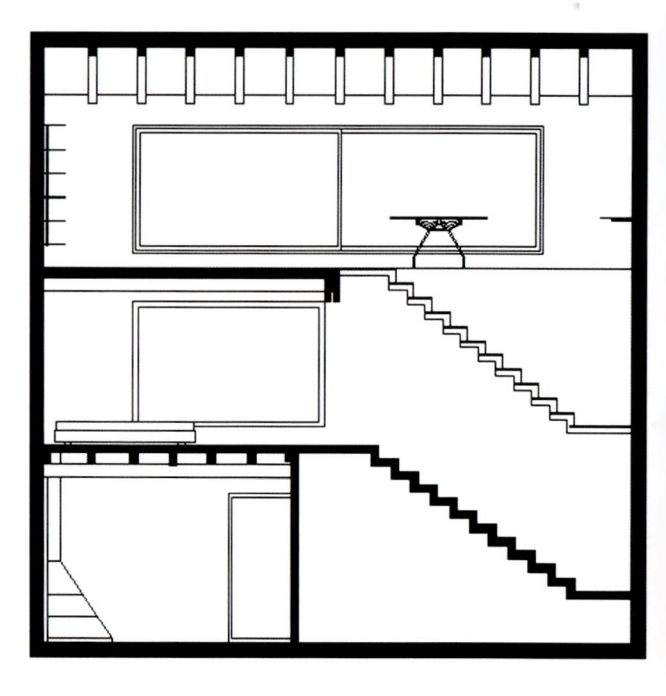

Longitudinal sections

124 Studio House in Montseny

Studio House in Montseny

This project respects and highlights the austere arrangement of a traditional rural building of the Lombardia region, close to Lake Varese. The architects created new links with the different spaces and reconsidered the relation between the porch and the overlapping exterior gallery with the rest of the house.

House in Lombardia

Architects: Studio Blumer
Photographer © Andrea Martiradonna
Location: Casciago, Italy
Completion date: 2003

Both the roof and the loft were severely deteriorated and were reconstructed and restored so as to be able to recover the three levels that existed beneath the tiled roof. These establish their own relationship with the exterior through the porch and the arched gallery that overlaps parallel to this.

In the porch, a large window covers the lights of the arches of the shorter façade, creating a visually open space in the courtyard. In the upper gallery, between the courtyard and the old straw loft, the arcade has been left open. In the same way that the façade has highlighted the importance of the arches, in the interior the different levels have been connected by way of a key element, this time a newly constructed one. A stone ramp, which starts in the hallway, rises to the upper floor, where it becomes a complex and linear structure. Lined with arches it follows an elliptical line and via radial beams becomes a point of support for the floor where the studio is located. This framework is also the supporting mesh for the glass box that is inserted diagonally in the vertex of the gallery. As well as joining the two wings of the building, this structure reaffirms its autonomy regarding the original aspects by connecting different conflicting elements. Rather than imposing on the existing harmony it unites the house through a chromatic contrast of the wood with the neutral tones of the walls and the green-grayish resin floor.

128 House in Lombardia

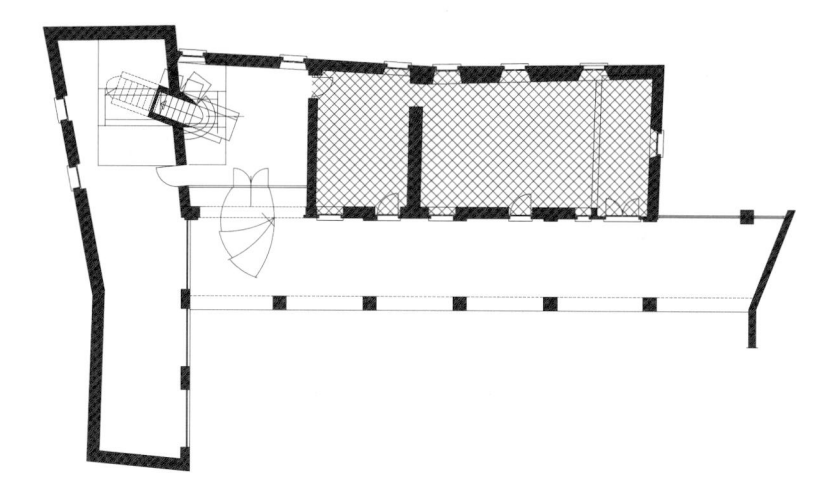

First floor

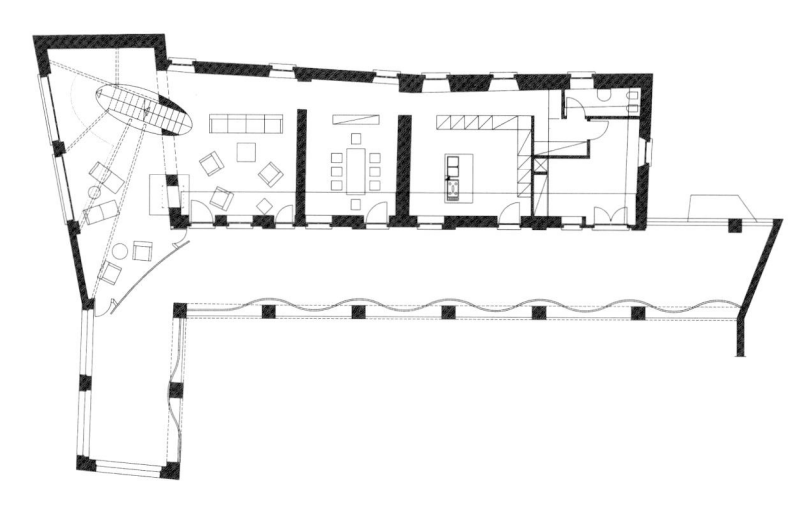

Second floor

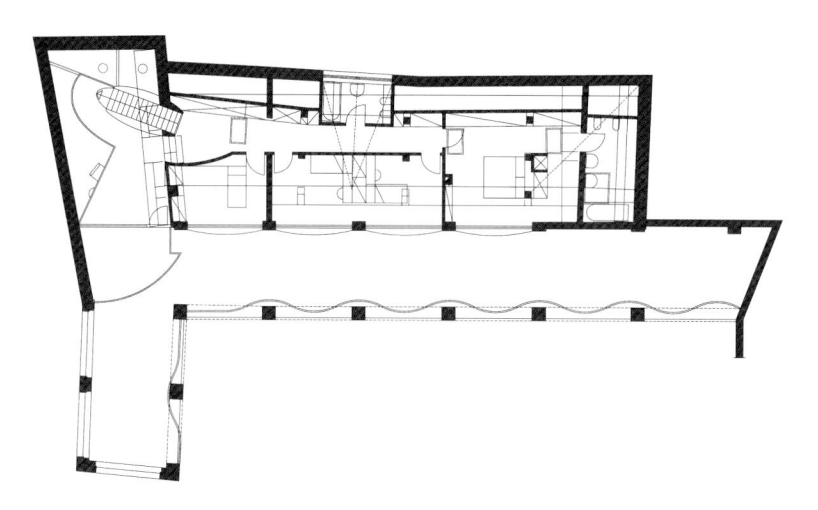

Attic

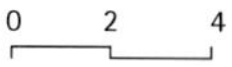

0 2 4

House in Lombardia 129

130 House in Lombardia

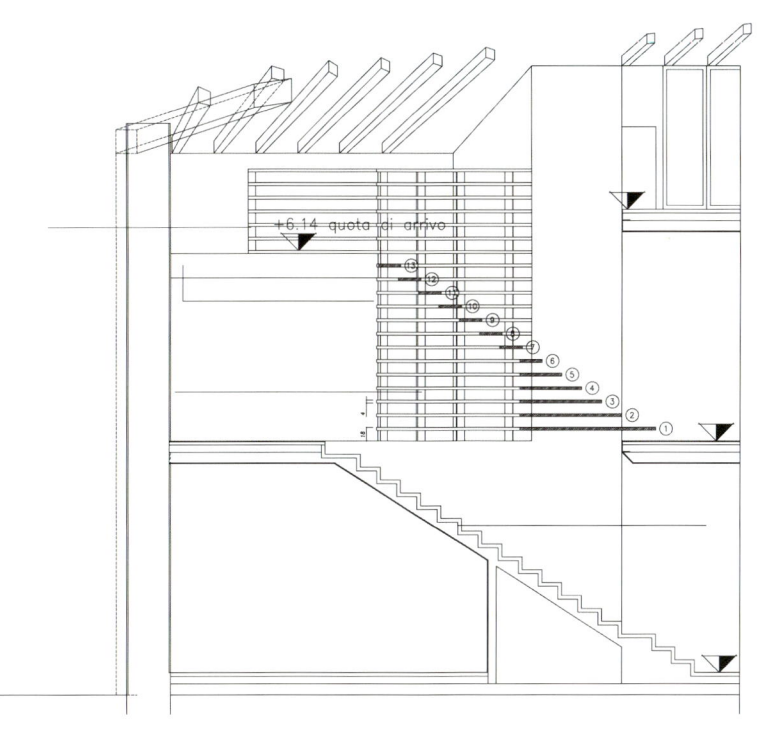

Detail of the stairs

House in Lombardia 131

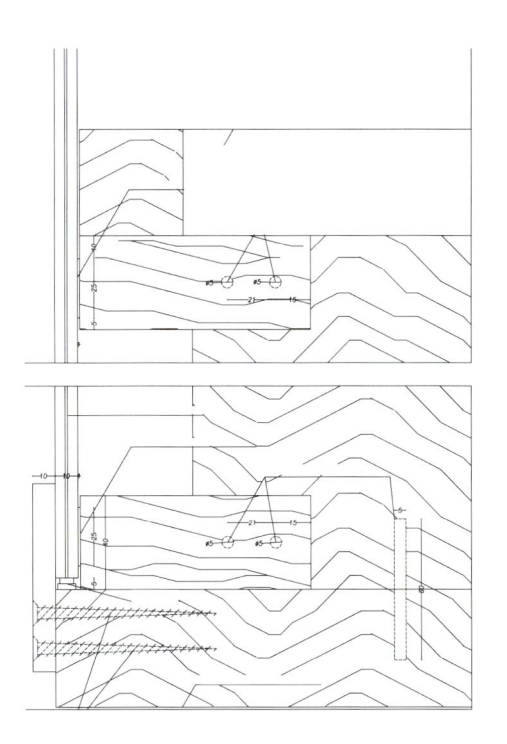

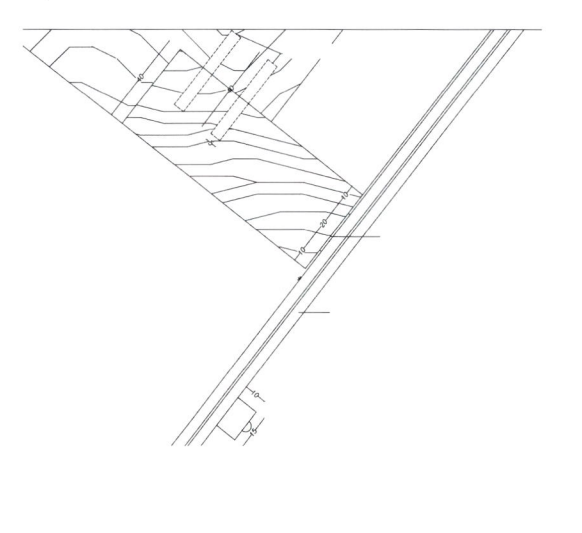

Details of the windows

Thanks to the original concept of the stairs, whose steps seem to float, the different levels are joined in such a way that the light travels unobstructed through the house.

134 House in Lombardia

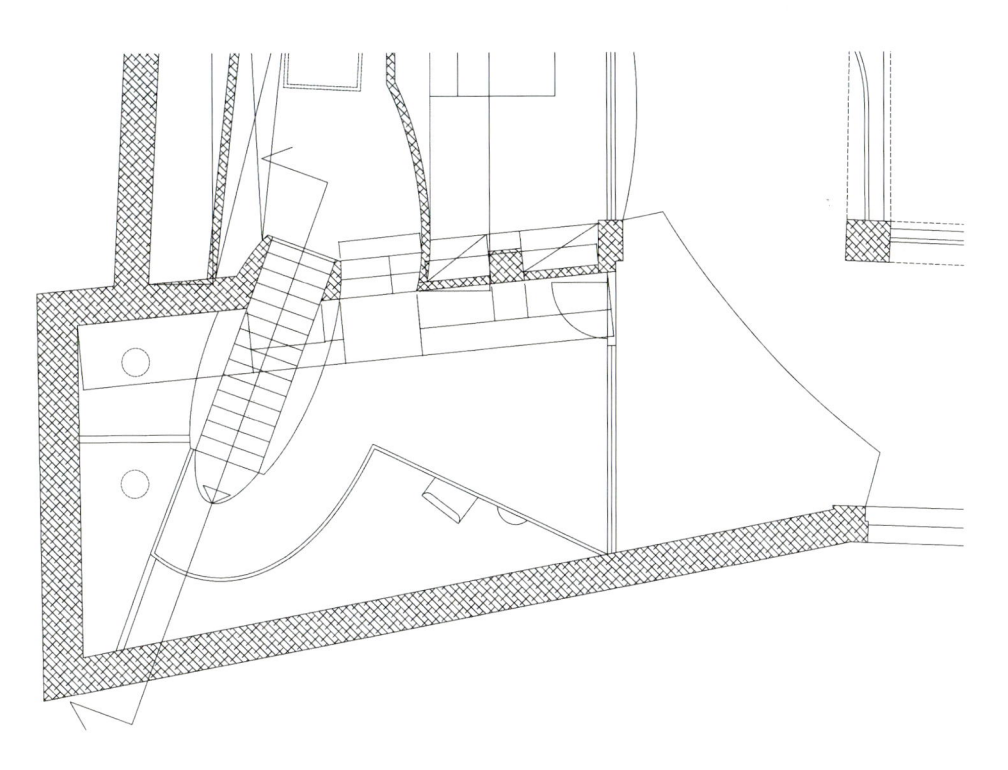

Detail of the attic stairs

Situated in the heart of the mountainous region of Styria, in the southeast of Austria and a few miles from the Slovenian border, this farm has been through a major transformation with the aim of improving it as a home and to implement its function as farm storage.

Farm in the Austrian Alps

Architect: Peter Zinganel
Photographer © Paul Ott
Location: Hart bei Graz, Austria
Completion date: 2004

The construction consisted of a stable located in front of the main south-facing house, a farm garage and a barn, distributed about a central courtyard.

In the main house two small family units were created, whose open plan feel was achieved through an opening in the flooring of the second floor. This means the living areas are double height. The interior staircase was redesigned and rebuilt, parallel to the central load-bearing wall, and interior and exterior openings were created to bring light to this part of the house. The work area on the top floor is also an open space. The extension of the terrace, which has been covered by a wooden lattice for creeper plants, affords space and clarity. Part of the exterior wall was replaced by large windows.

The old wooden cladding was removed from the exterior and the volumetry was restructured to open new light entries and provide the façade with greater clarity. The old garage was converted into agricultural storage with a cold store. The cellar located beneath the house was divided in two to house a dry area to protect the harvest from damp. The central courtyard was restructured and a part of the land was prepared for its possible use to grow fruit and vegetables. A rainwater collector was also built for agricultural and industrial use.

These pages show the transformation of the house's exterior and the extension of the terrace, which acquires great importance for the volumes conceived throughout the restorative process.

Farm in the Austrian Alps 139

Situation plan

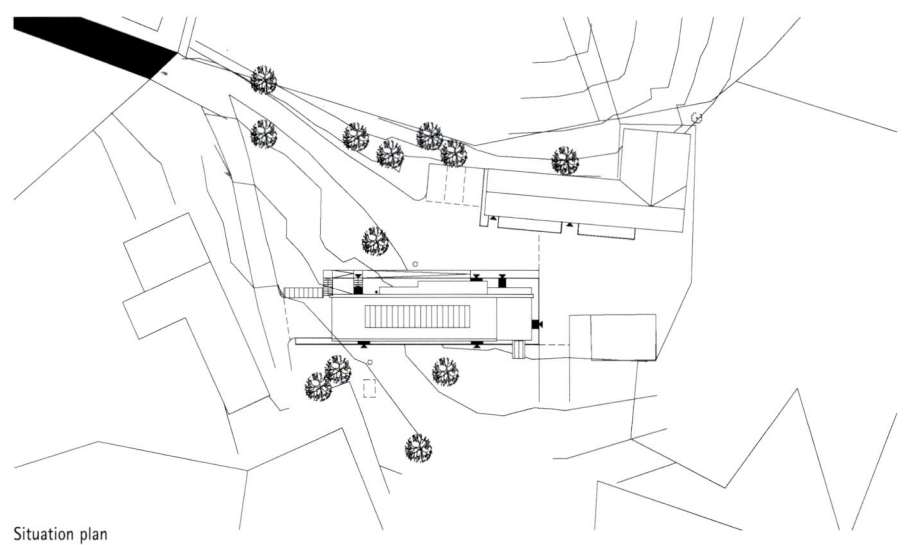

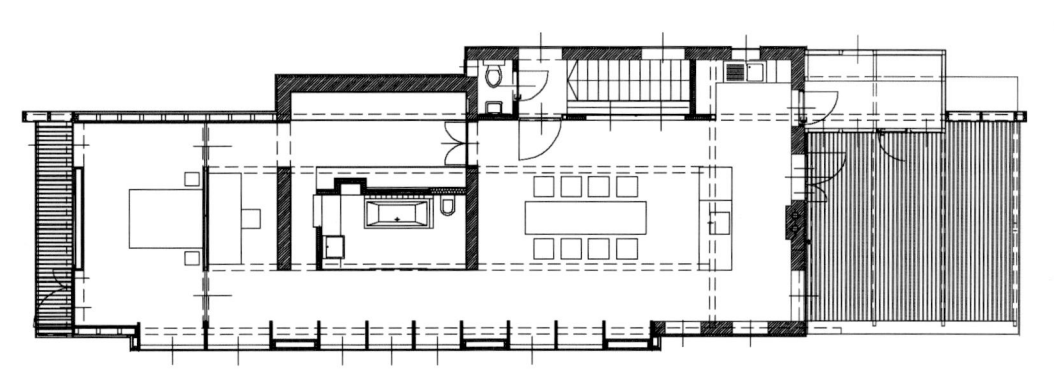

First floor

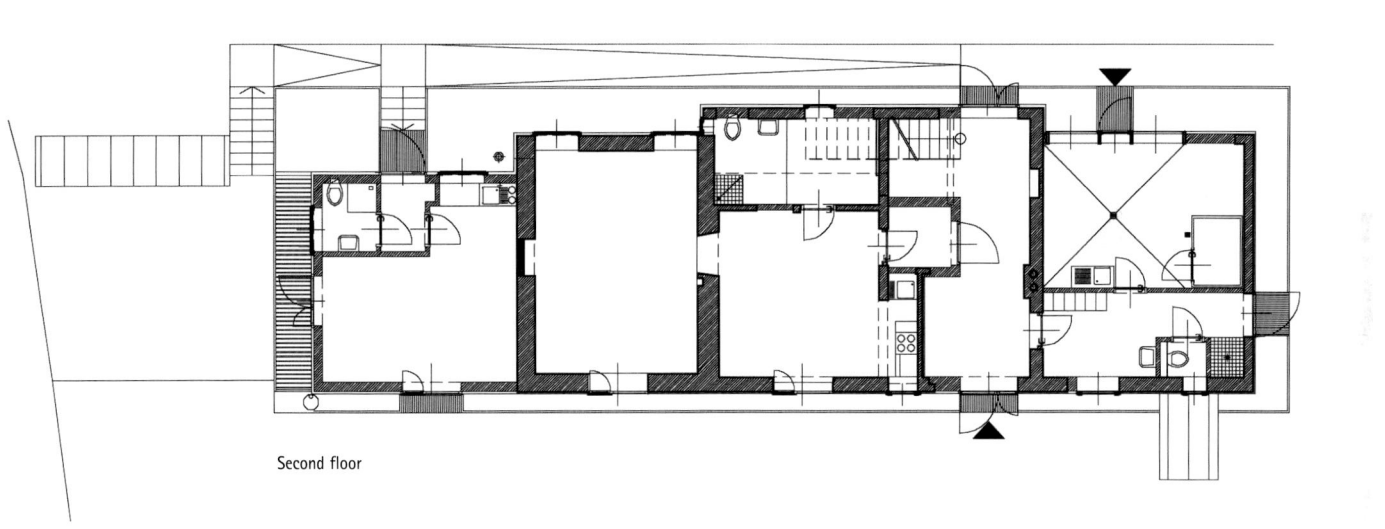

Second floor

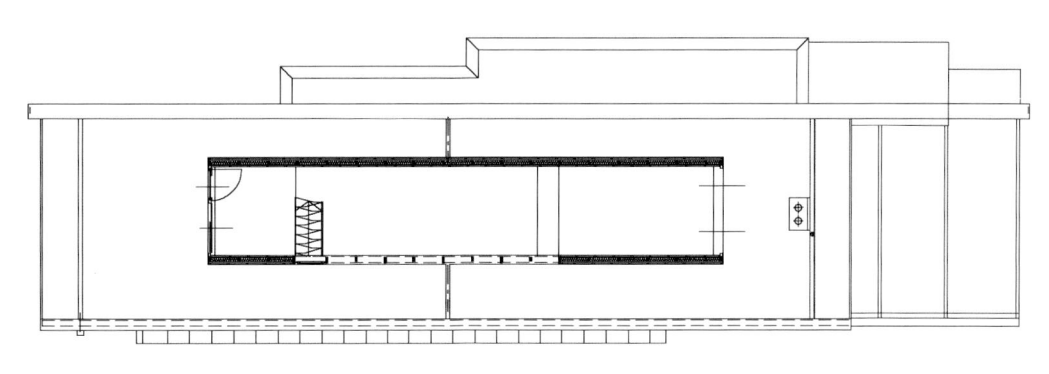

Roof

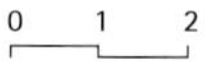

0 1 2

Farm in the Austrian Alps 141

Left side elevation

Front elevation

142 Farm in the Austrian Alps

Transversal sections

Farm in the Austrian Alps 143

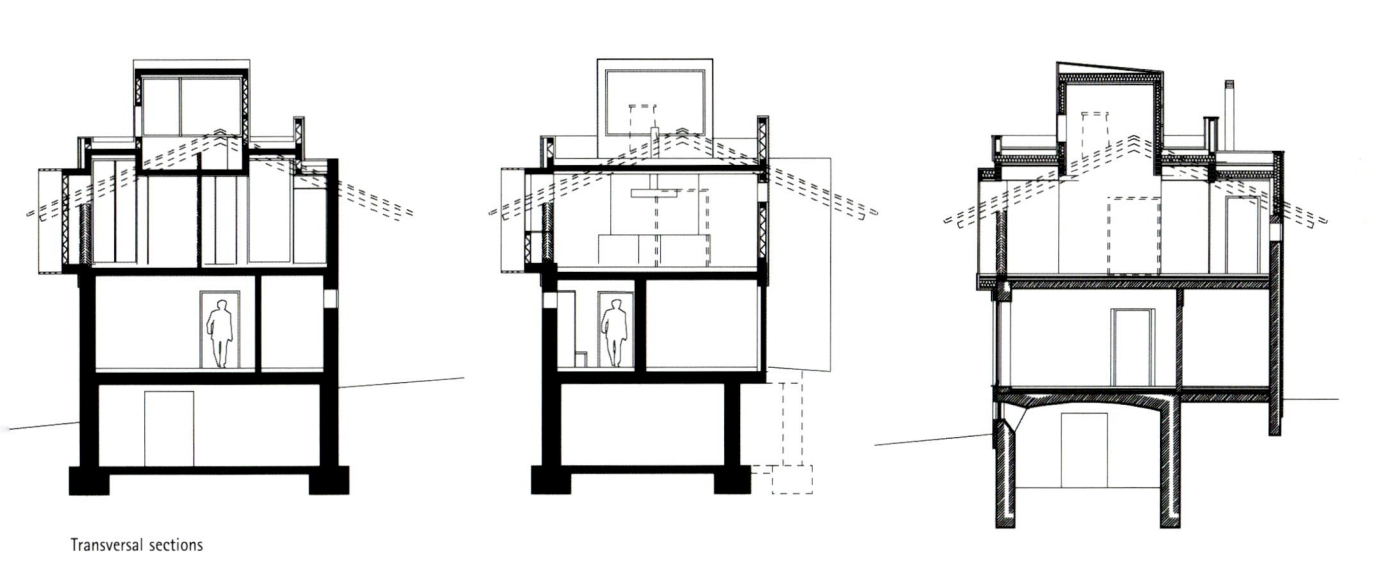

144 Farm in the Austrian Alps

Farm in the Austrian Alps 145

In a pine forest on the island of Formentera, a small, single-story house and farmyard have been transformed into a contemporary, open-plan space, which integrates perfectly with its surroundings.

Can Pujoleta

Architect: Víctor Beltran
Photographer © Lourdes Grivé
Location: Formentera, Spain
Completion date: 2006

This construction is situated in the middle of a small pine forest, typical of the western Mediterranean coastline. It is composed of a small house with a rectangular floor plan and farmyards. The intervention consisted in annexing the farmyards to the house and increasing the vertical surface area via the construction of a second floor on top of one of the volumes. The restoration included the adjustment of the orientation of the main axis in accordance with the inclination of the land and the plot's rectangular shape. The existing construction and the new annex are connected via a hallway, an accordion style piece that joins the entire home and has been designed as an empty circulation space.

In the house, the lounge has openings in the two opposite walls, offering views in the summer and making the most of the sunlight in the winter. The bedrooms, distributed in a two-story cubic volume, form the second body that constitutes a vertical counterpoint to the composition. The entire building has been carried out within a perimeter, with no intervention outside of this. The surrounding forest therefore wraps around the house without the interruption of a garden. A wall extends towards the access visually organizing the different elements and orienting the visitor.

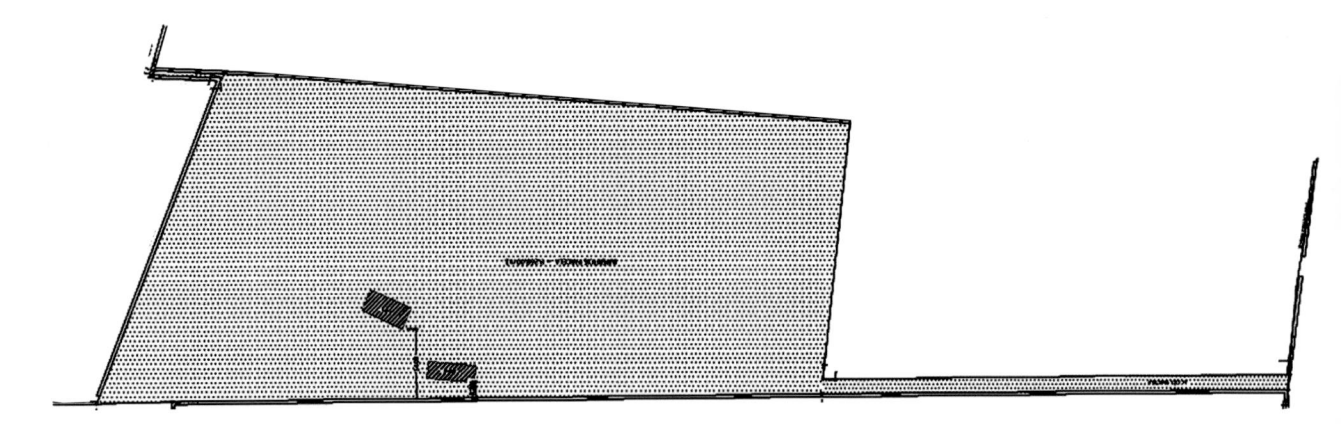

Plan of previous situation

Plan of new situation

148 Can Pujoleta

The structure of the main door, which filters the sunlight, provides a cool, shady space inside the hallway.

Second floor

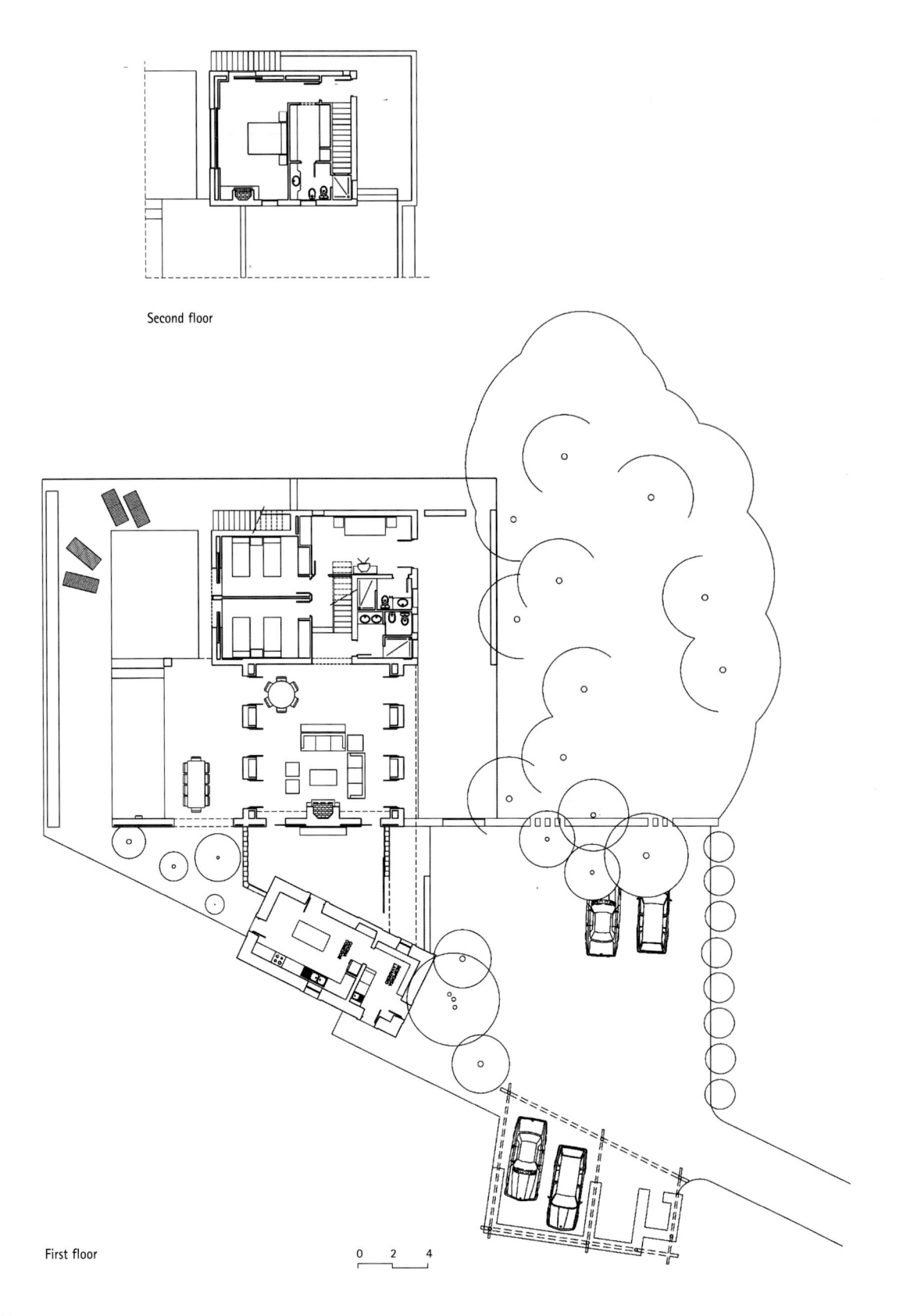

First floor 0 2 4

150 Can Pujoleta

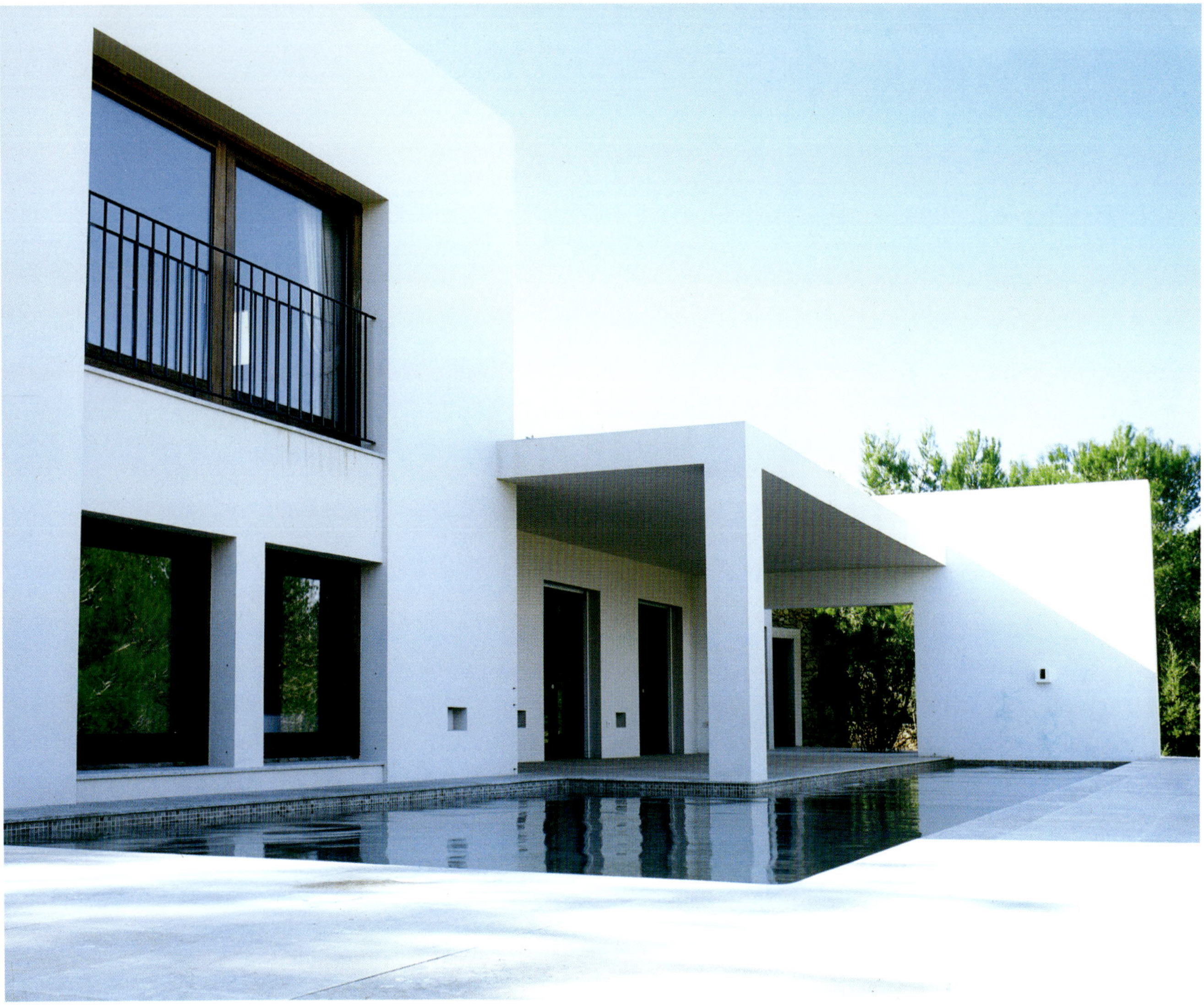

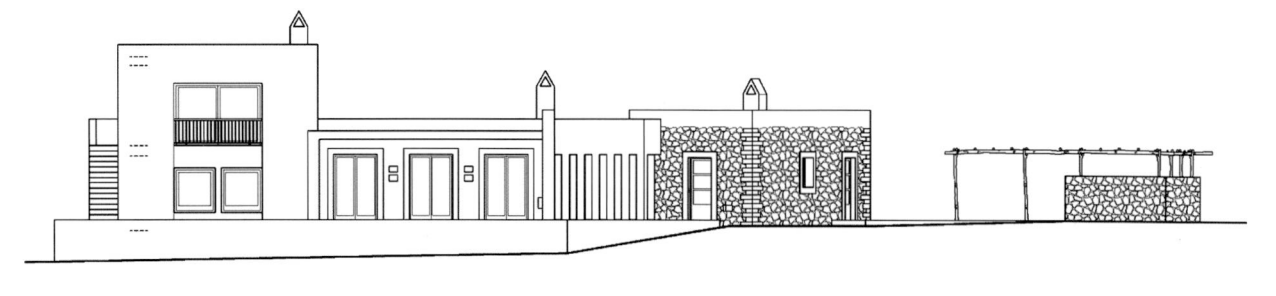

Front elevation

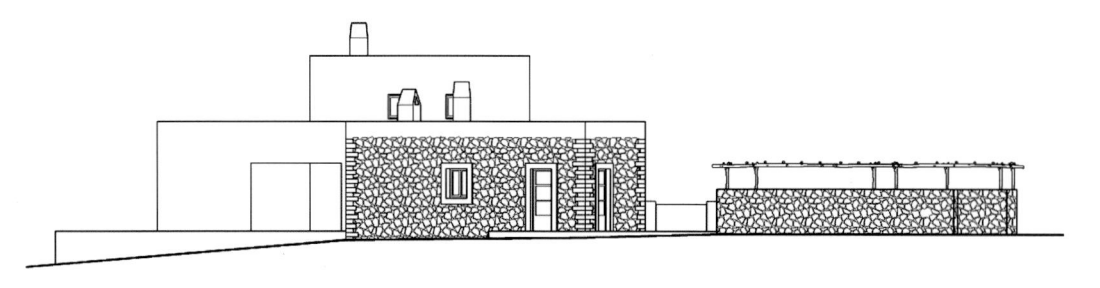

Right side elevation

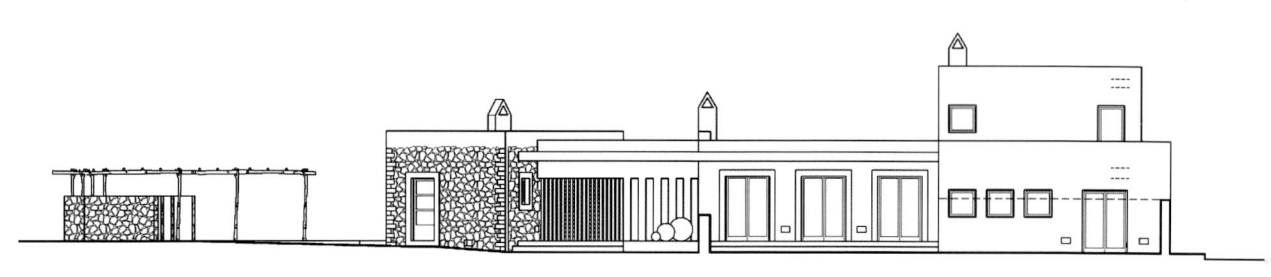

Rear elevation

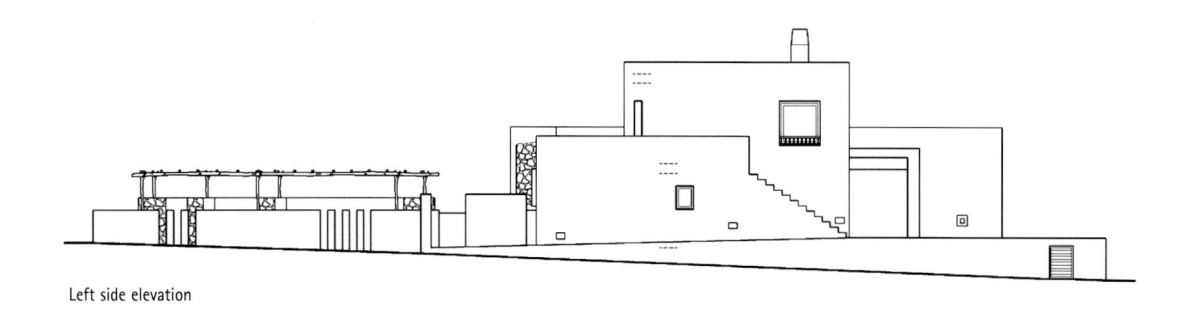

Left side elevation

Can Pujoleta 153

Left side section

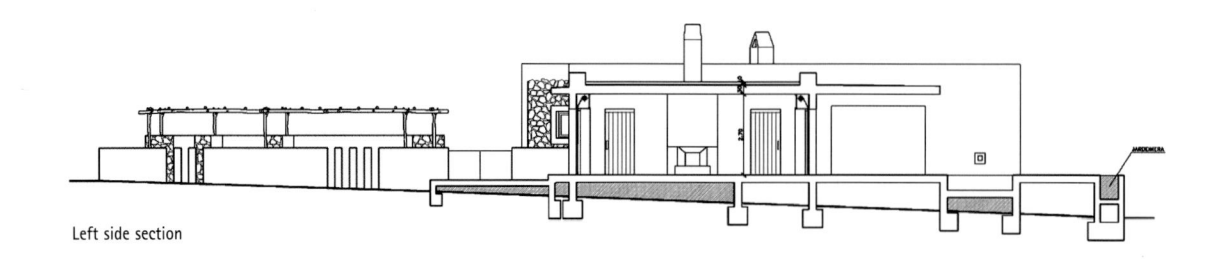

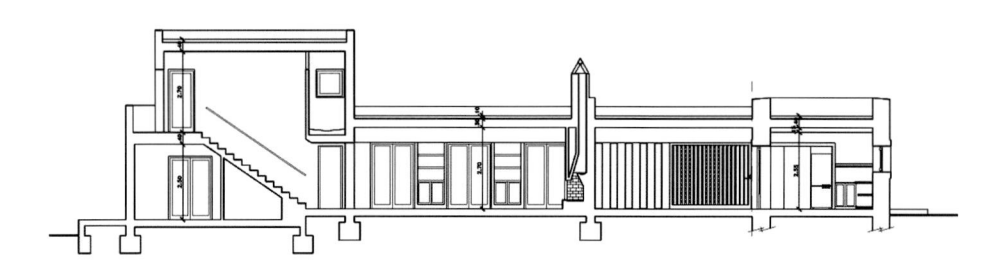

Front section

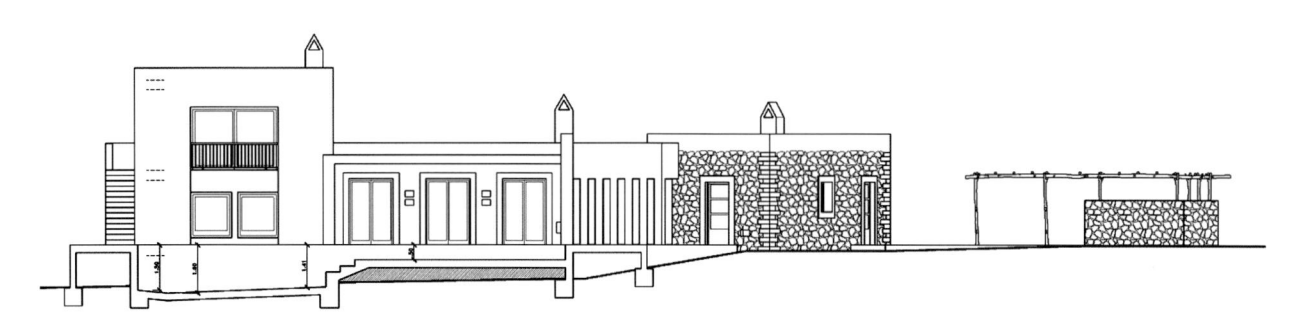

Swimming pool section

The contemporary and the traditional form a dynamic combination. In the hallway, framed by the innovative façade with vertical openings, is a pedestal on which an old woodcarving welcomes the visitor.

This house is located in Nossa Senhora da Guía, in an area dedicated to the cultivation of the albariño grape, to produce the prestigious Vinho verde. The restoration sought to preserve the structural elements and enhance the finishes with natural materials from the region.

Holiday Home on the Costa Verde

Architects: Francisco Portugal e Gomes
Photographers © Luís Ferreira Alves,
Luís Oliveira Santos, Jorge Garcia Pereira
Location: Peñafiel, Portugal
Completion date: 2005

The land is located to the north of the city of Peñafiel, close to the Nossa Senhora da Guía chapel. The house stands on a small hill that constitutes the highest part of the farm. The existing structure is composed of granite, the area's dominant material, and is formed by two volumes situated next to a central core, which used to form a single building. The building had severely deteriorated and a small construction annexed to the house had to be demolished. From the outset it was decided to keep within the building's existing boundaries and not to carry out any kind of extension, while respecting the geometry of the floor plans and tiled roofs. The interior was projected from a vigorous complementary structure, designed to structurally add the different volumes so as to integrate the whole project. This offered the possibility of creating a large central interior courtyard, defined by the shadows projected from the sloping roofs.

The restorative project was extended at a later date to include interventions on the walls, the design of an exterior access staircase, the recovery of the granite floor, the construction of a slate overhang and new wooden panels to cover the openings to the exterior.

Situation plan

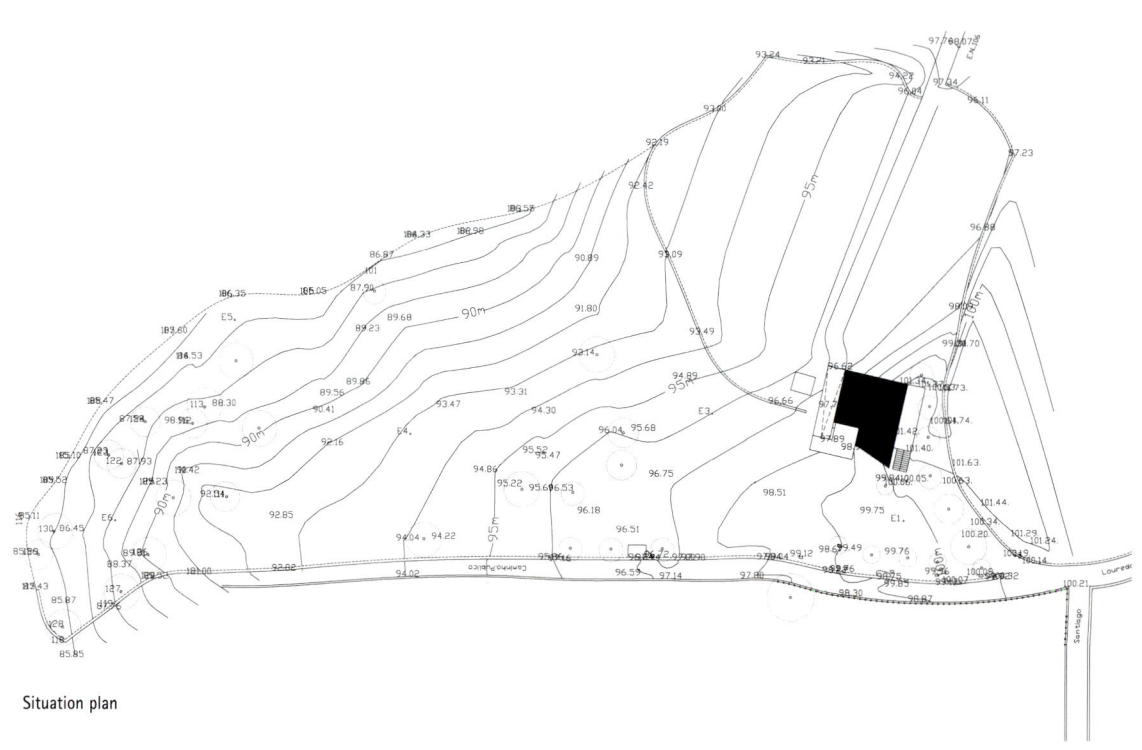

158 Holiday Home on the Costa Verde

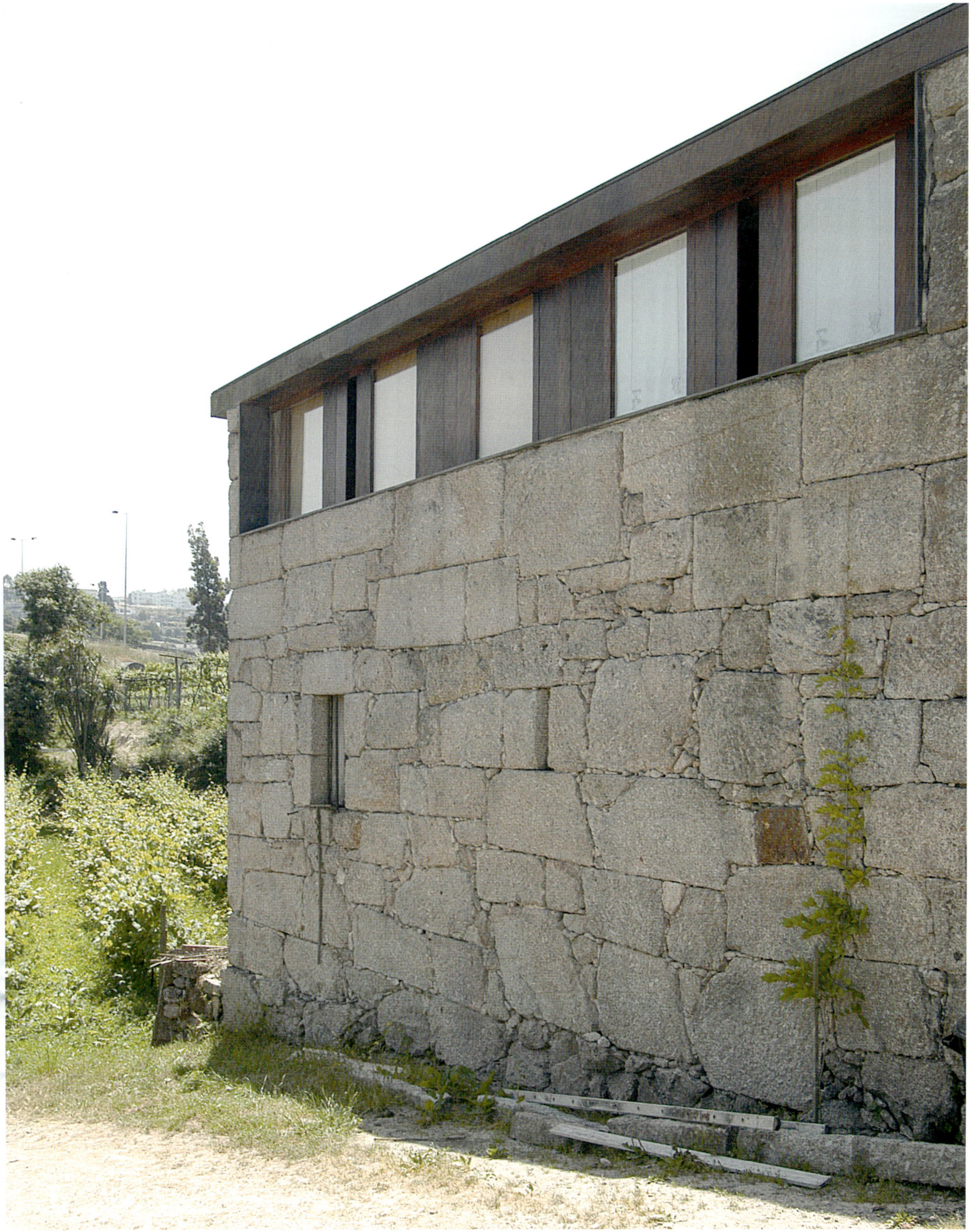

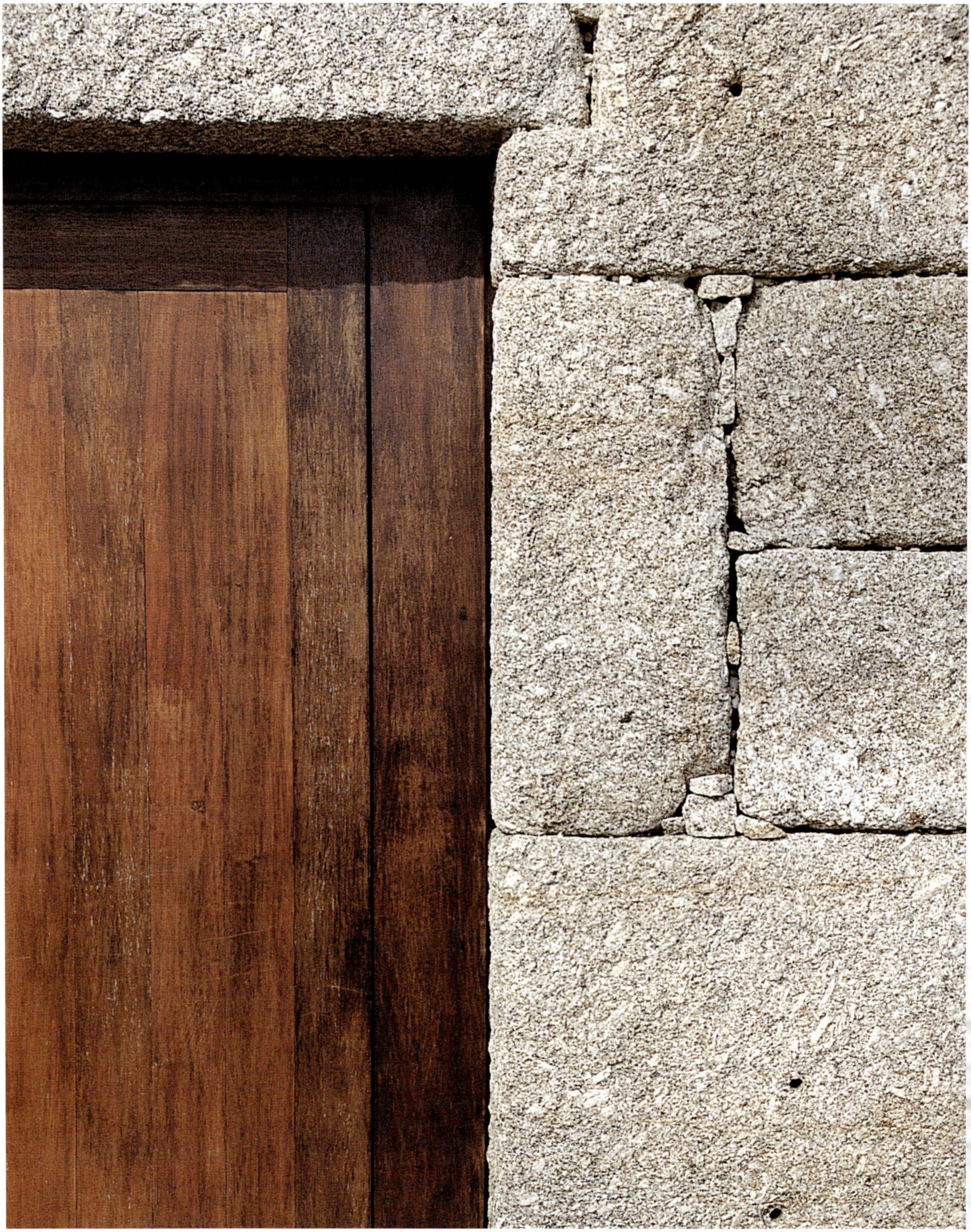

Holiday Home on the Costa Verde

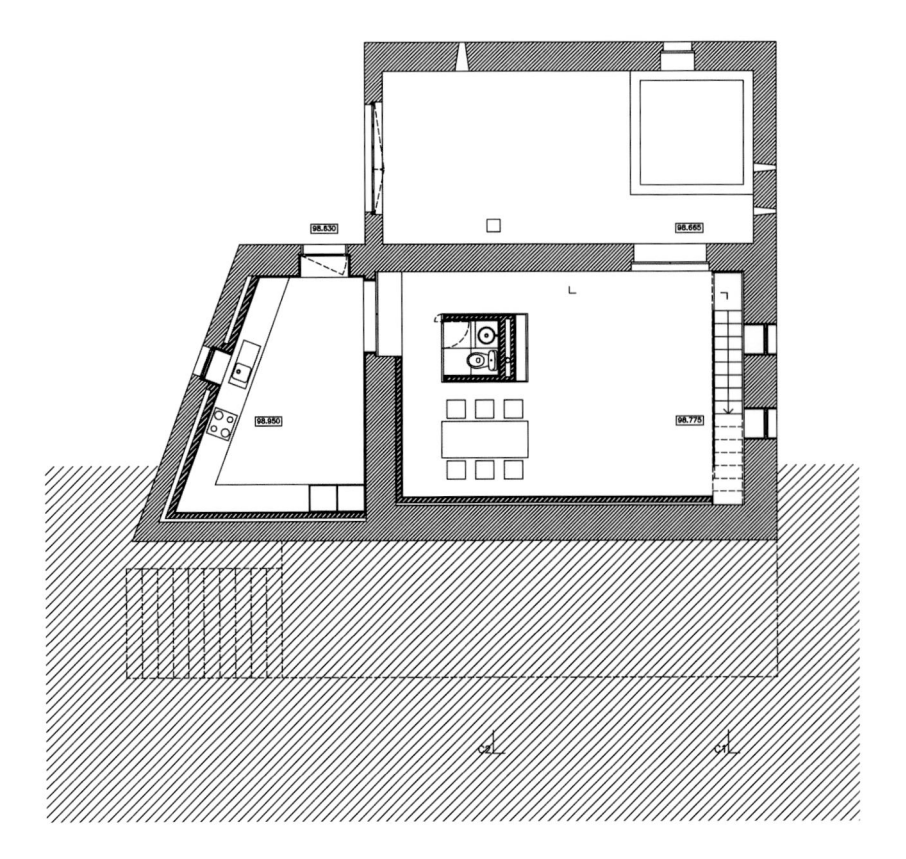

First floor

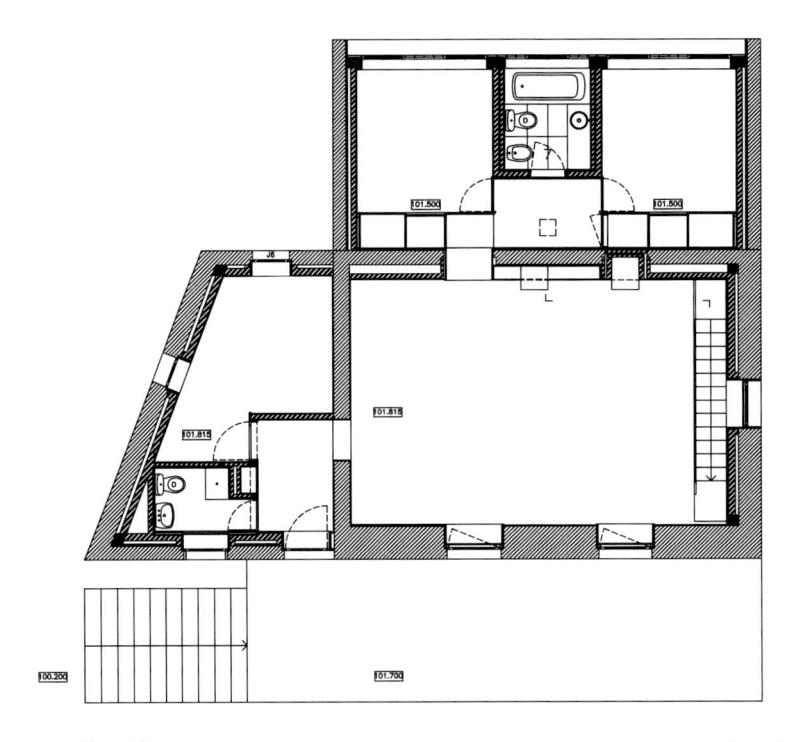

Second floor

0 1 2

162 Holiday Home on the Costa Verde

In contrast to the surroundings, far from any kind of urban center, the interior of the house has sought an eminently contemporary form, opting for pure lines and smooth surfaces.

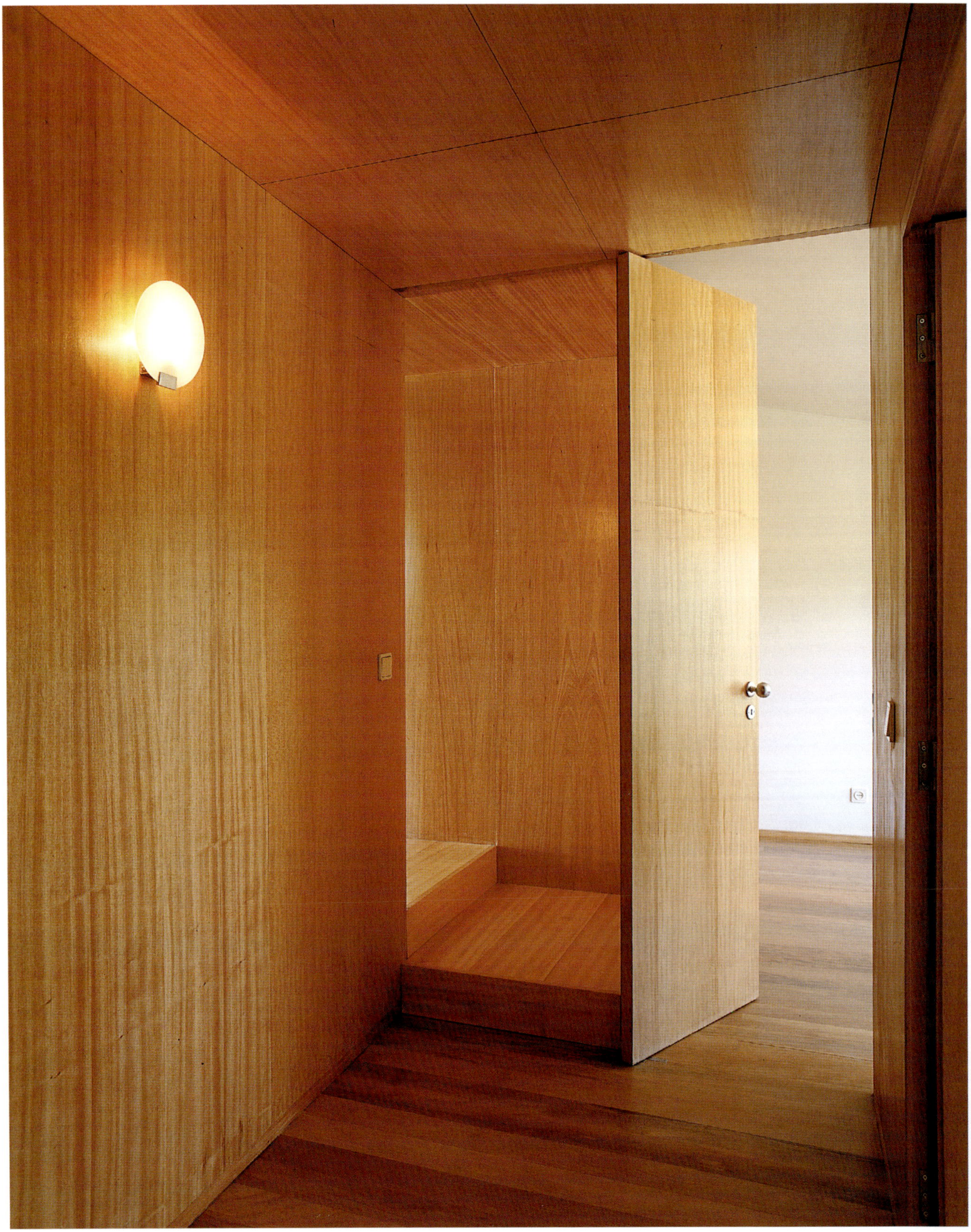

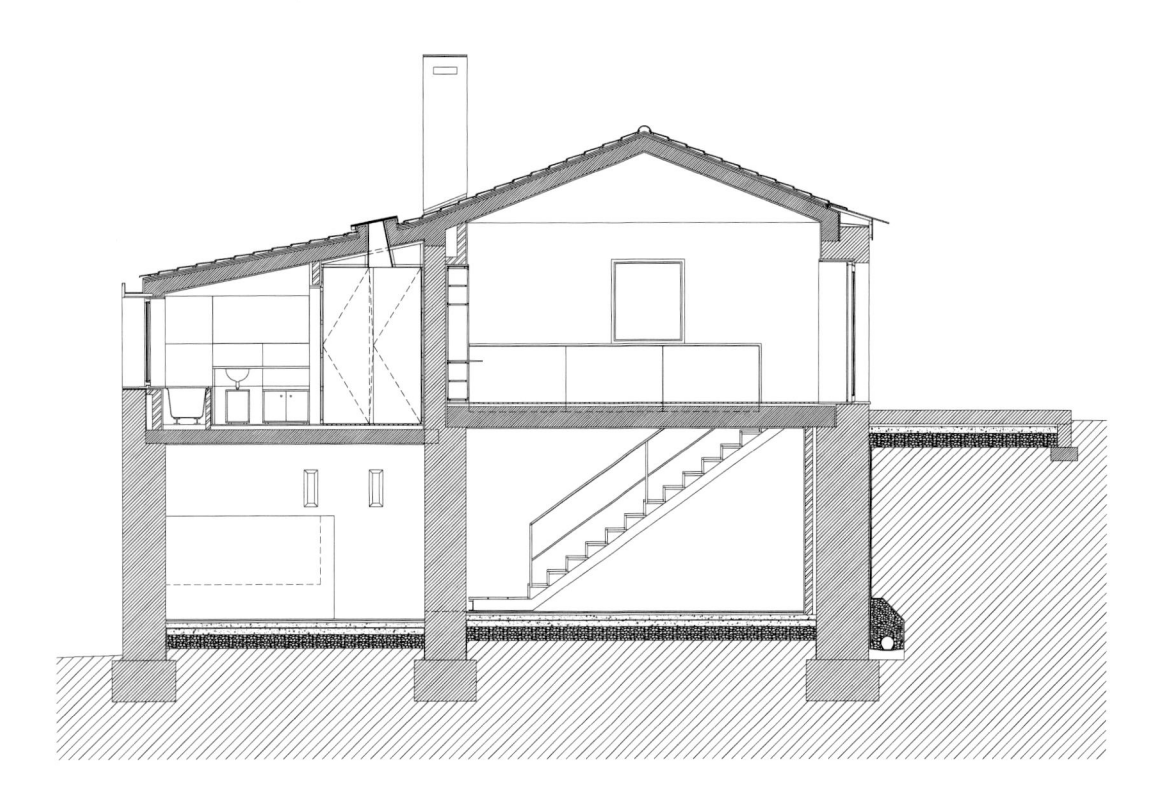

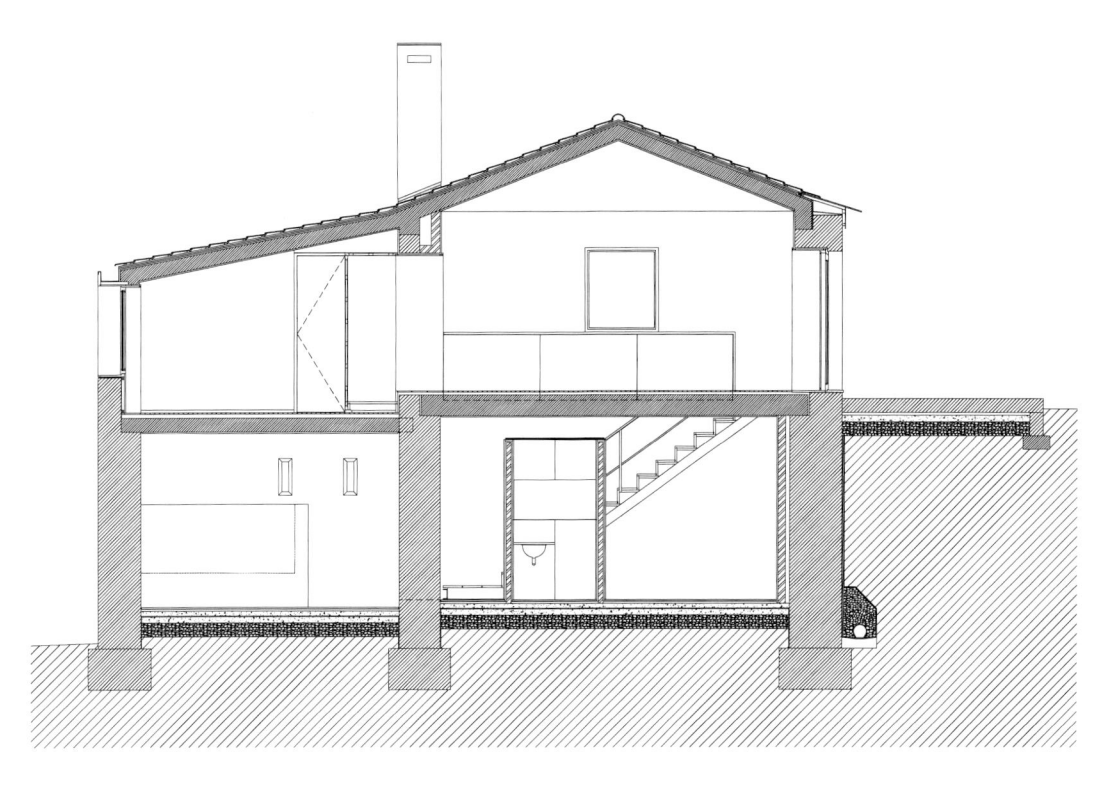

Transversal sections

A house in the small village of Veneto was subjected to a thorough restoration, which consisted in completely reorganizing the house, making the most of the space, recovering its original rural character and adapting it to be used as a home in a semi-urban setting.

House in Schio

Architects: Studio Zerbato Santacatterina
Photographer © Andrea Martiradonna
Location: Schio, Italy
Completion date: 2006

The house had been renovated in the 80s preserving the original dimensions and structures, in such a way that the separation between the areas for farm use and the home was still very much visible. A covered porch was given a tiled roof in the original center of the house. The project arose from the need to readapt the existing spaces to convert a rural house into a house for a large family. The restoration included the reorganization and extension of the house's program, a renovation of the façade and the construction of a pool. "Traditional" external elements were removed from the original volume, and the porch and the wooden fences were removed. The stone and concrete walls have been thickly whitewashed. The depth of the openings for the windows has been accentuated thanks to an increased thickness of the walls. The exterior walls have been surfaced with bronze laminates. The annex consists of a stainless steel laminated box, like the old agricultural containers, closely connected to the main house but without mixing with it. The new kitchen has been installed here, integrated with a dining area and an area for amenities in the basement. The flooring is oak, and in both houses volumes, woodwork, equipment and finishes have been custom designed.

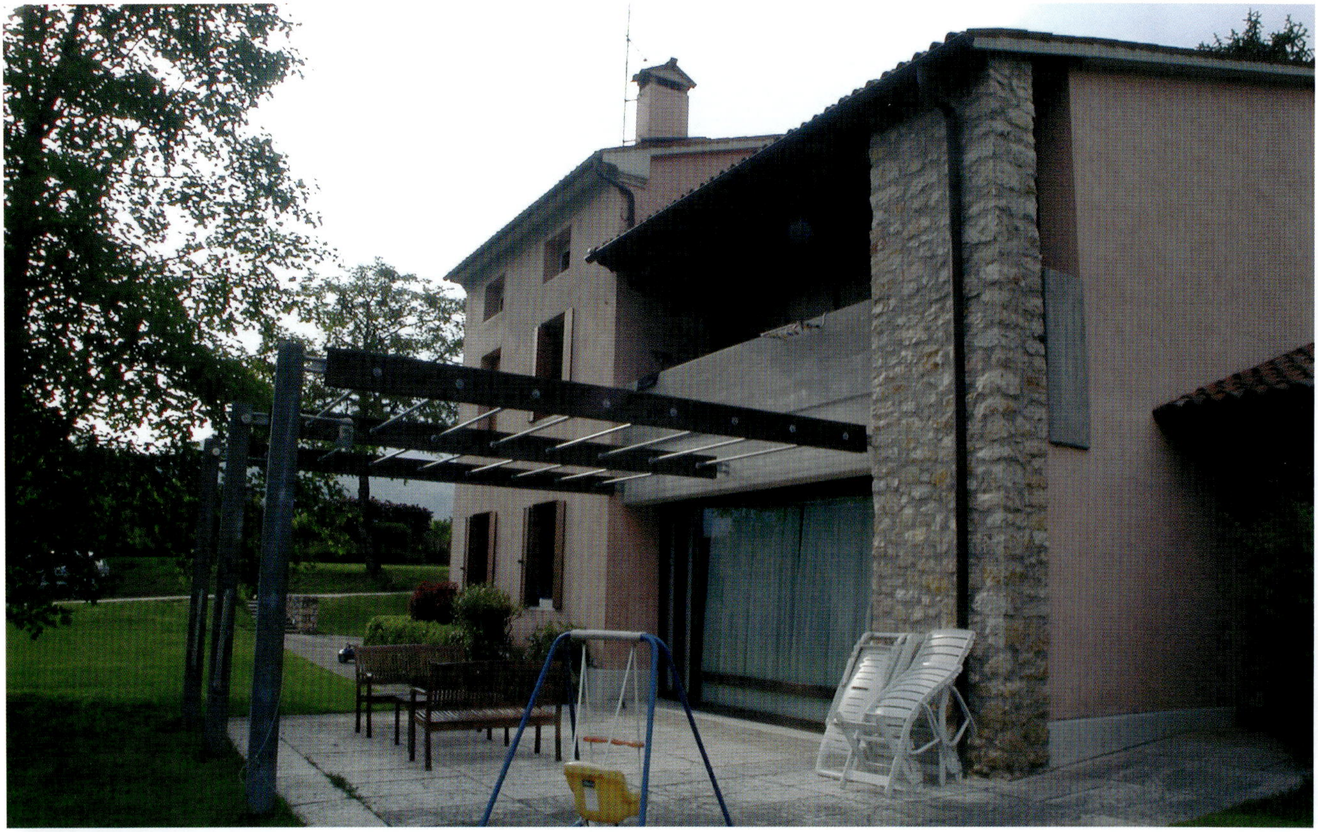

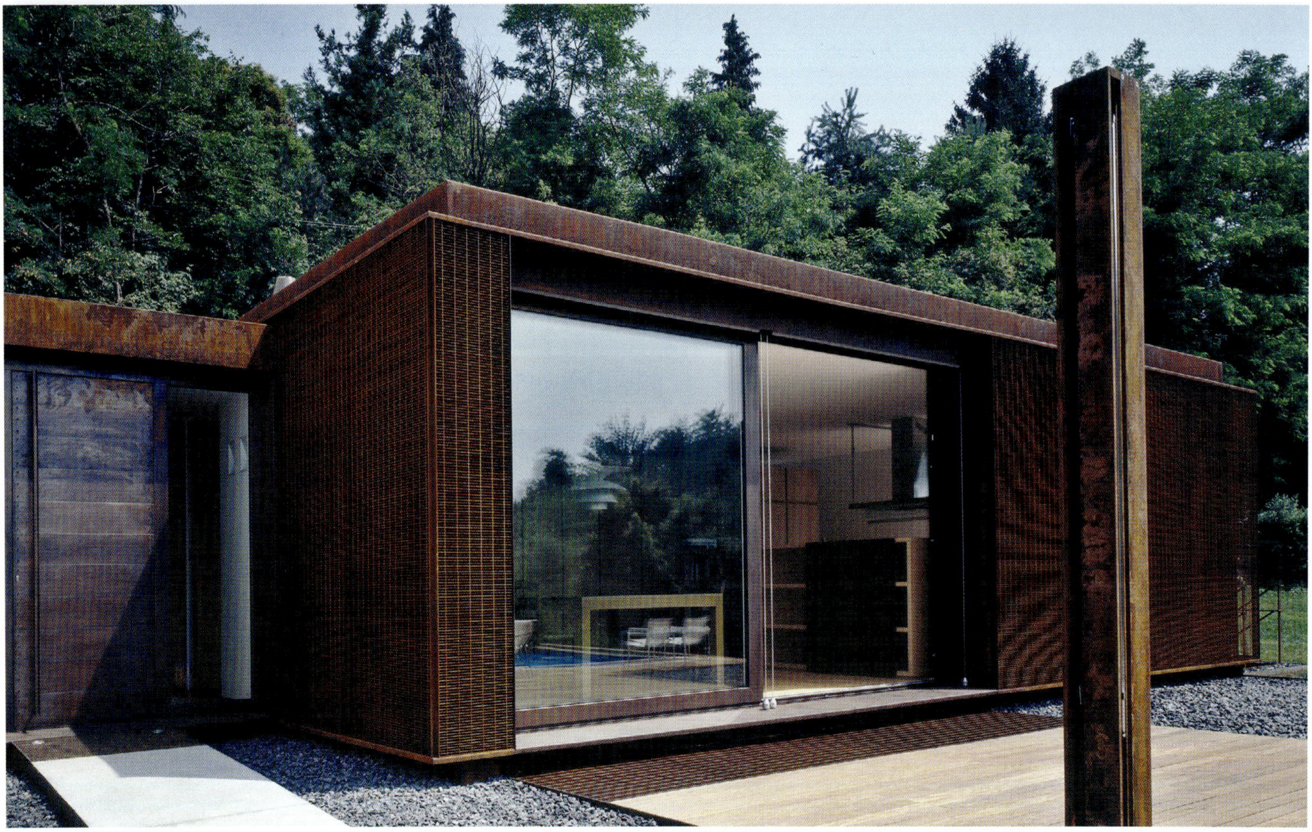

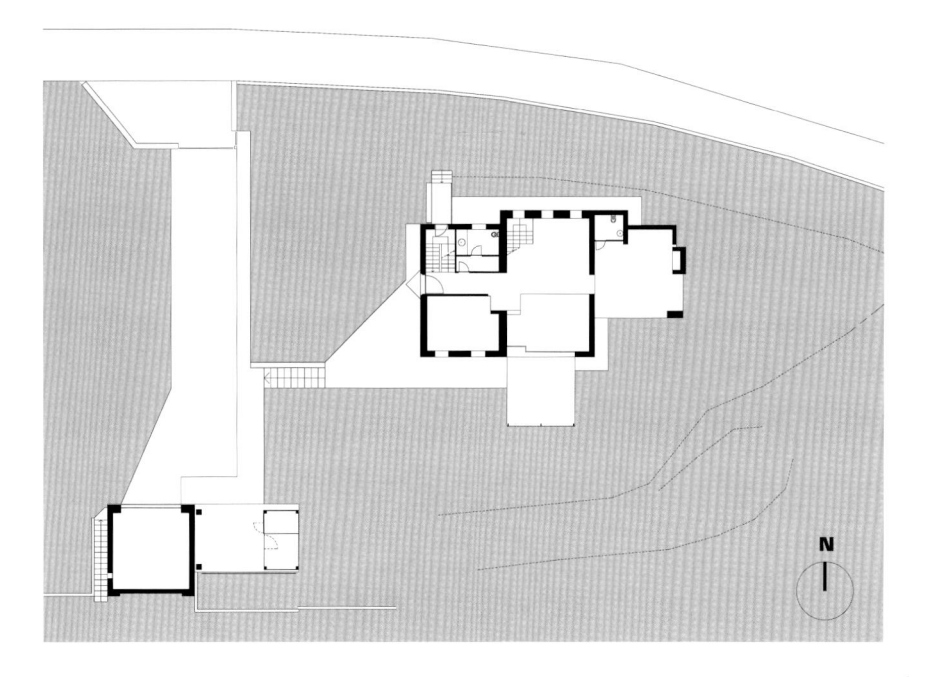

Previous plan

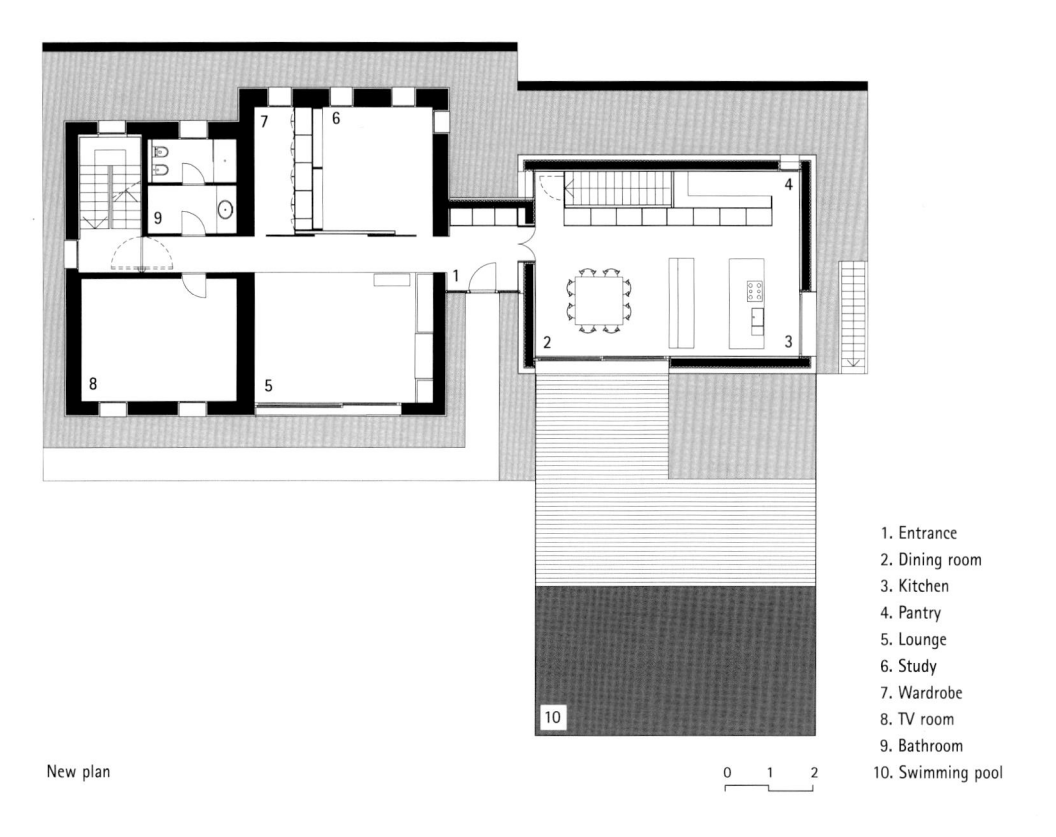

New plan

1. Entrance
2. Dining room
3. Kitchen
4. Pantry
5. Lounge
6. Study
7. Wardrobe
8. TV room
9. Bathroom
10. Swimming pool

As well as the extension of the space and the renovation of the exteriors, the project includes the reorganization of the house's internal structure.

House in Schio 171

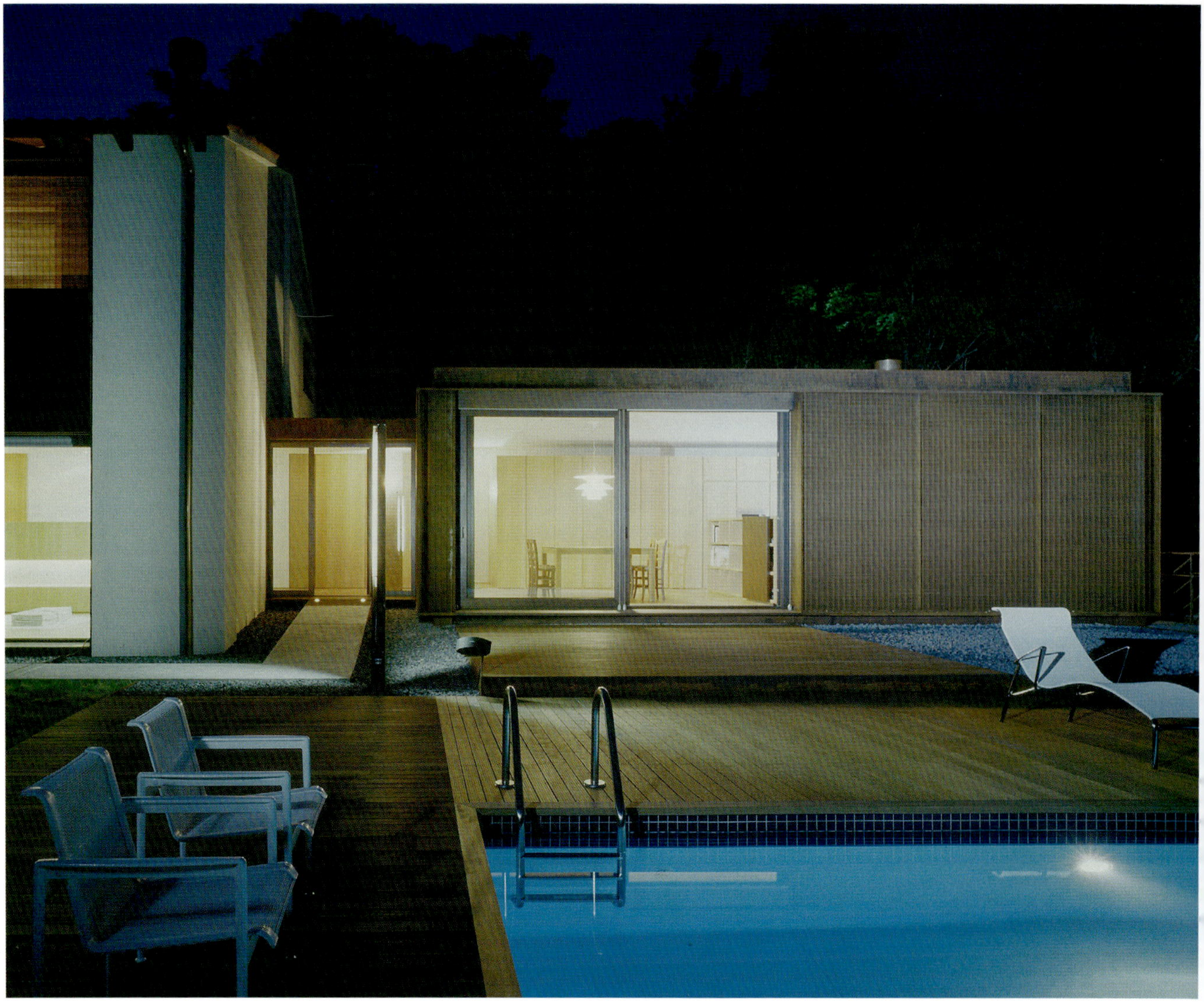

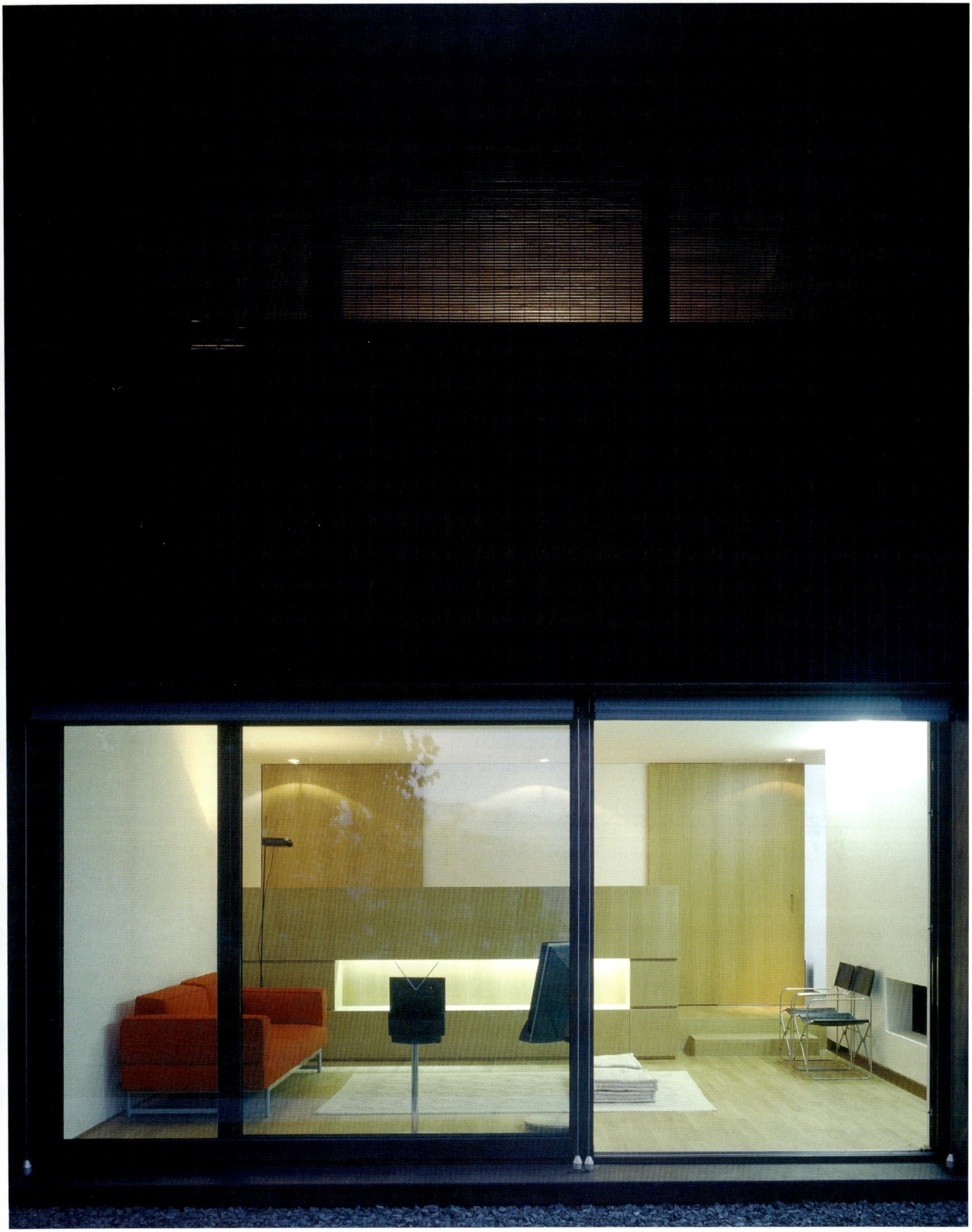

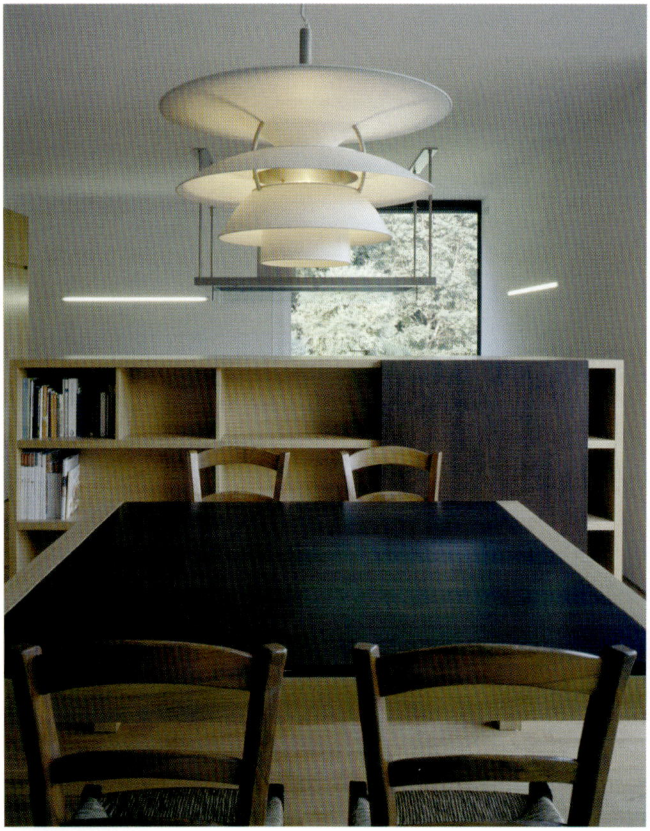
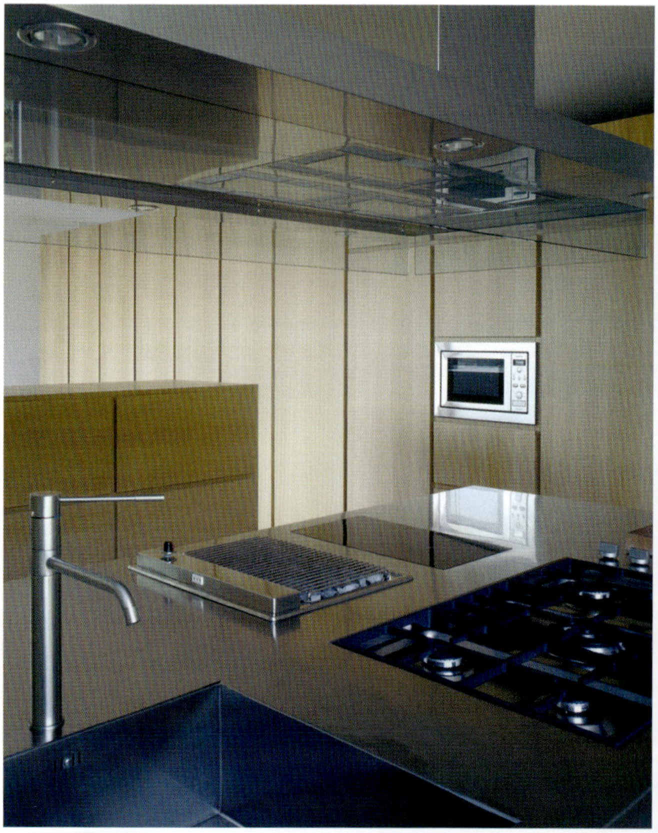
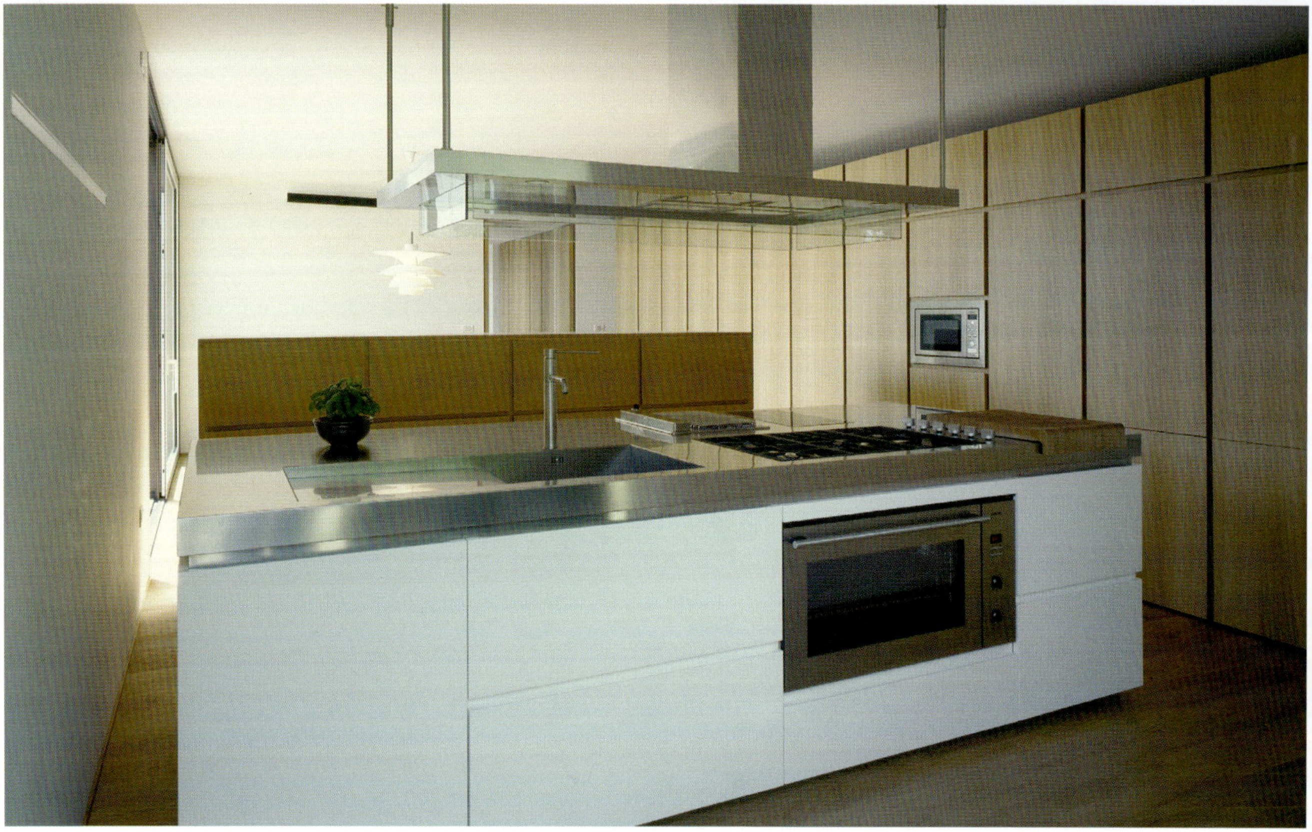

Previous south elevation

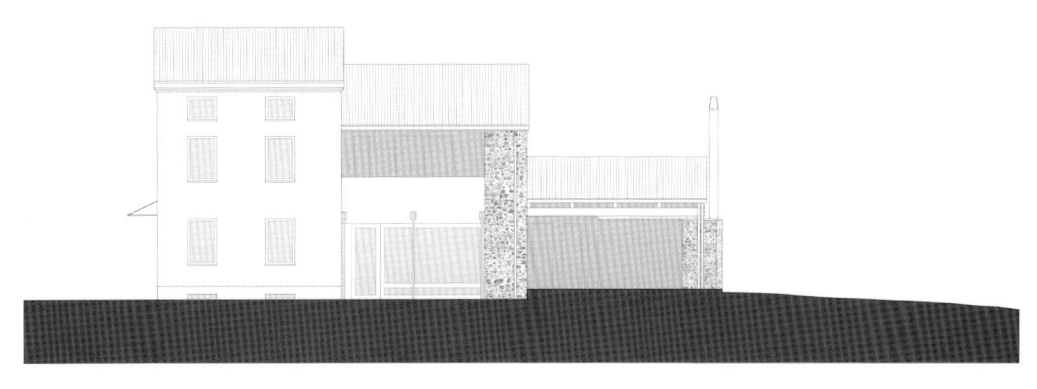

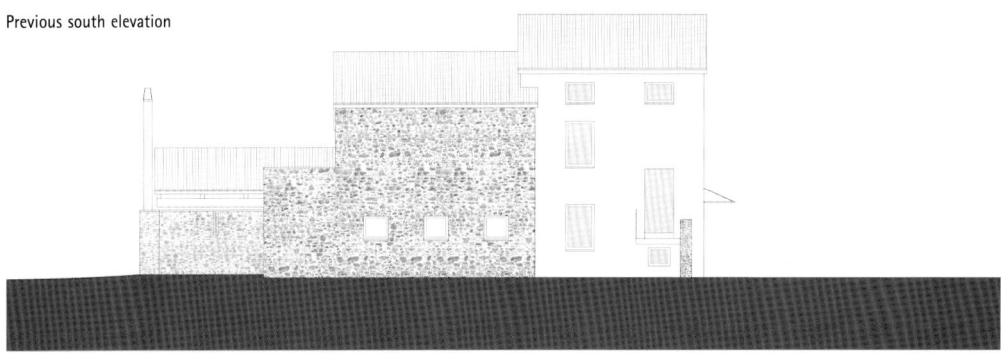

Previous north elevation

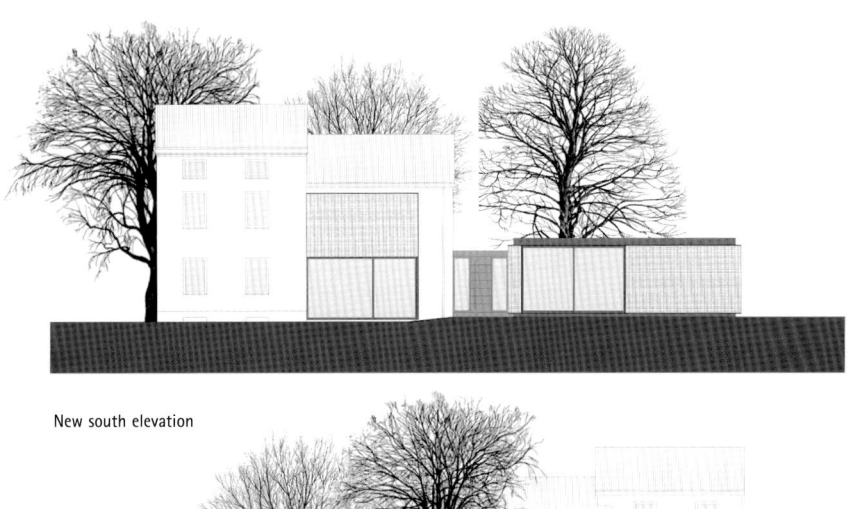

New south elevation

New north elevation

House in Schio

Built on medieval foundations next to a 7th century parochial church, the house, despite being in ruins, showed signs of its original functions at the end of the 12th century, such as the old kitchen or the drying terrace, which were preserved in the same positions.

Ca la Paua

Architects: Lizarriturri Tuneu Arquitectura
Photographer © José Luis Hausmann
Location: Empordà, Spain
Completion date: 2006

The architectural studio proposed a conservationist reform of the region's typically austere style, which required somewhat delicate interventions. Many of the whitewashed walls were preserved, restored using products that respected the original textures of the house. Some of the roofing was redone without dismantling the existing beams or the beam spacing, by way of a mechanism of steel pieces positioned along the old beams allowing the roofing to be redone from above.

The heating was resolved using recycled cast radiators, which date back to the beginning of the century, whose raised thermal inertia allows for operation with water at low temperatures, thereby reducing energy consumption. All these systems operate through domotics which, via a modem, allows the system to be operated from anywhere in the house. On the flat roof is a water tank tempered by a small heat pump that ensures hot water in the middle of winter with highly reduced energy consumption.

The flooring has been covered with tiles of local stone on the top floor and with a combination of polished concrete and oak on the ground floor. Between the two rooms of the ground floor the idea of the bookcase as a secret door has been revived and becomes one of the most interesting parts of the house. The project manages to preserve the essence and austerity of the region's architecture, but also responds to the needs of the 21st century.

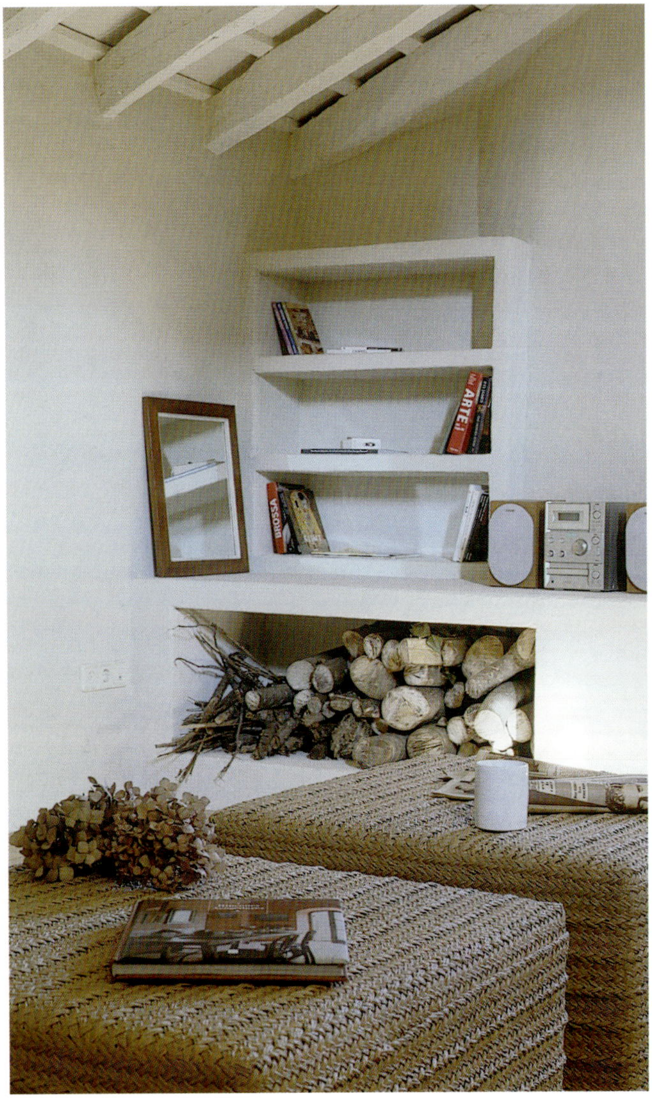

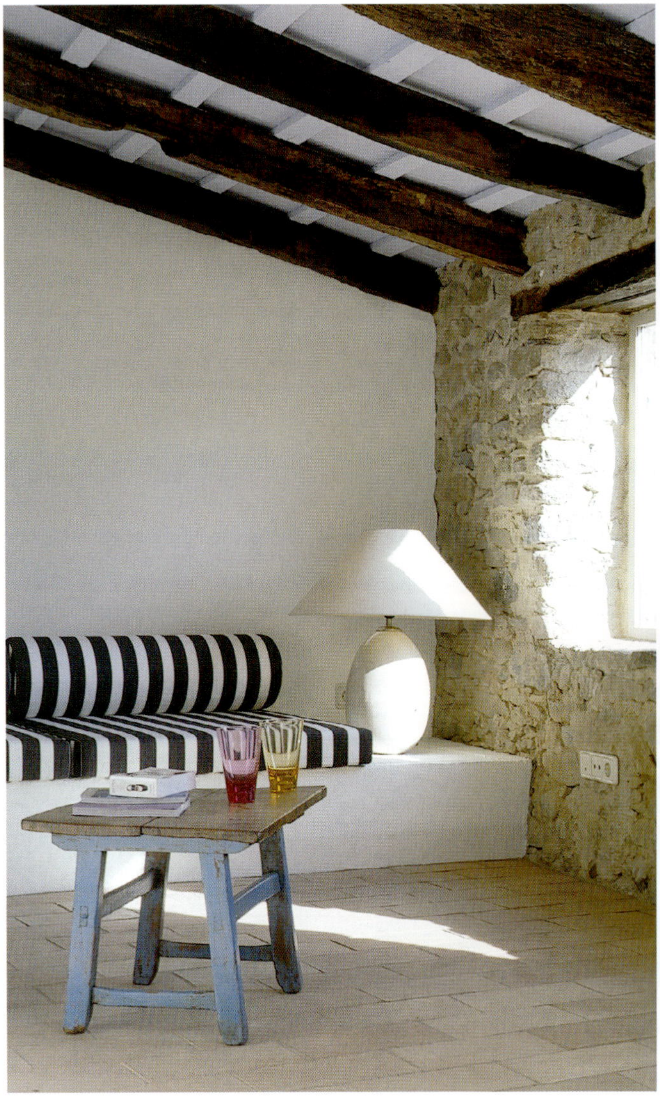

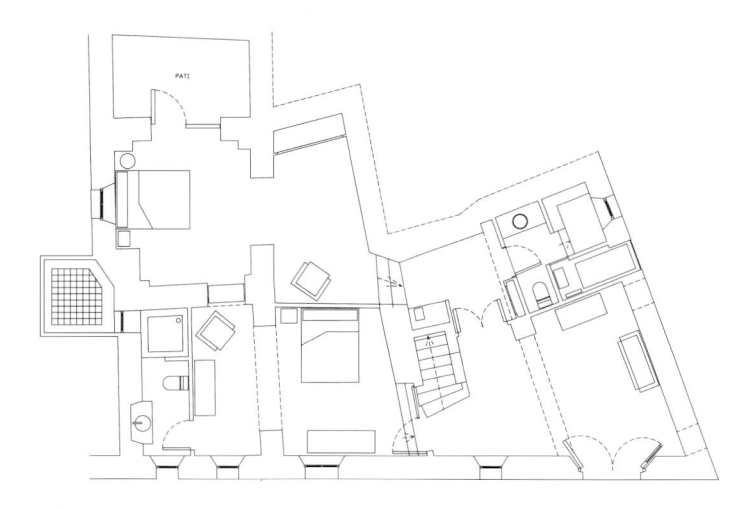

First floor

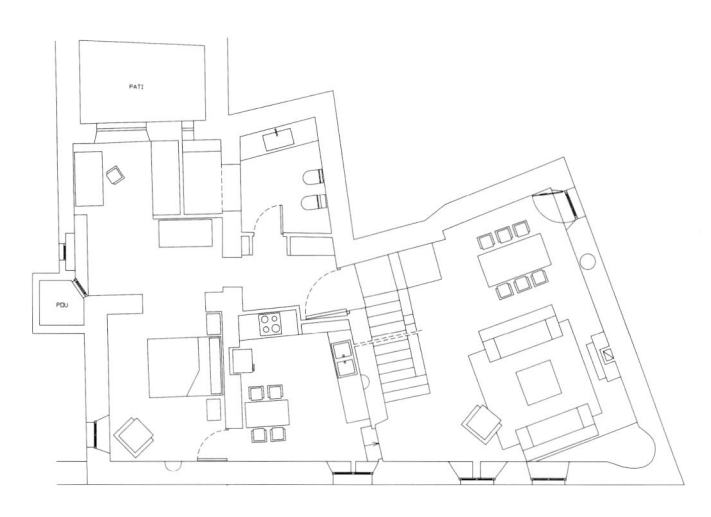

Second floor

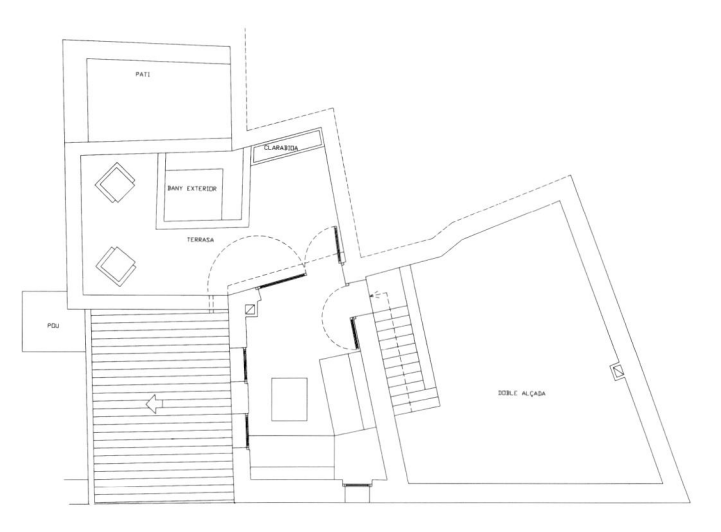

Attic

0 1 2

Ca la Paua 179

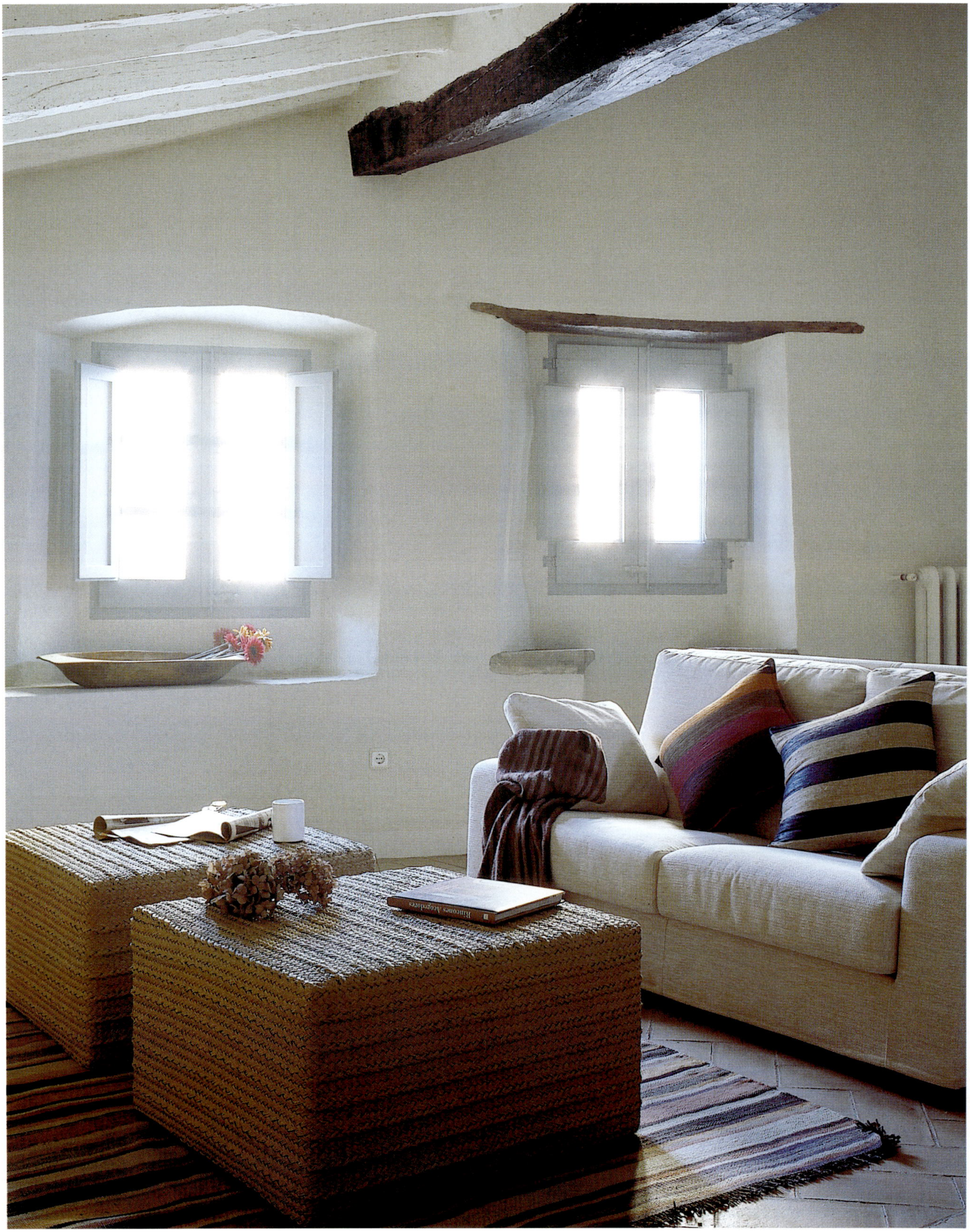

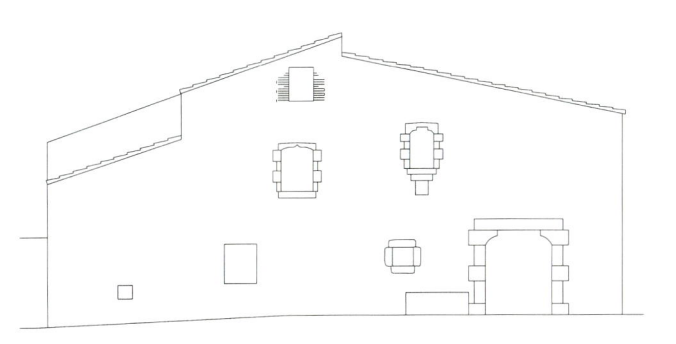

Previous north-south elevation

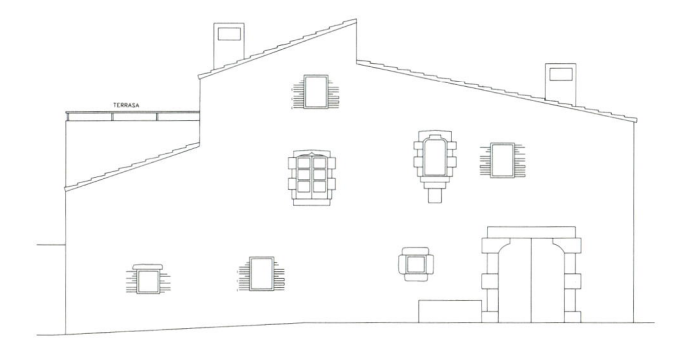

New north-south elevation

Ca la Paua 181

The project has preserved the whitewashed wall and the original structure of the arches. The different textures and the diverse materials form counterpoints, revealing the complexity of the house's architectural landscape.

Previous east-west section

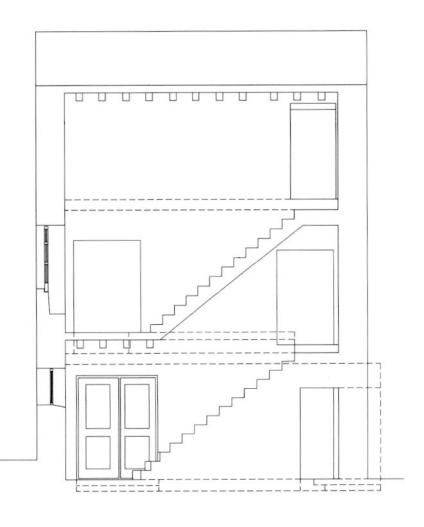

North-south section

New east-west section

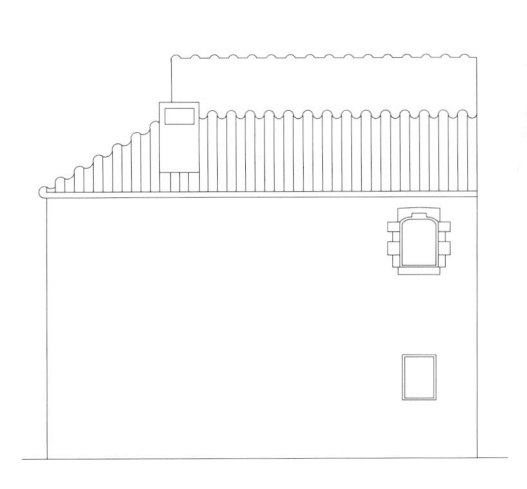

West elevation

184 Ca la Paua

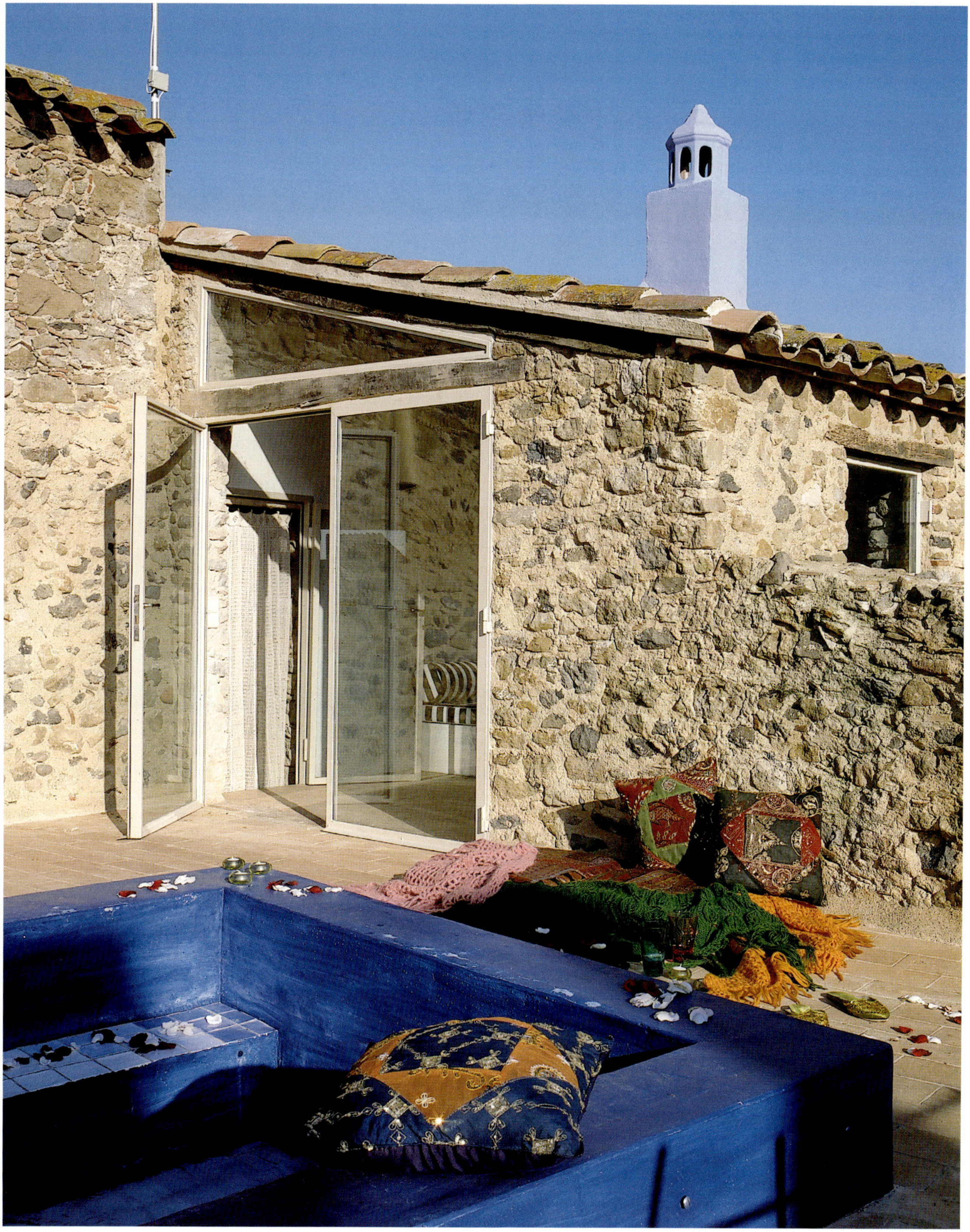

This old water tower, which had been in disuse for sometime, is surrounded by forest. In order to preserve its structure and integrate it with the surroundings, few materials were used for its restoration with very basic textures and colors.

Moereels Tower

Architects: Crepain Binst Architecture
Photographer © Sven Everaert
Location: Brasschaat, Belgium
Completion date: 2002

This water tower, built to supply water to a farm and several annexed buildings, is one of the first buildings to have been built from concrete and was operating up till 1937, before falling into decades of disuse. Finally the local town council decided to sell it and it was restored for private use. The tower's structure consisted of a filter bowl at ground level and four 13 x 13 ft platforms supported by pillars, on top of which is the 13-ft-high cylindrical water tank. Metal stairs lead up the entire height of the tower. The restoration restructured the tower to function as a private home, which incorporated the existing platforms. The ground floor structure is wider than the tower and leaves the four pillars visible. The walls were clad in a double layer of concrete and another floor was added thus creating a large duplex. A living area was incorporated with a kitchen that looks to the exterior, as well as a lounge that faces a small stream and the surrounding forest. In the structure's new floor is the bathroom and a dressing room, and the roof now includes a terrace. The old stairs have been replaced by other similar ones of galvanized metal. The upper platforms accommodate the main bedroom, the guest room, the study and on the highest there is a winter garden. Three sides of the tower are clad in translucent Reglit. The south side, which is less visible, has been double-glazed and on each of the platforms metal balconies have been installed. A variety of local species of vegetation have been planted in the garden, such as ivy and honeysuckle, which in time will cover the lower volume and integrate the building into its surroundings.

188 Moereels Tower

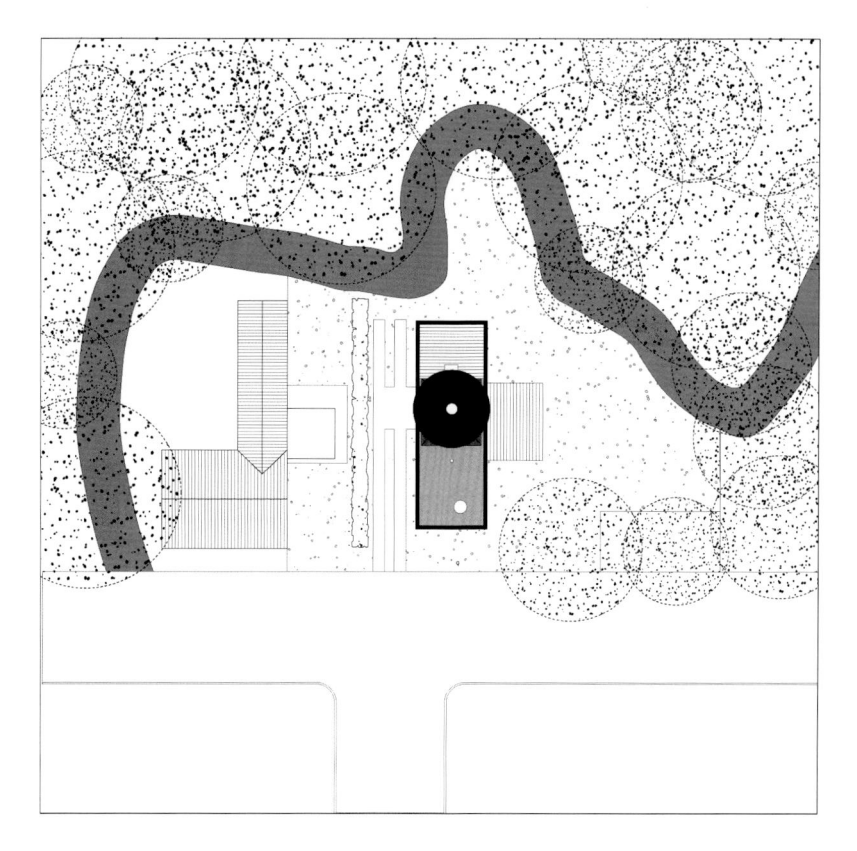

Situation plan

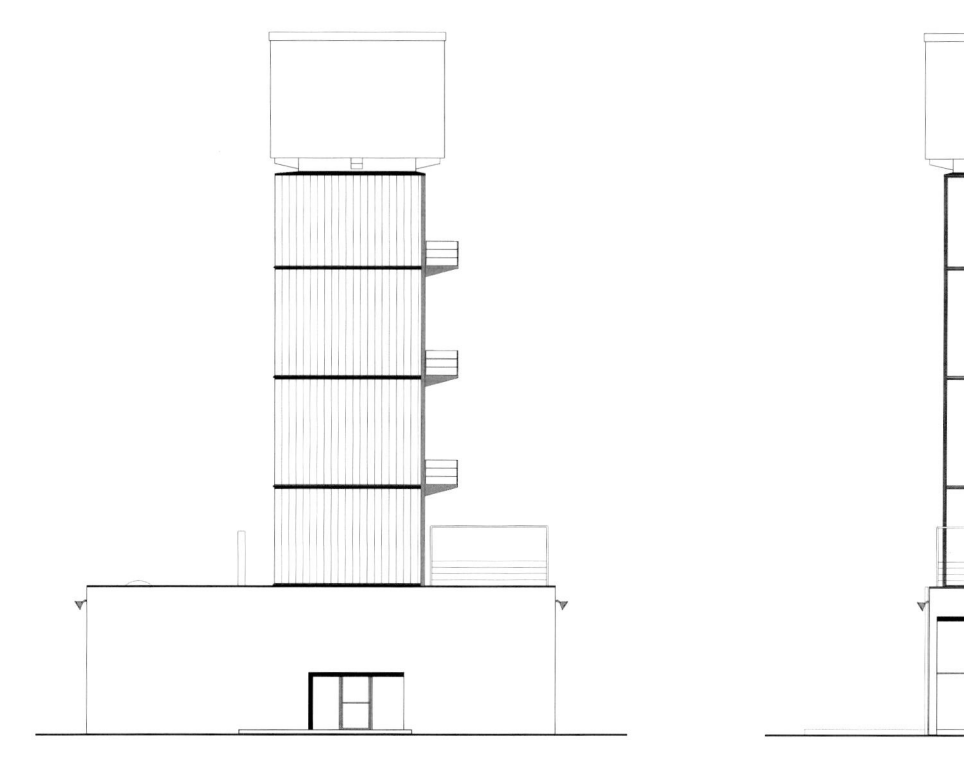

West elevation

South elevation

Moereels Tower

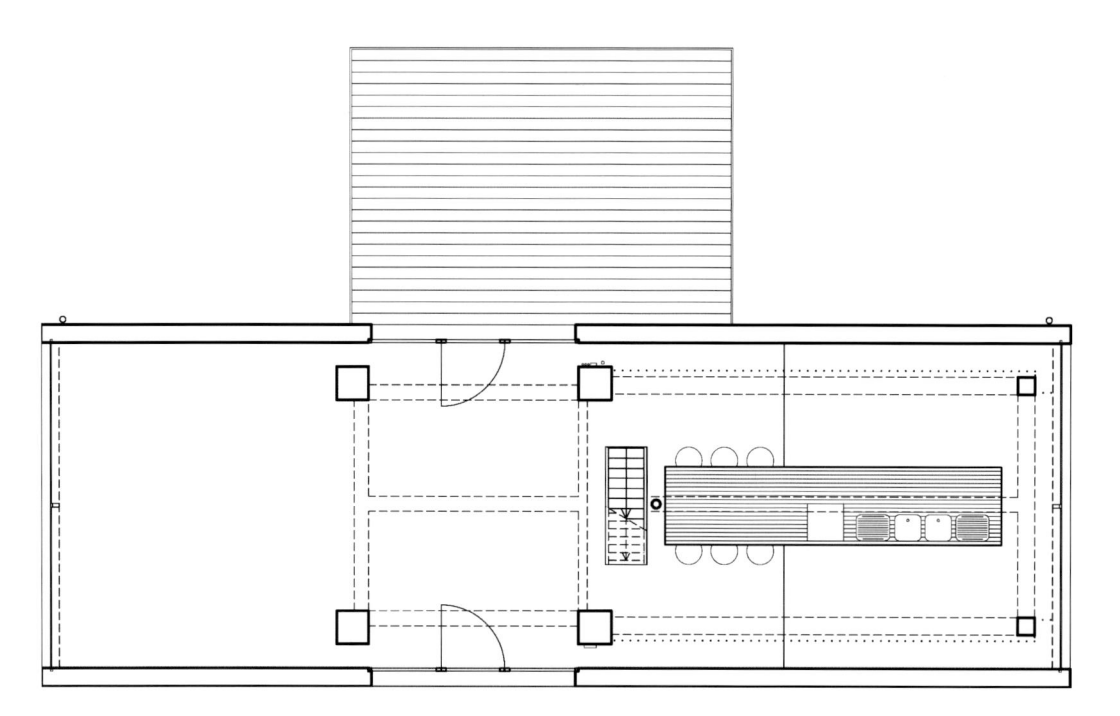

First floor

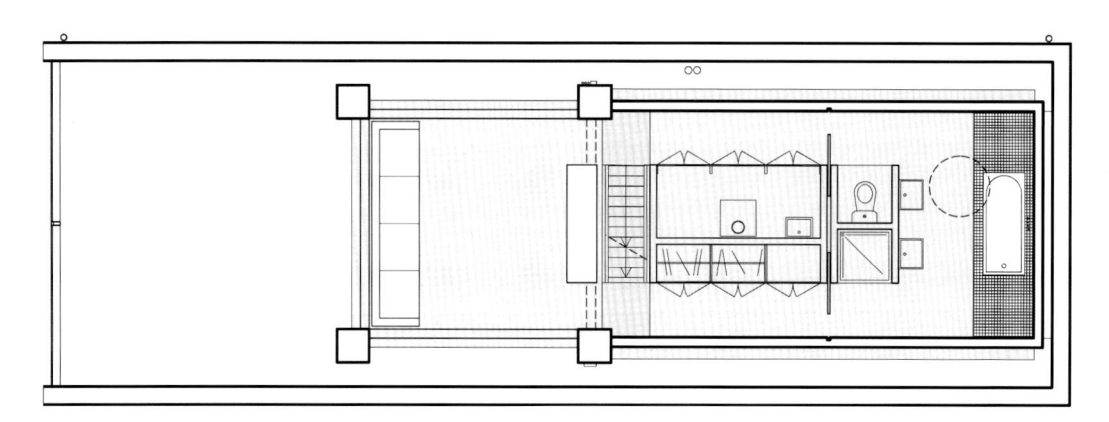

Second floor

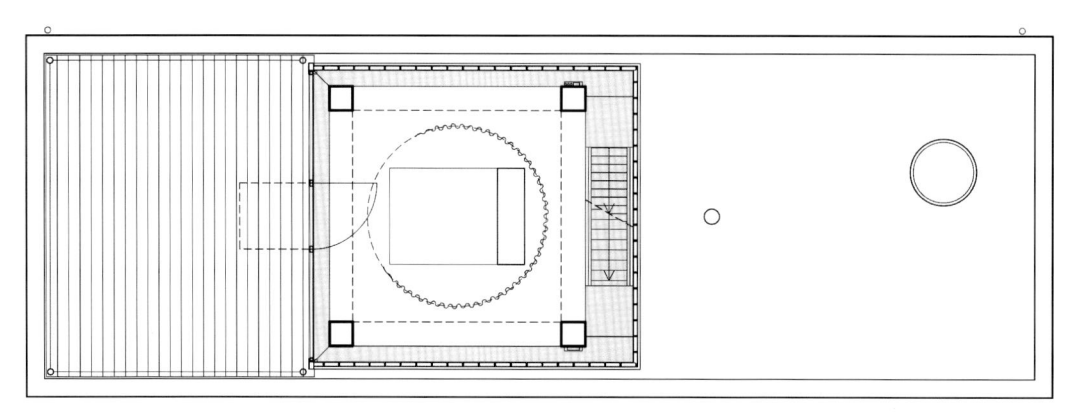

Third floor

0 1 2

190 Moereels Tower

The tower's south façade faces the forest and is more hidden from the exterior. The architects therefore chose to use double-glazing instead of translucent Reglit for its surface.

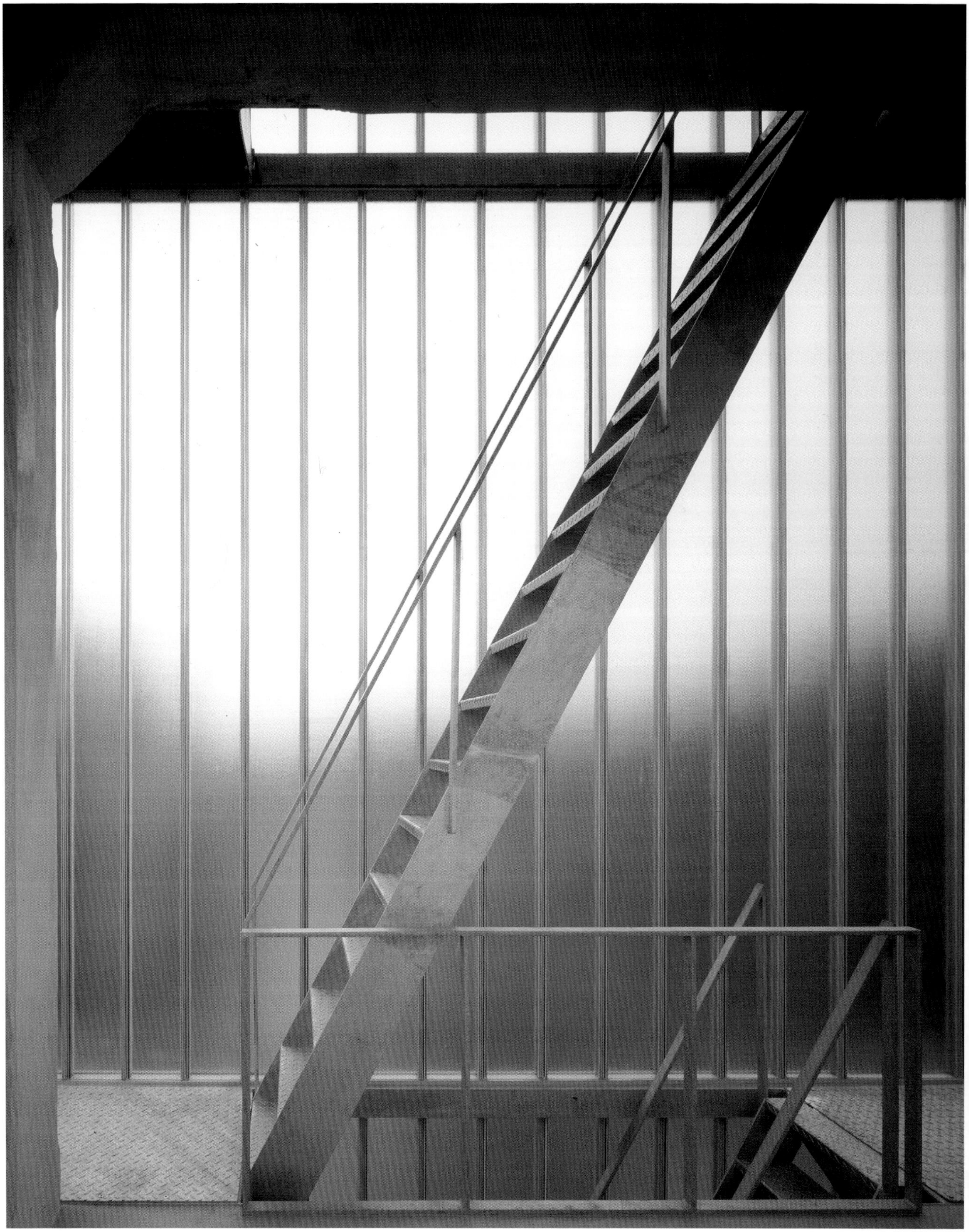

Moereels Tower 193

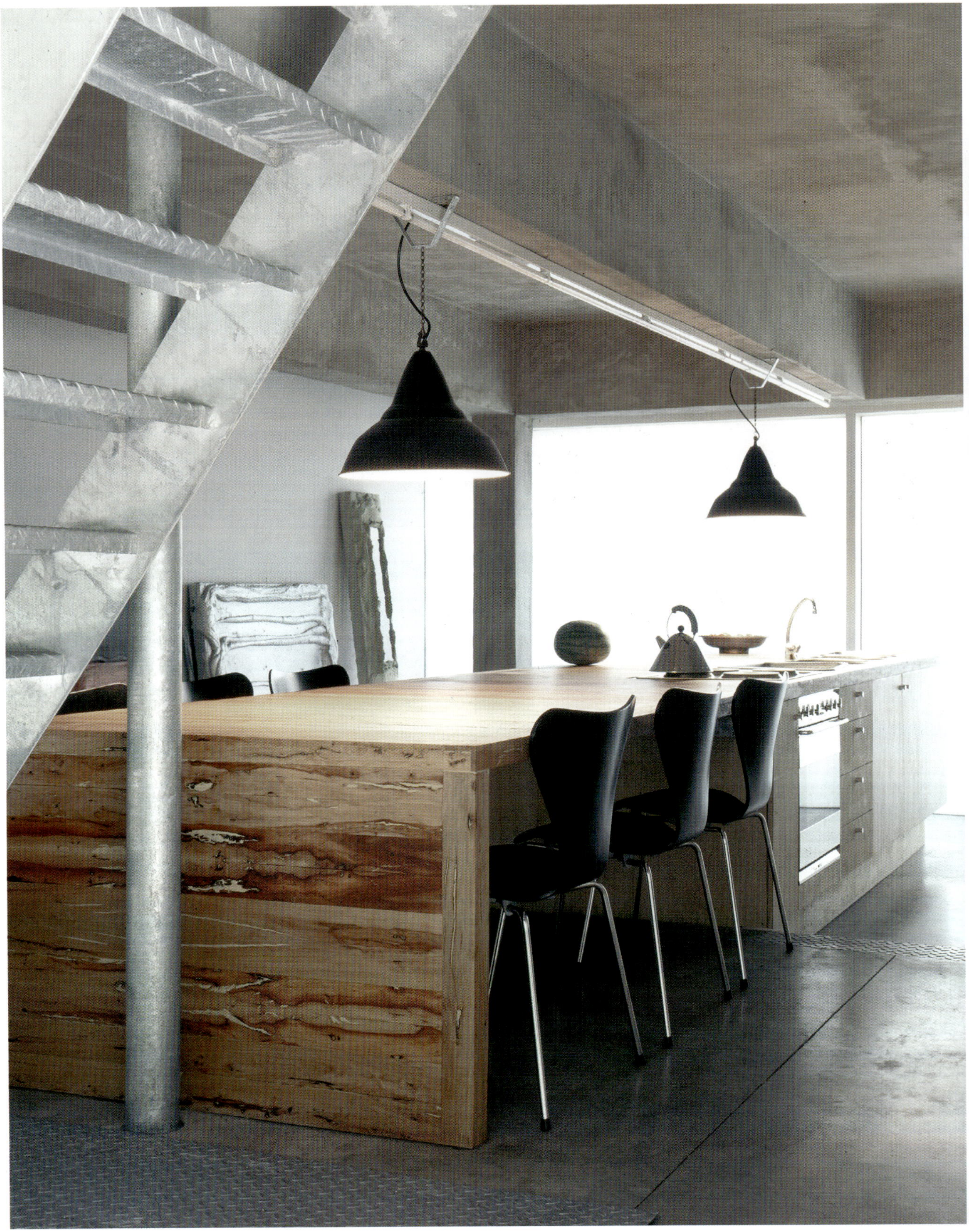

Moereels Tower

The building on which this restoration was projected is an old forge, whose origins date back to the 18th century, and which has been built with stones from an old gunwale. The date 1801 has been engraved onto the primitive lintel, which, 200 years later, has been transported to the interior of the new house to serve as the base for the fireplace.

House in Cerdanya

Architects: Arturo Frediani Arquitectos
Photographer © Eugeni Pons
Location: Lles de Cerdanya, Spain
Completion date: 2003

For the restoration and extension of the gunwale construction materials were used which are typical of the area, such as wood, stone and Arabic tiles. These were always applied directly and left exposed. The original 30-inch-thick walls were incorporated into the project and the same was applied to the new dividing walls. The steel structure and the wooden framework of the façades and interiors draws on the constructive principal of the Steinway & Sons grand pianos, which due to a metallic harp in their interior were able to produce a cleaner and more finely tuned sound. In a similar way the intention was for the metal structure to withstand the test of time and maintain the dimensional stability of the wooden walls.

Oregon pine, which had been dried for three years, was used to cover the main façade and also for the sliding shutters. These operate by way of a system used by the motor industry for the sliding doors of vans. A mechanism was developed that would allow 75 ft^2 shutters weighing up to 290 lb to be mechanically opened, without any human effort. The pieces fit perfectly into the doorways and windows and disappear when the house is shut. Once designed these pieces and their mechanism were installed onto the façade. The floor plan has the shape of a figure of 8 with two sectors connected by a 6.5 ft-wide gallery. The main sector contains the main bedroom and both have independent stairs to access the second floor.

Although the openings are much bigger than those that are traditional for the area, the obligatory use of shutters has been respected thanks to the development of a mechanism that allows large surface areas to be easily moved.

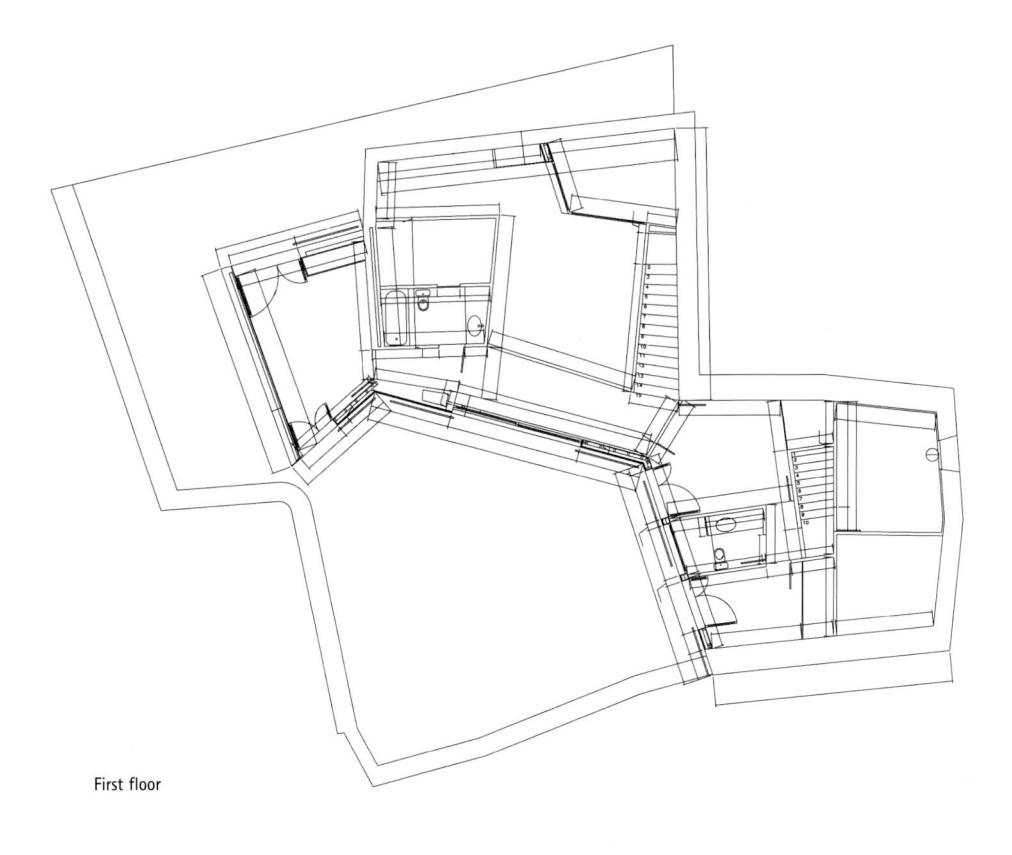

First floor

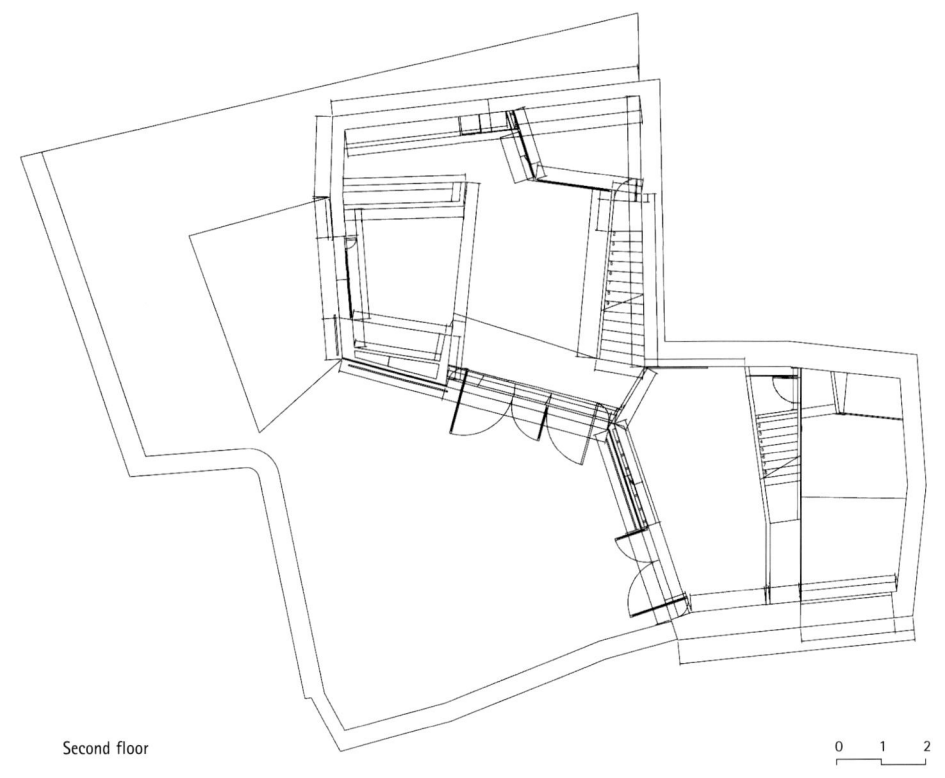

Second floor

0 1 2

House in Cerdanya 199

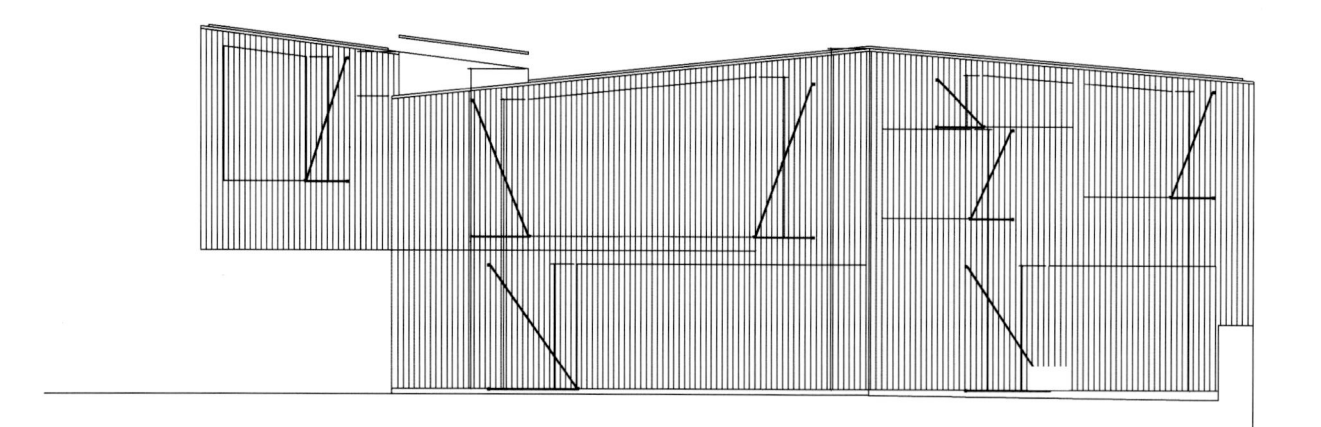

Front elevation (Shutters closed)

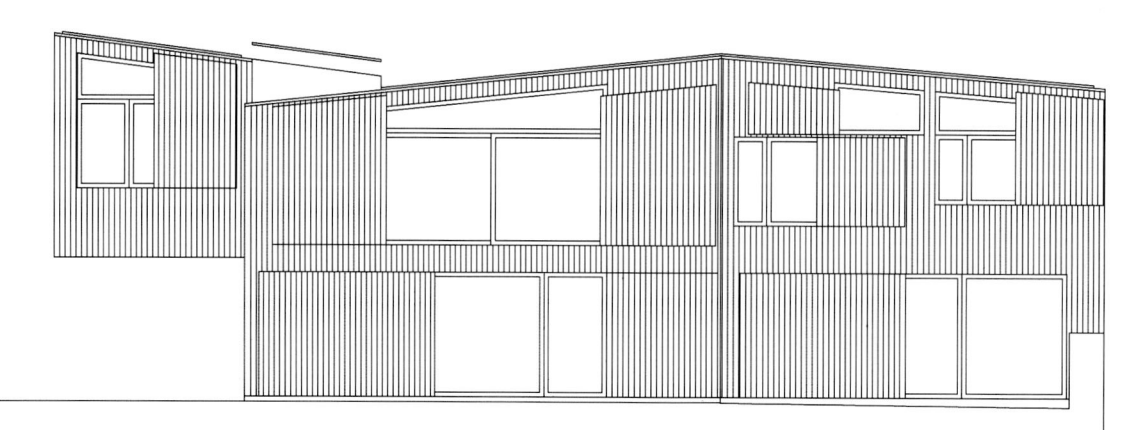

Front elevation (Shutters open)

House in Cerdanya 201

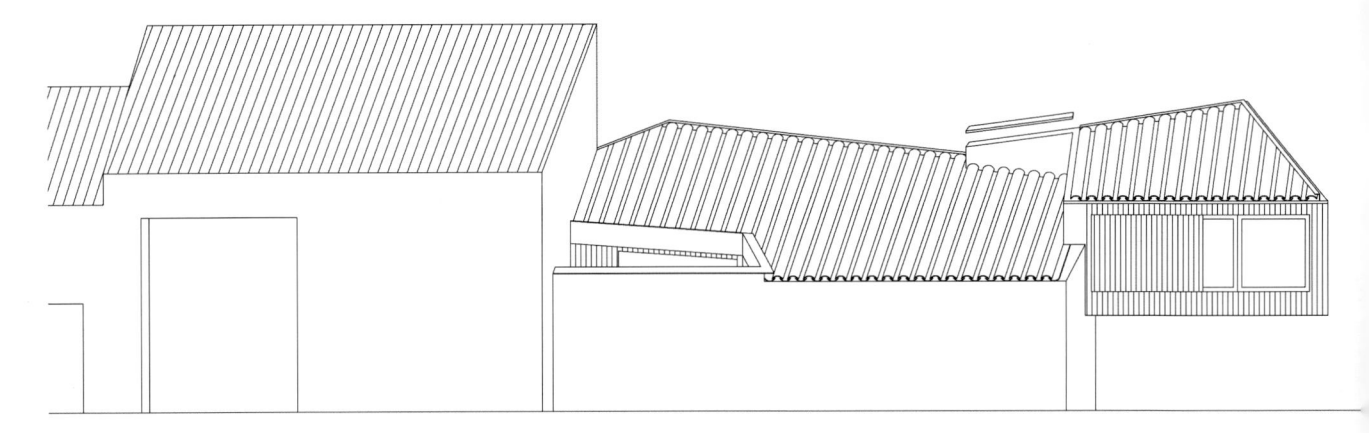

Longitudinal section

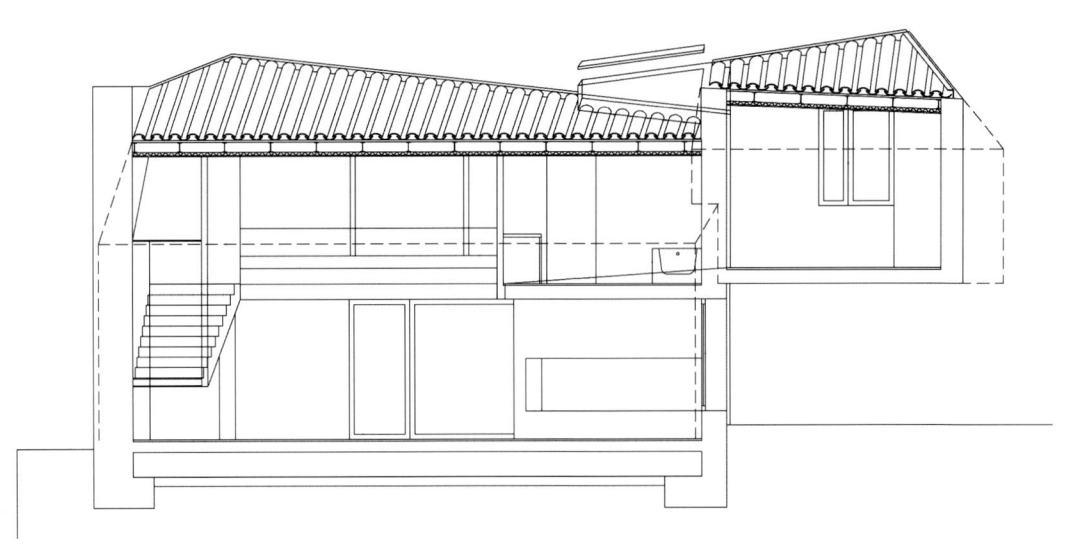

Transversal section

House in Cerdanya 203

204 House in Cerdanya

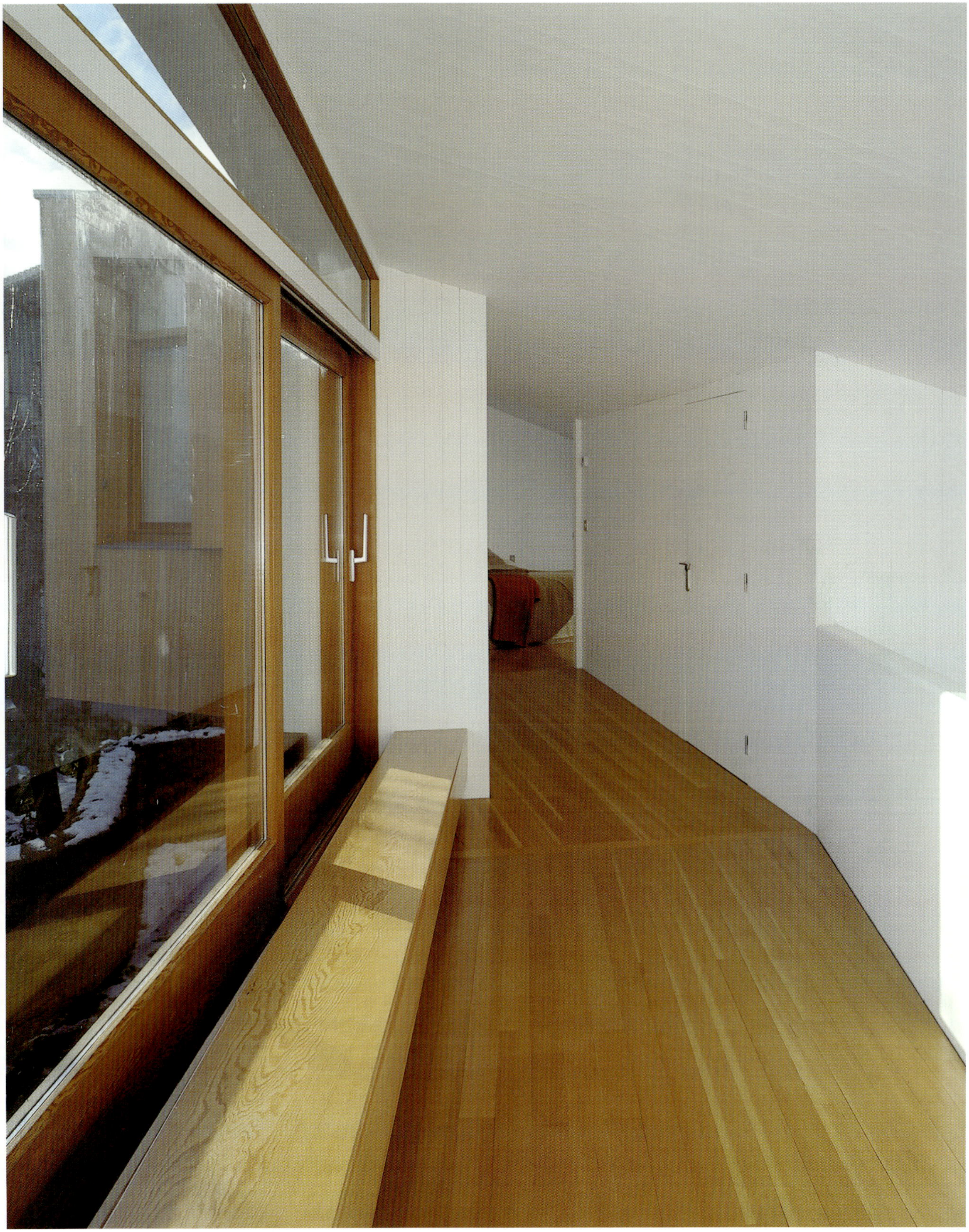

Póvoa de Lanhoso is a village situated in a region of outstanding landscapes, close to the city of Braga, in the north of Portugal. The original farm consisted of an old farmhand's house, which included an annexed stable and barn. The constructions stood on a rocky, sloping plot.

House in Taide

Architects: Topos Atelier de Arquitectura
Photographer © Xavier Antunes
Location: Póvoa de Lanhoso, Portugal
Completion date: 2005

The land, surrounded by crops, was ideal for being restored as a home, since it is protected from the northerly wind, the rains from the southeast and the orange groves and olive trees provide shade.

The project maintains the floor plan's situation, orientation, volumetry and organization, which had already been established, based on the climate conditions. The plant life was preserved as a much as possible. The farmhand's house, built from granite on the perimeter, was restored and returned to its original state. The oil press, barn, pens and stables were all included, along with the spaces in the house used for practical functions, such as the garage, the kitchen and the rooms for technical work.

From the granite volume a new building was projected on the same level and in place of the annexed constructions. This building contains the bedrooms and the living areas. The old rules laid down by the master builders were followed where possible and the farm workers' traditions also, maintaining a link between the present and the past. The result is a heritage from years gone by that can be found today in this house in the country.

The house is the result of both an interaction between the past and the present and a respect of the wisdom of the old masons and farmhands.

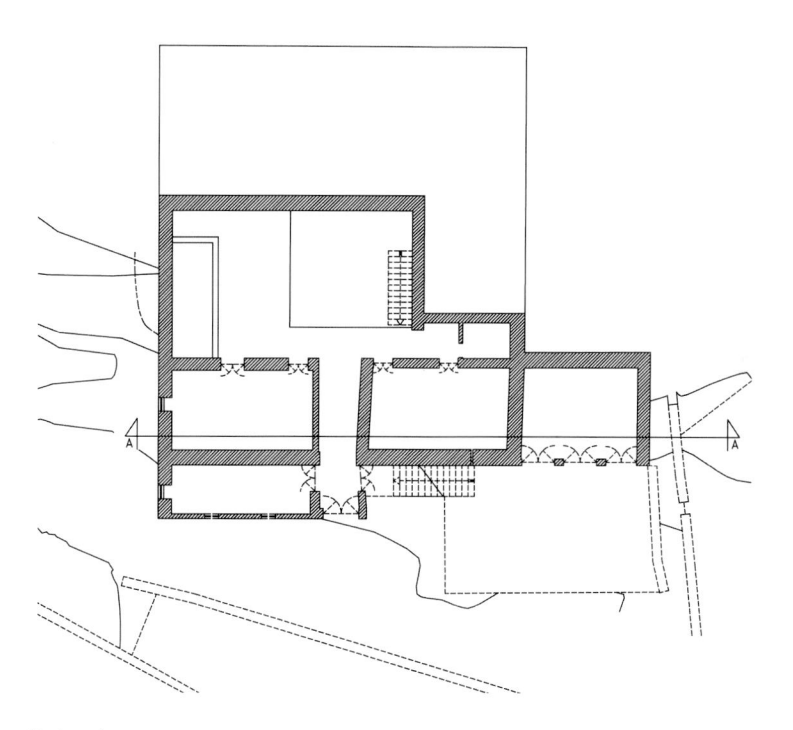

Previous plan

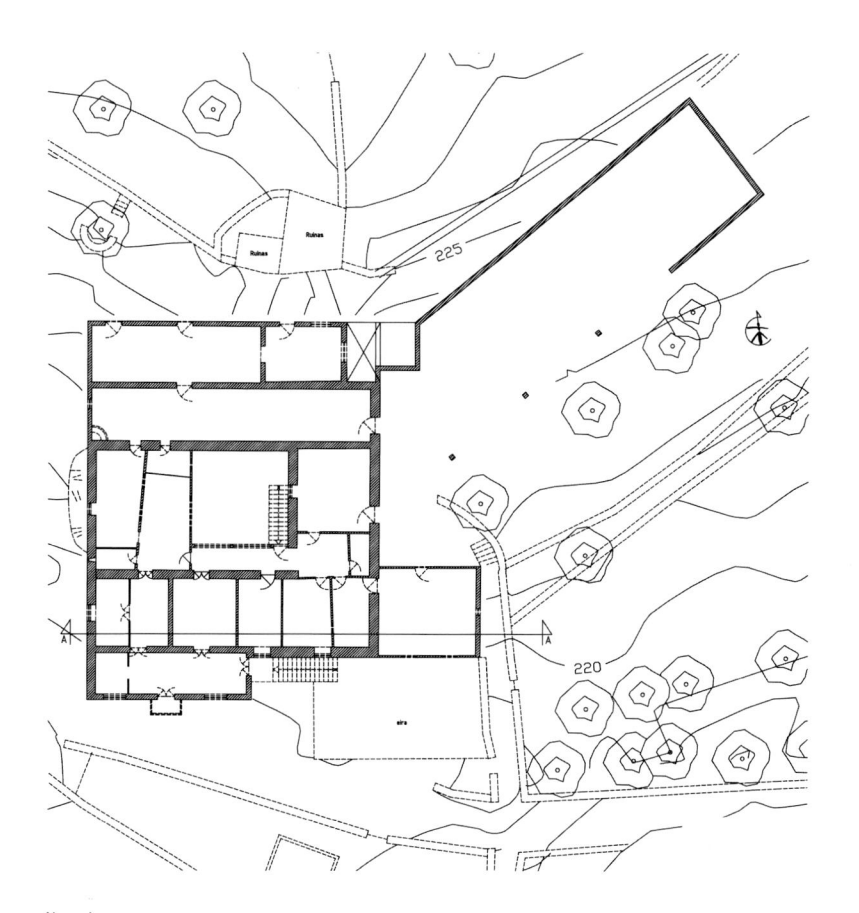

New plan

House in Taide 209

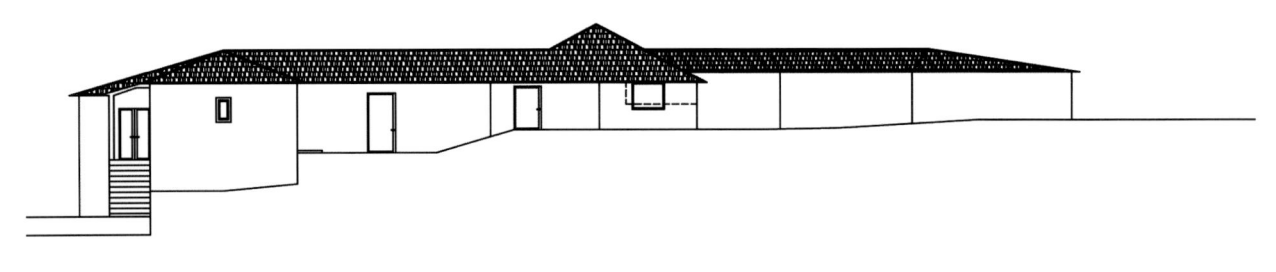

East elevation

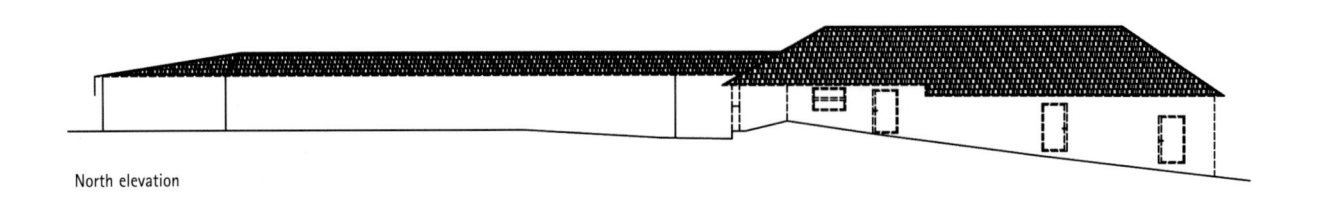

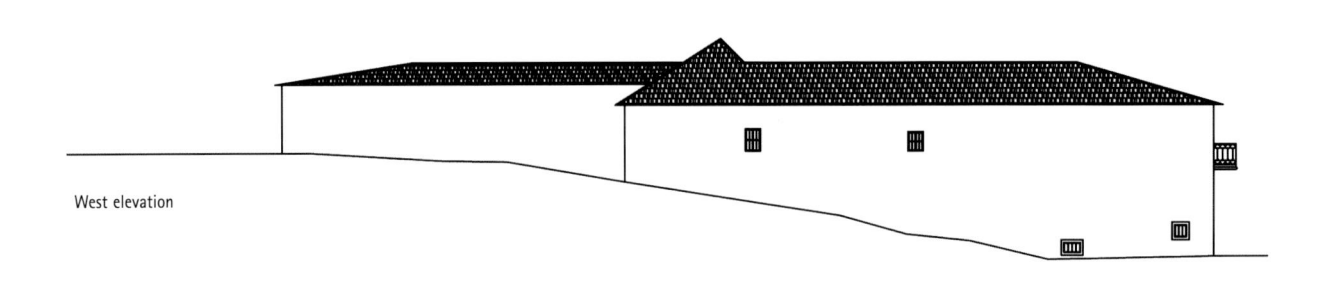

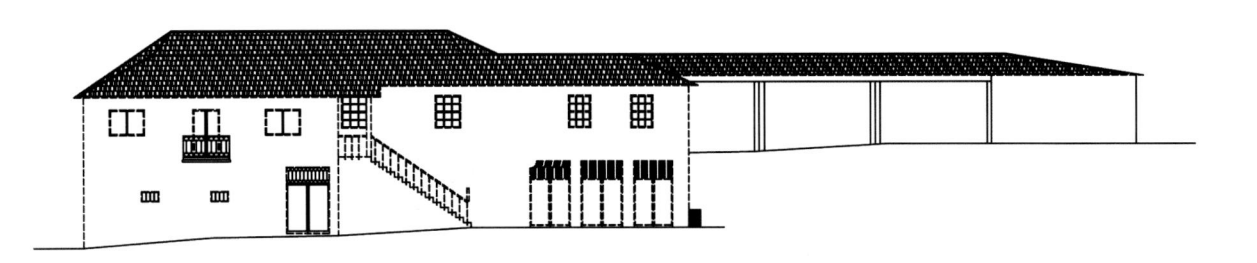

North elevation

West elevation

South elevation

210 House in Taide

Sketch

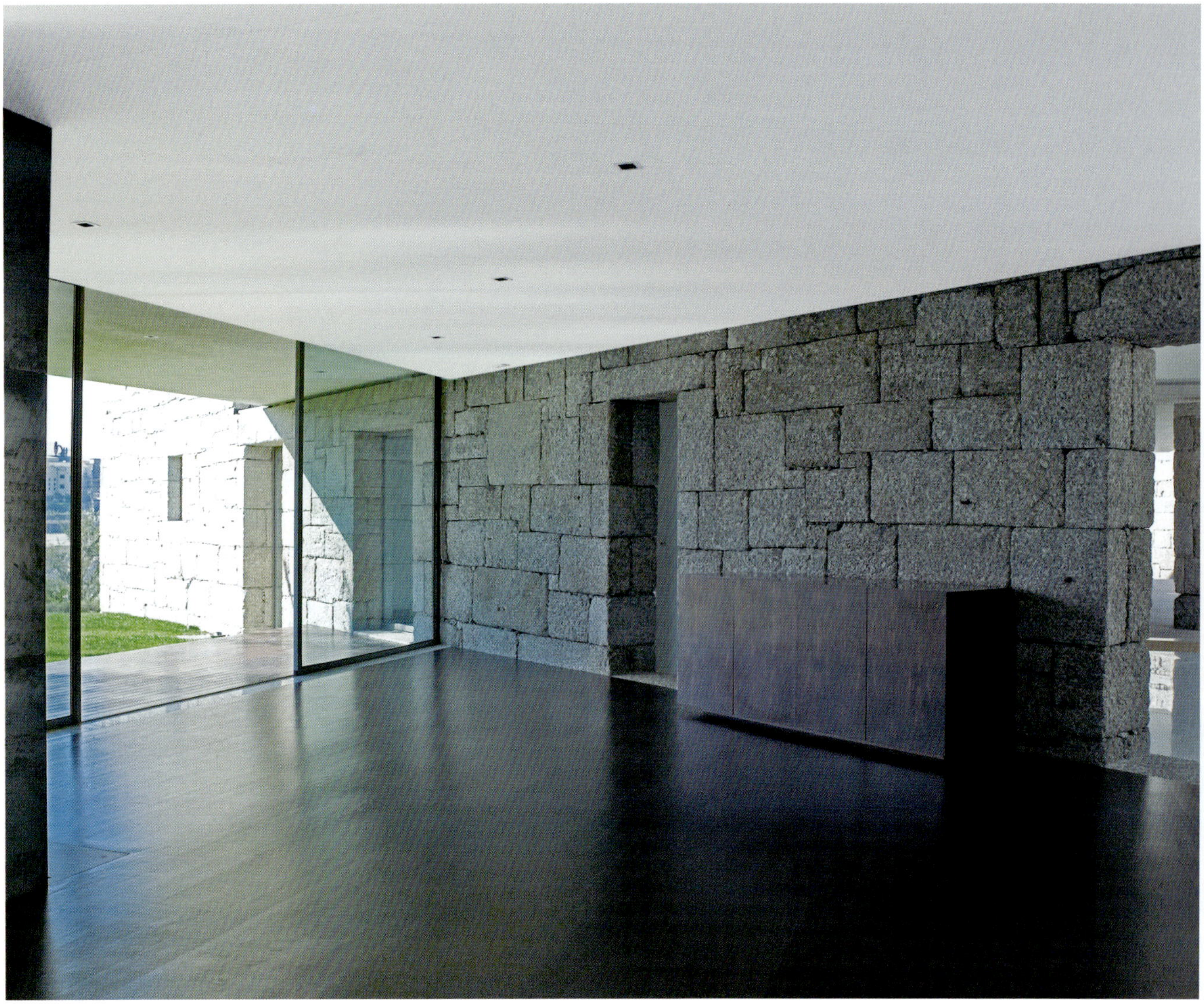

House in Taide

These old stables situated in the outskirts of the small city of Volkach, in lower Franconia, consisted of six buildings with a front courtyard used for agriculture, livestock and wine production; all activities which continue today.

Stables in Bavaria

Architect: Reinhold Jäcklein
Photographer © Stefan Mayer
Location: Volkach, Germany
Completion date: 2005

The restoration project consisted of the transformation of one of the old farms into a house and office. The original group of buildings has remained in tact, although the property has been divided among various members of the family. Architect Reinhold Jäcklein divided the building corresponding to the stables and barn into four areas with different functions. The most was made of all the space and height, so as to create a fluid living and work space. The northern part of the building, facing the vineyards, was converted into a two-story architectural studio. The spaces of the home were situated in the southern part, where the large stable entrance had once been located. The interior spaces are open and connect via stairs, so that they are perceived as areas with different functions joined beneath the large roof. Two exterior stairways, which give access to the work and living areas, have been situated parallel to each other on the eastern side of the building. The areas which house the pigpens and the stables had to be completely redone and were whitewashed. The woodwork of the entire building was restored to recover the original appearance. The floors were laid with double thickness oak floorboards. On the upper floors the window openings were enlarged, but always considering the preservation of the character of the old stable. For practical reasons birch has been used for the shutters and window frames, which fuse with the exterior façade, clad in triple-layer colored laminates of the same material.

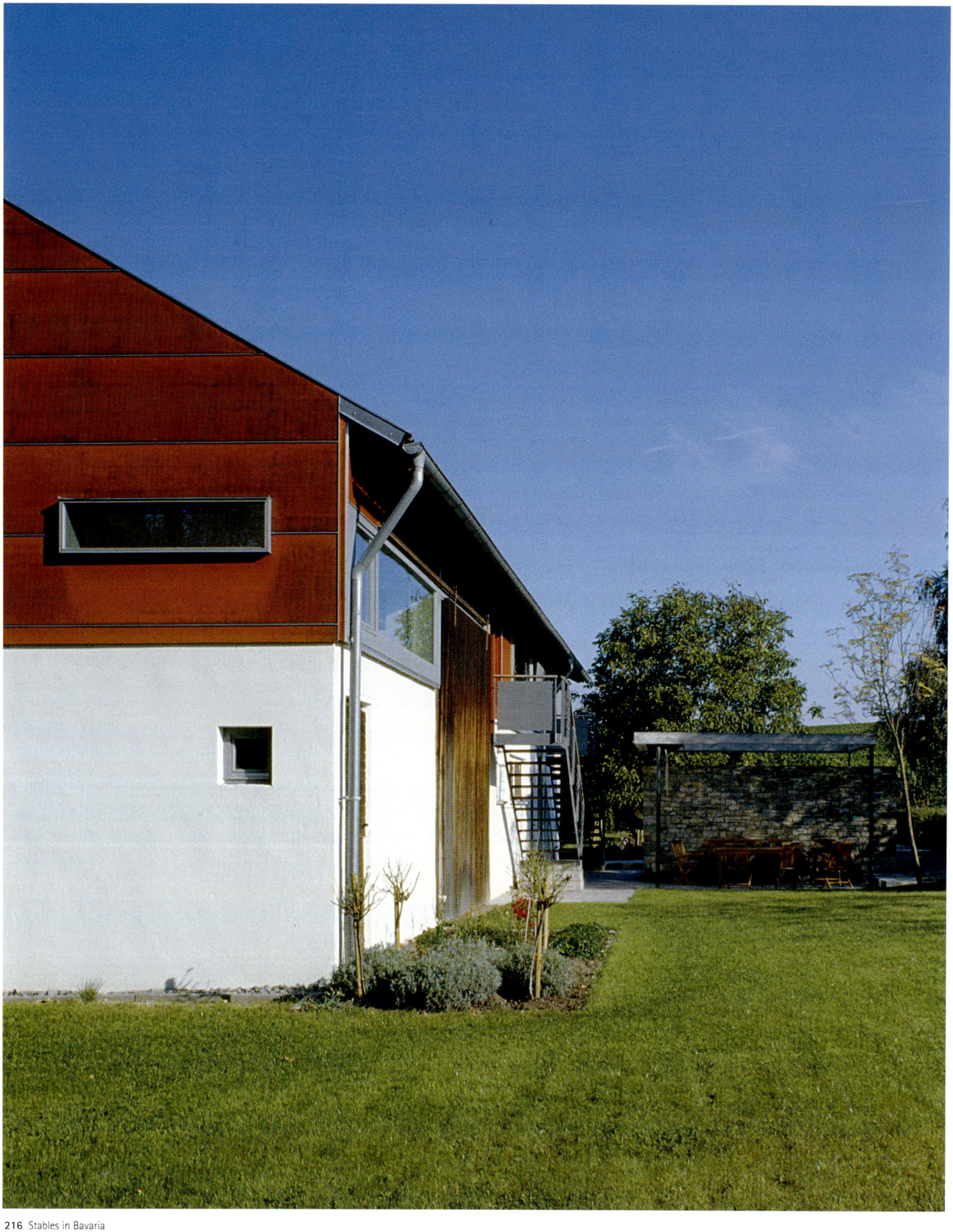

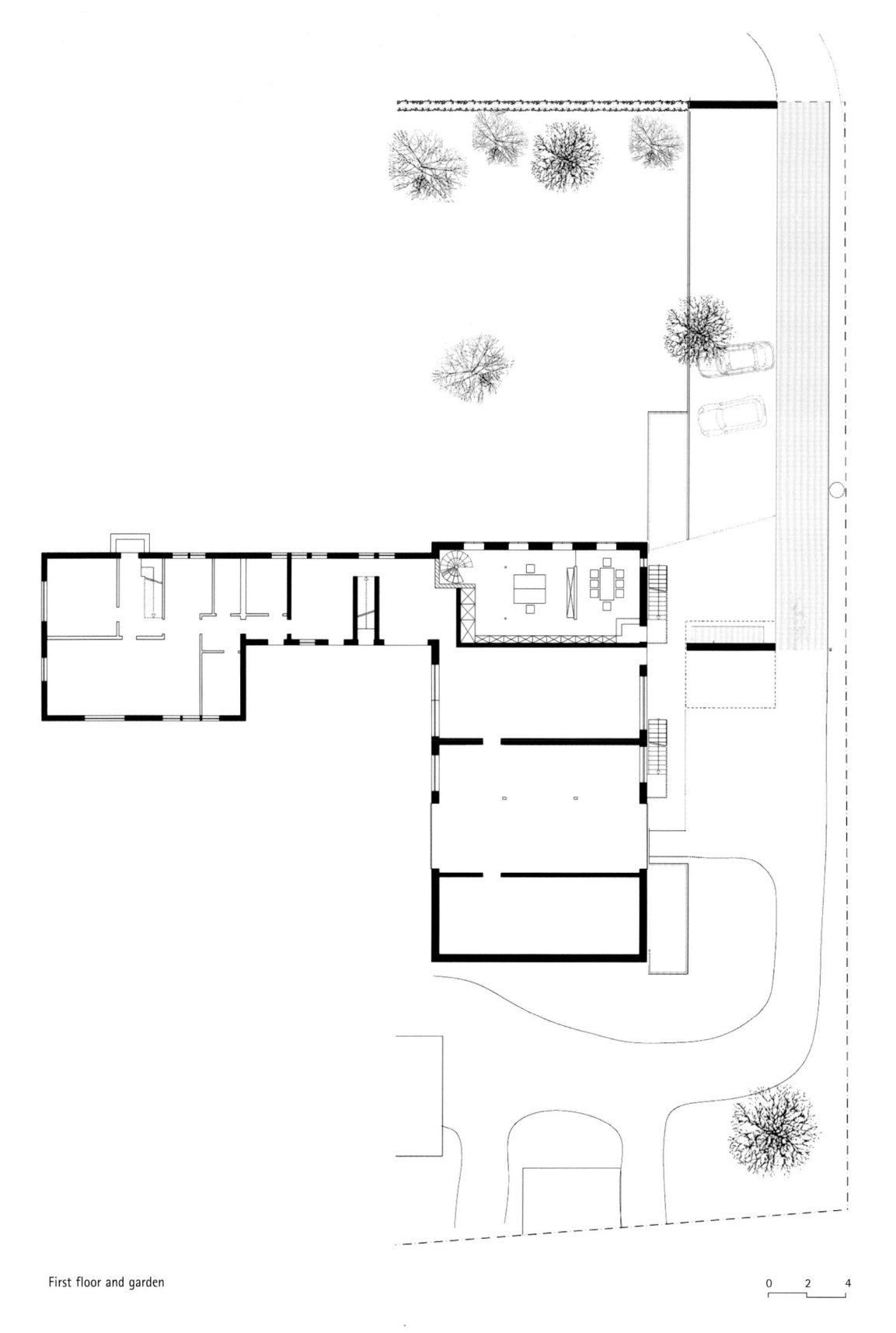

First floor and garden

0 2 4

Stables in Bavaria 217

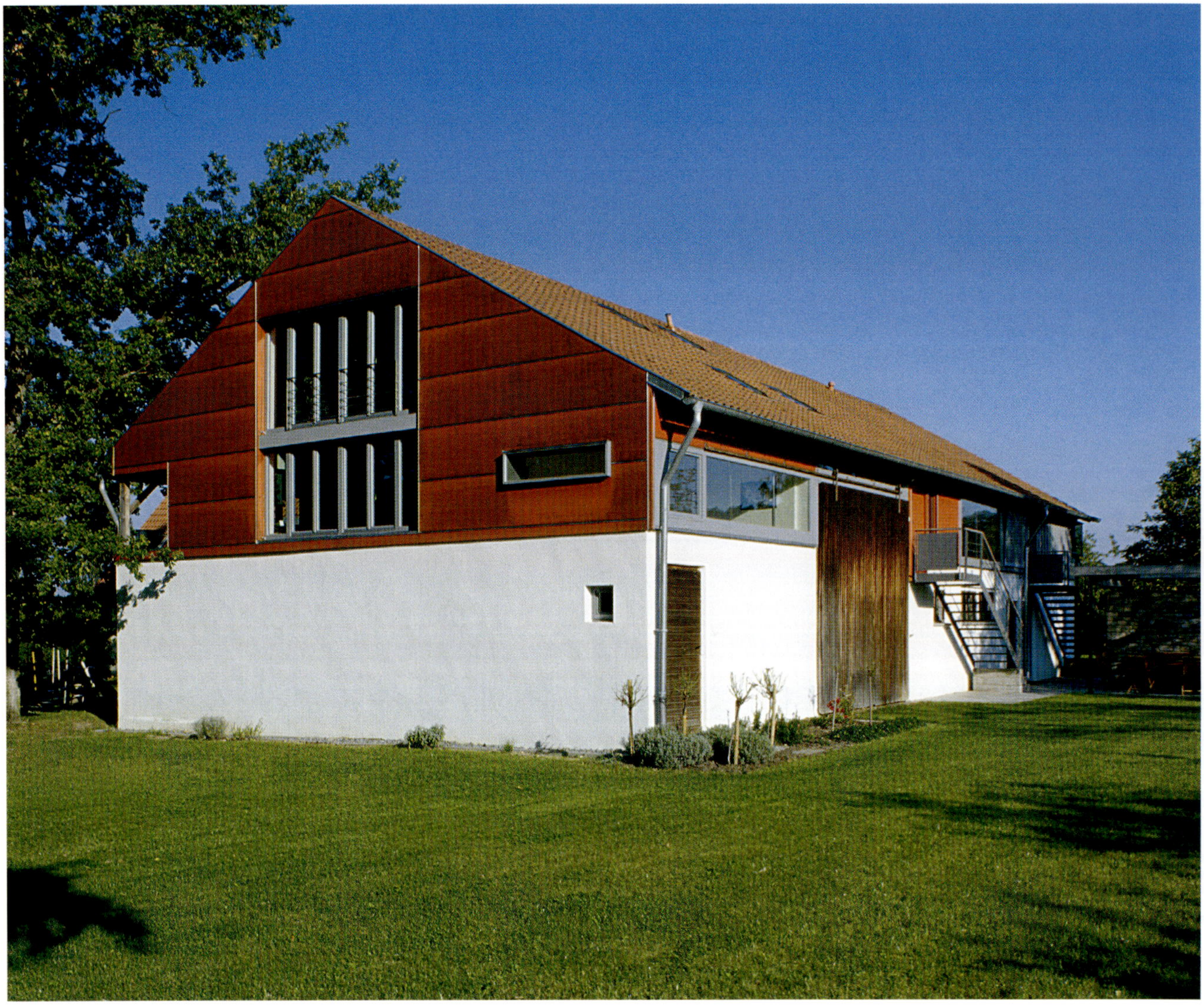

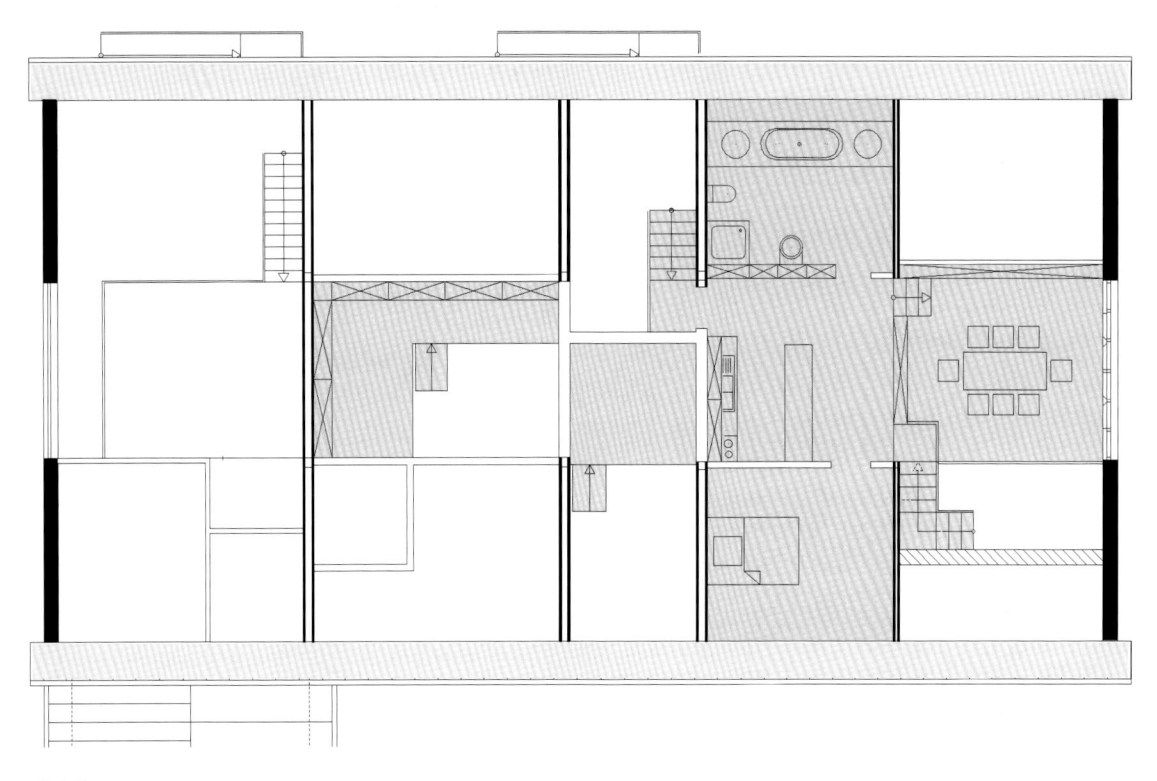

First floor

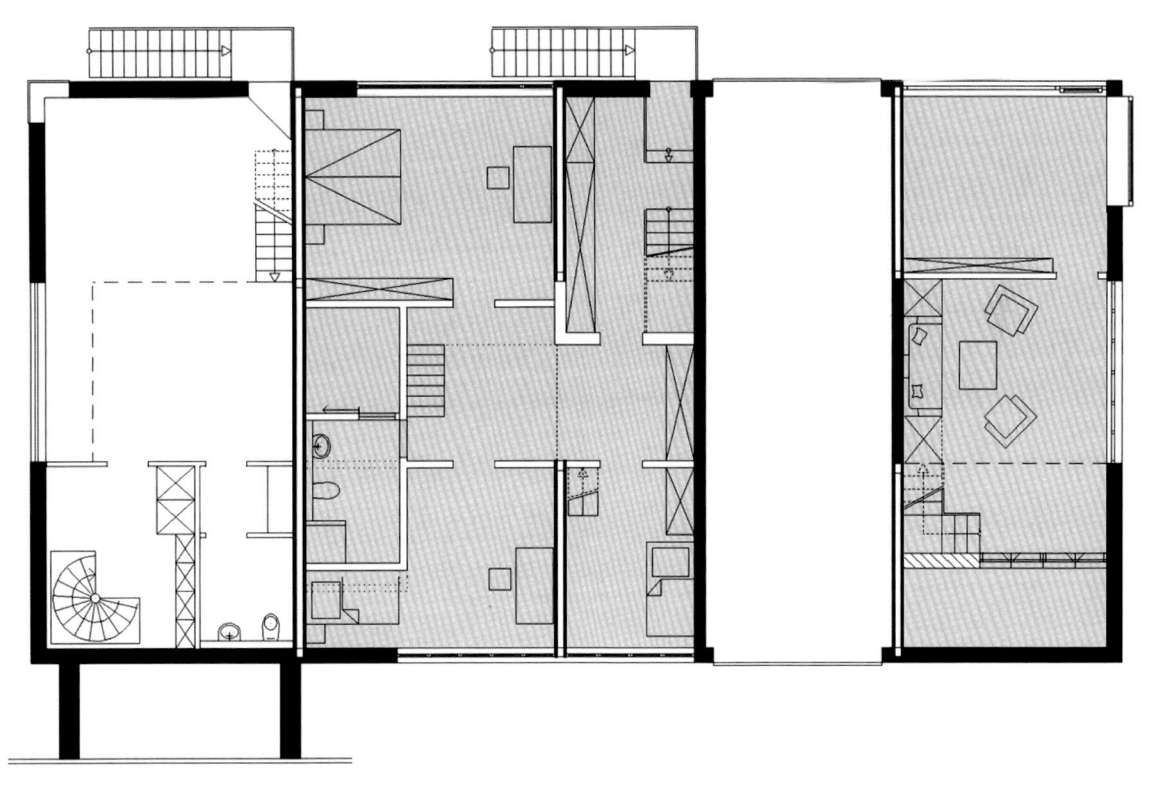

Second floor

Stables in Bavaria

One of the essential concepts of this renovation was to afford the house maximum light entry through the enlargement of the windows and the creation of new openings.

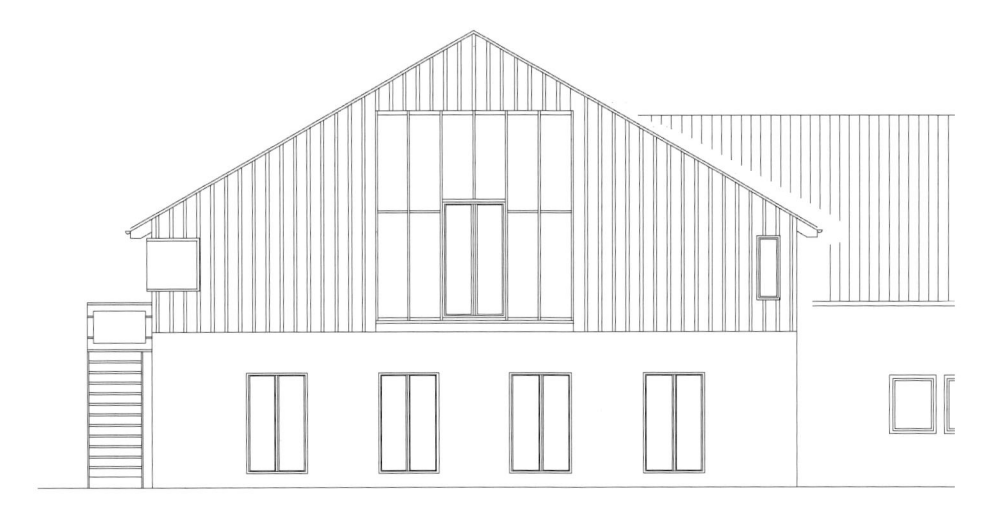

North elevation

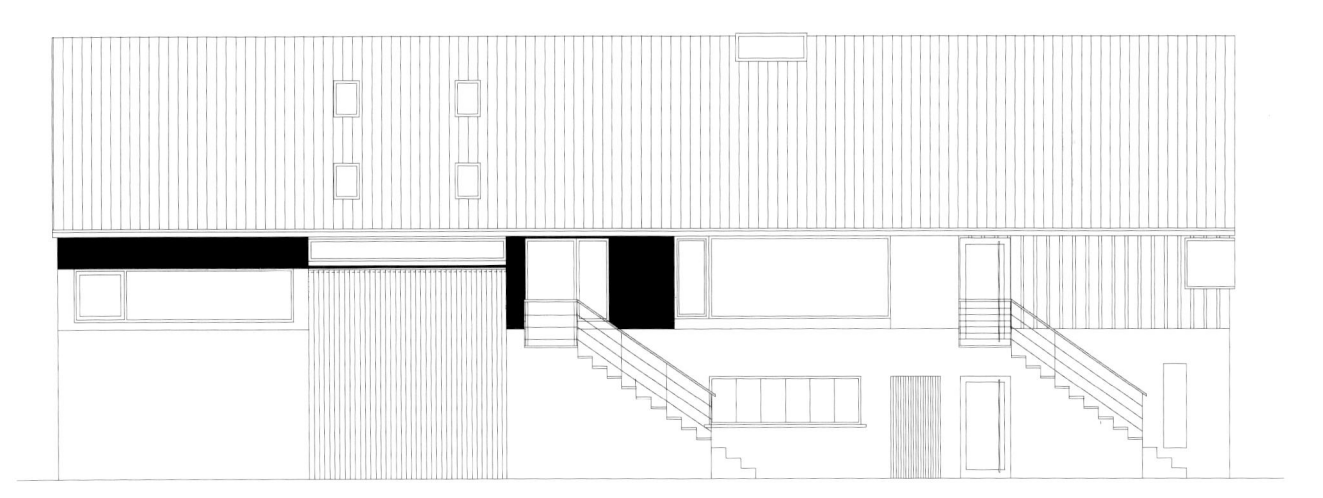

East elevation

South elevation

Stables in Bavaria 221

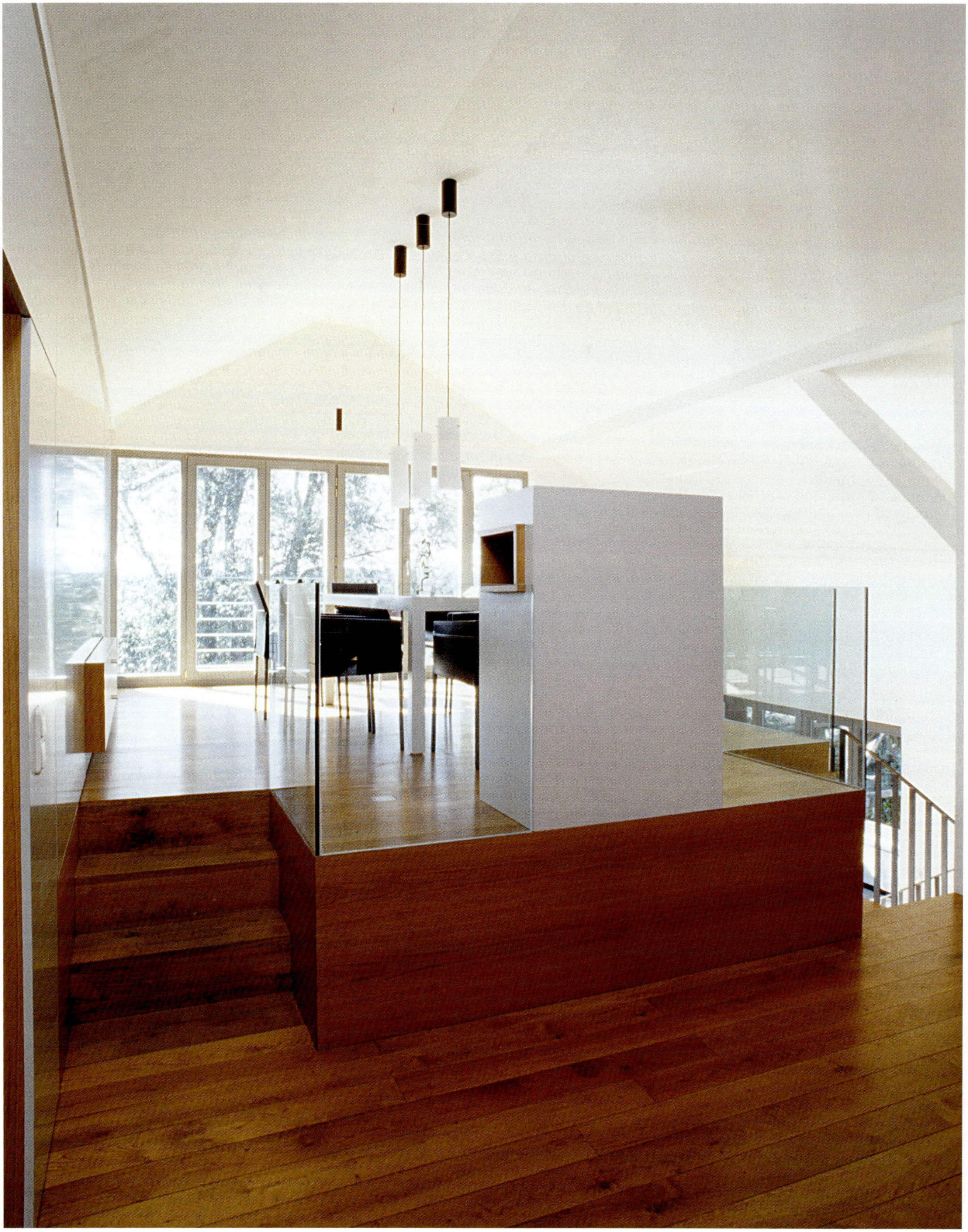

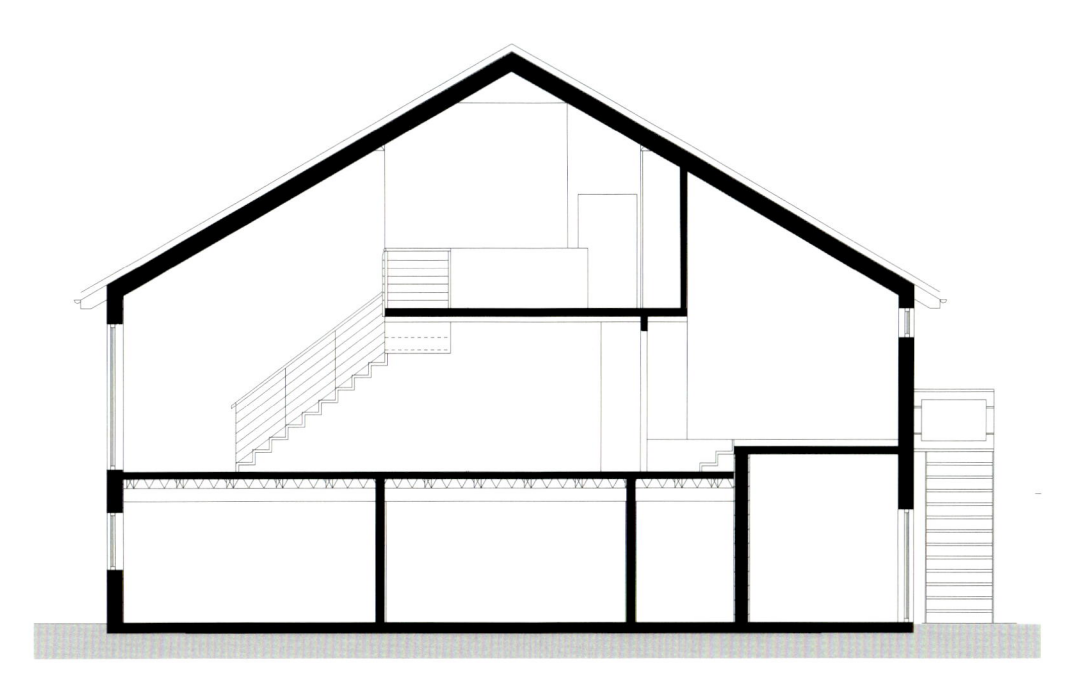

Transversal section

Stables in Bavaria 223

This old shepherds' building, situated in a beautiful spot of the Algarve, has been extended and reconstructed, preserving the typical elements of the region, and transformed into a home and a house for rural tourism.

Monte dos Mosqueiros

Architects: BFJ Arquitectos
Photographer © Daniel Malhão
Location: Portimão, Portugal
Completion date: 2006

The position of the old construction at the top of a small valley and its northeast orientation offer spectacular views of the Sierra de Monchique. It was an agricultural building that was used as a home by a shepherd and as a refuge for the flock. The openings are therefore positioned to offer the possibility of surveying the valley, used for crops. The restoration was considered with rural tourism in mind and included an extension that would also accommodate a home. The existing building was reconstructed preserving and enhancing its most characteristic aspects.

The extremely thick exterior walls were preserved, as well as the existing openings, which presented a highly harmonious sequence and proportion. Annexes that had been added were demolished since they were in very bad condition and detracted from the overall balance of the main construction. The natural inclination of the hillside was used as foundations for the new construction, offering support for the pool and the terrace. The extension from the excavation was the same size as the pre-existing construction. Structural reinforcements were added on the exterior walls, which required a new structure of concrete pillars inserted into the existing wall, adhering to a crown beam. The wall was finished in brickwork to offer uniformity to the interior surface and improve the thermal insulation. Local techniques and materials were used for the surfaces, such as the whitewashed walls and ceilings, the red clay tiles for the floor and limestone from the Monchique region, which was used for a variety of finishes in the bathrooms and the kitchen.

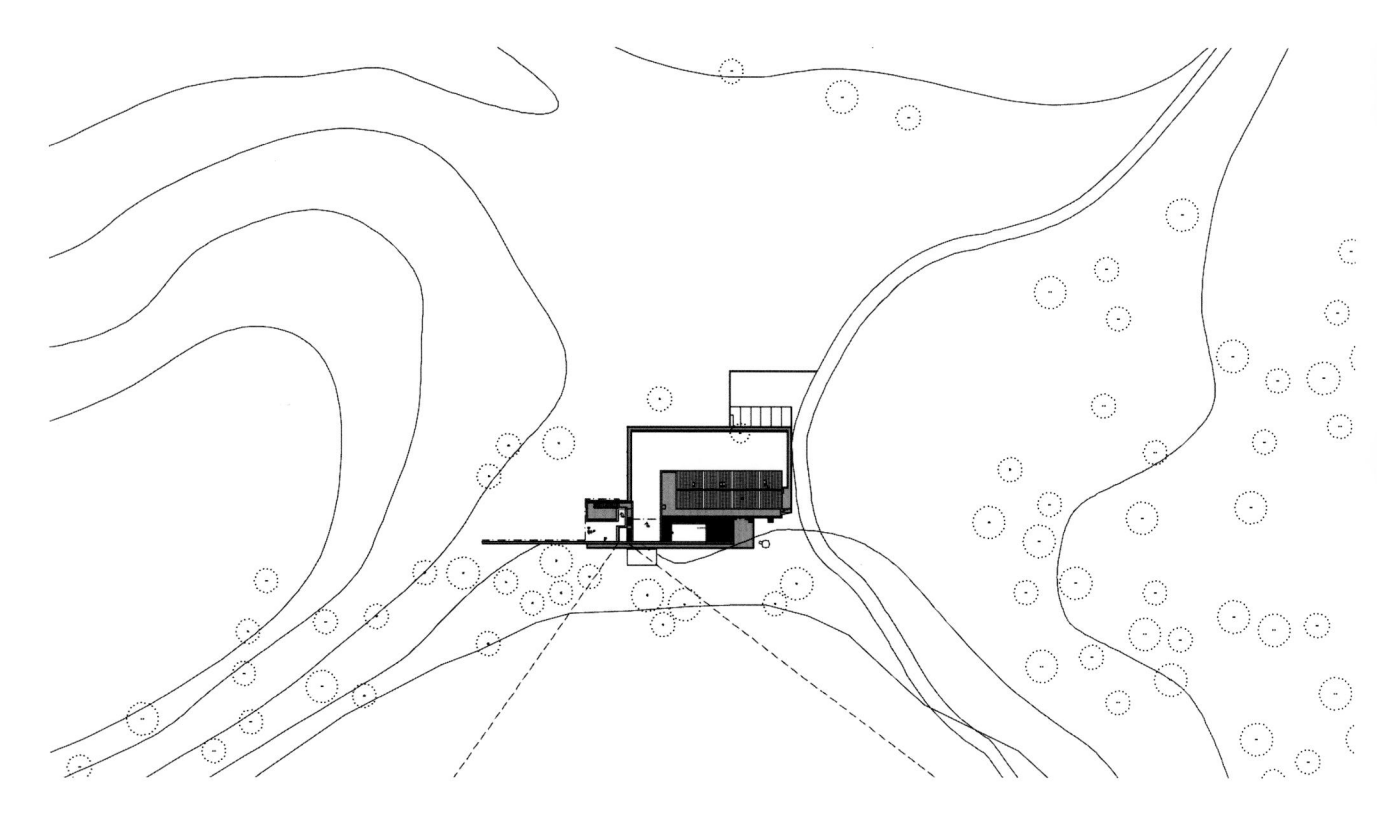

Situation plan

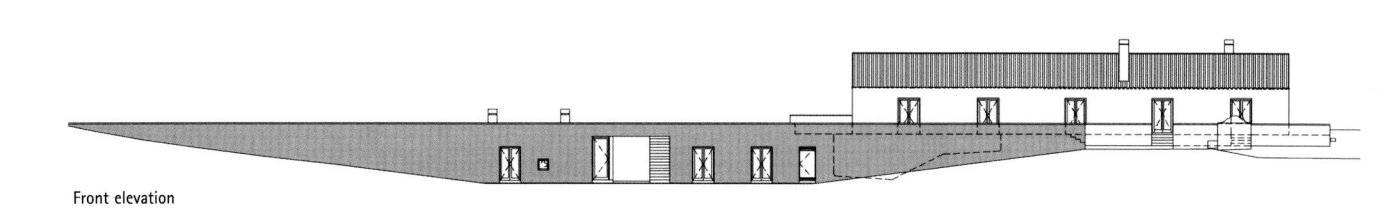

Front elevation

226 Monte dos Mosqueiros

Monte dos Mosqueiros 227

Previous floor plan

Sections of the extension

228 Monte dos Mosqueiros

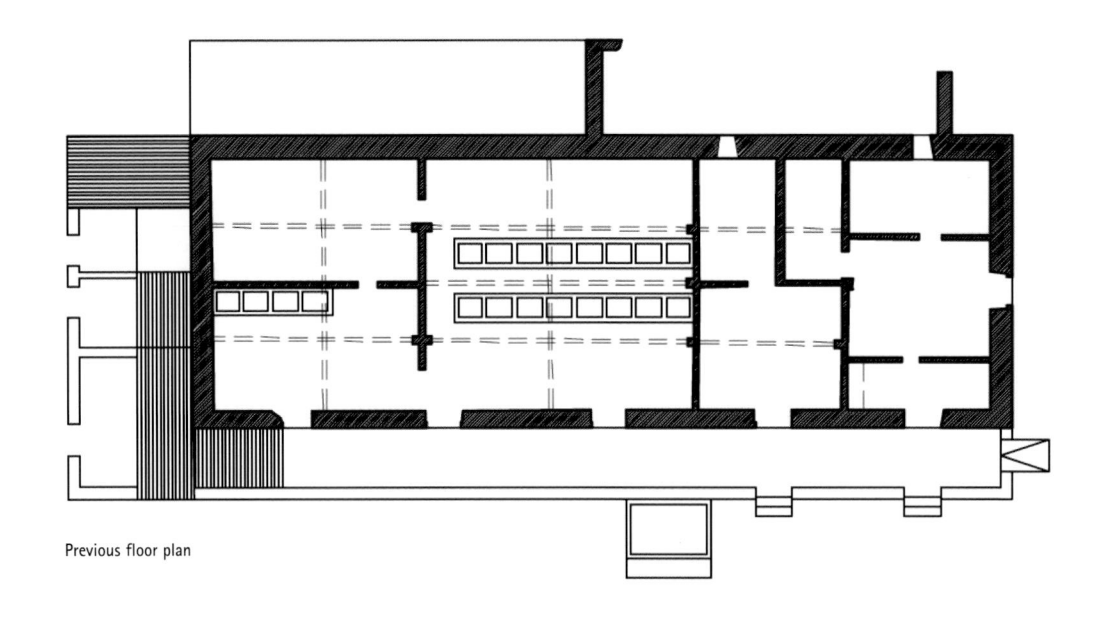

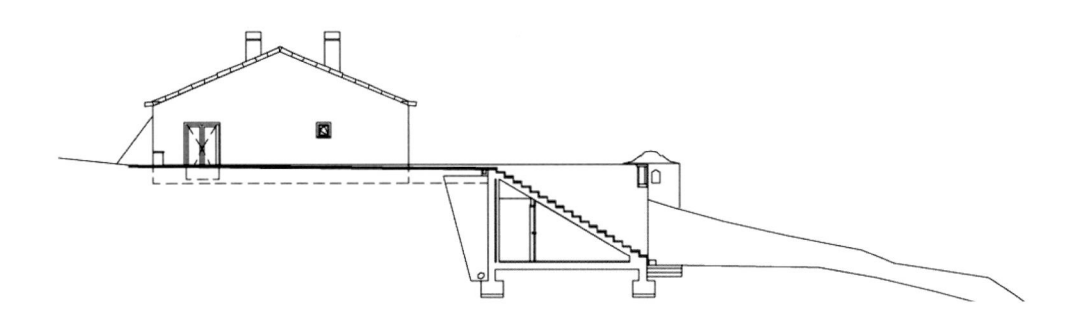

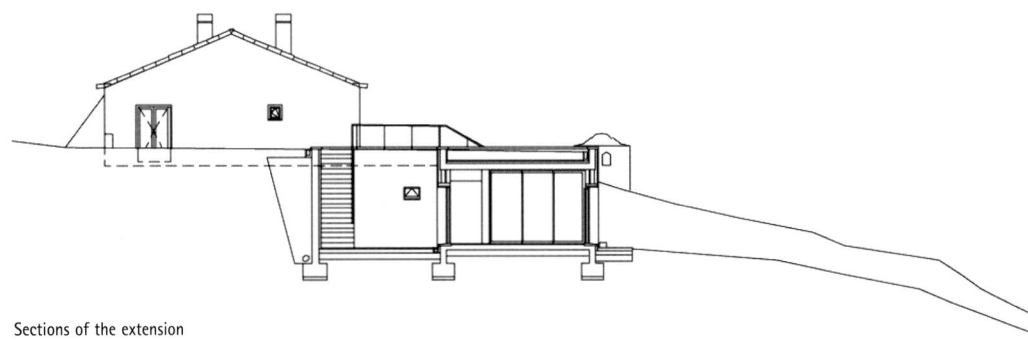

The house can be accessed via the stairs, which connect the interior with the exterior crossing the different levels of the land, or through the southeast facing interior courtyard.

1. Entry
2. Dining
3. Living
4. Kitchen
5. Bedroom
6. Bath
7. Pool
8. Old oven
9. parking
10. Machinery room
11. Patio

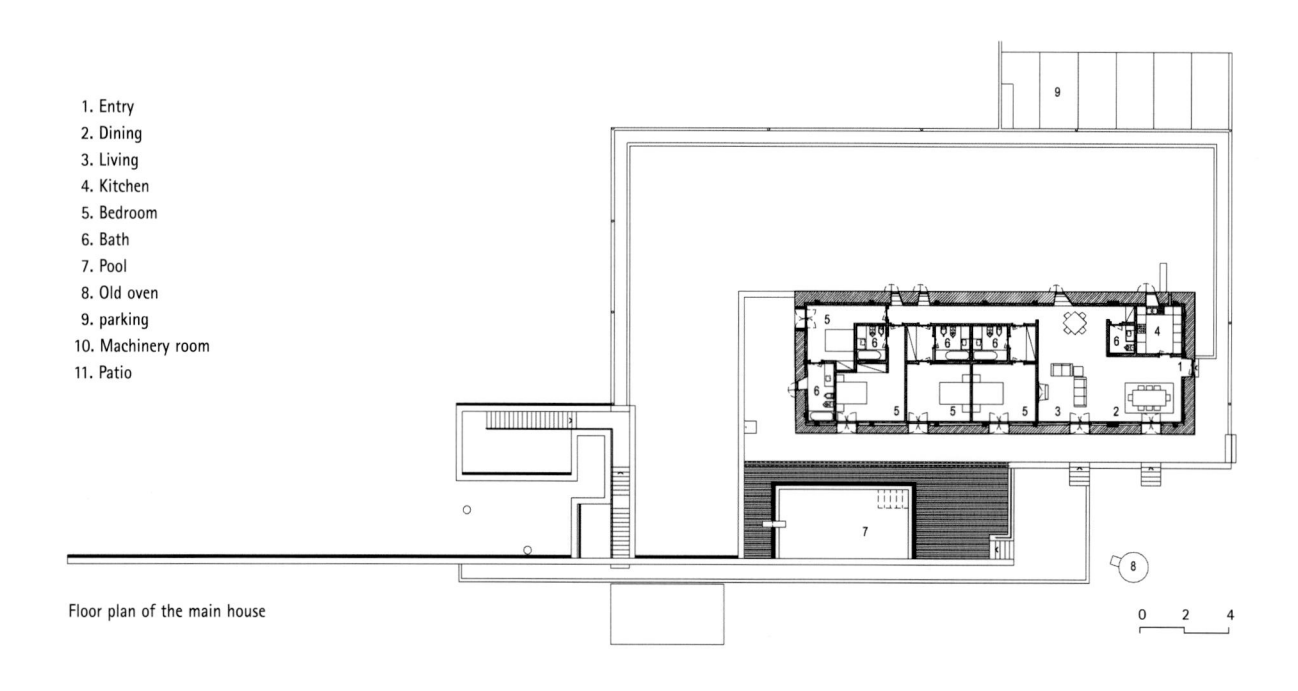

Floor plan of the main house

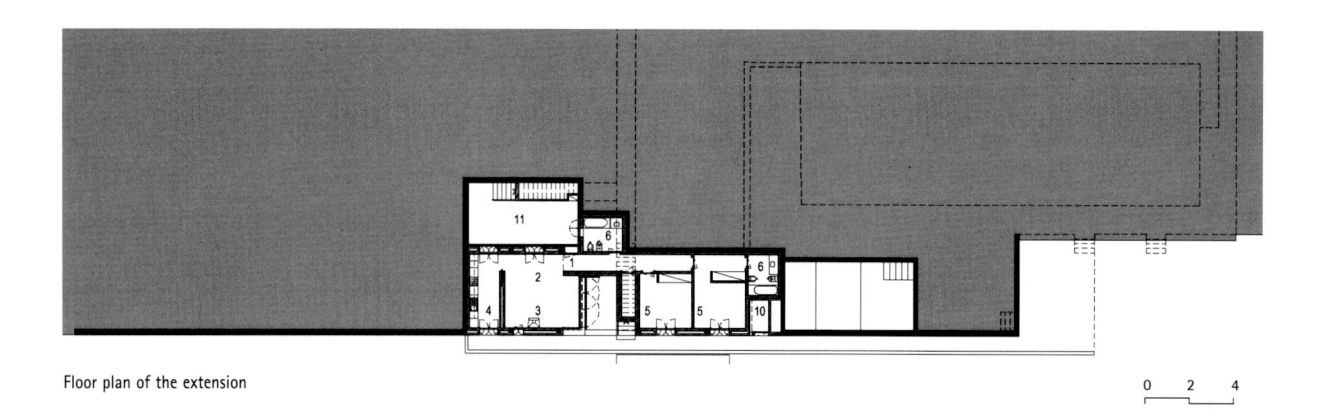

Floor plan of the extension

230 Monte dos Mosqueiros

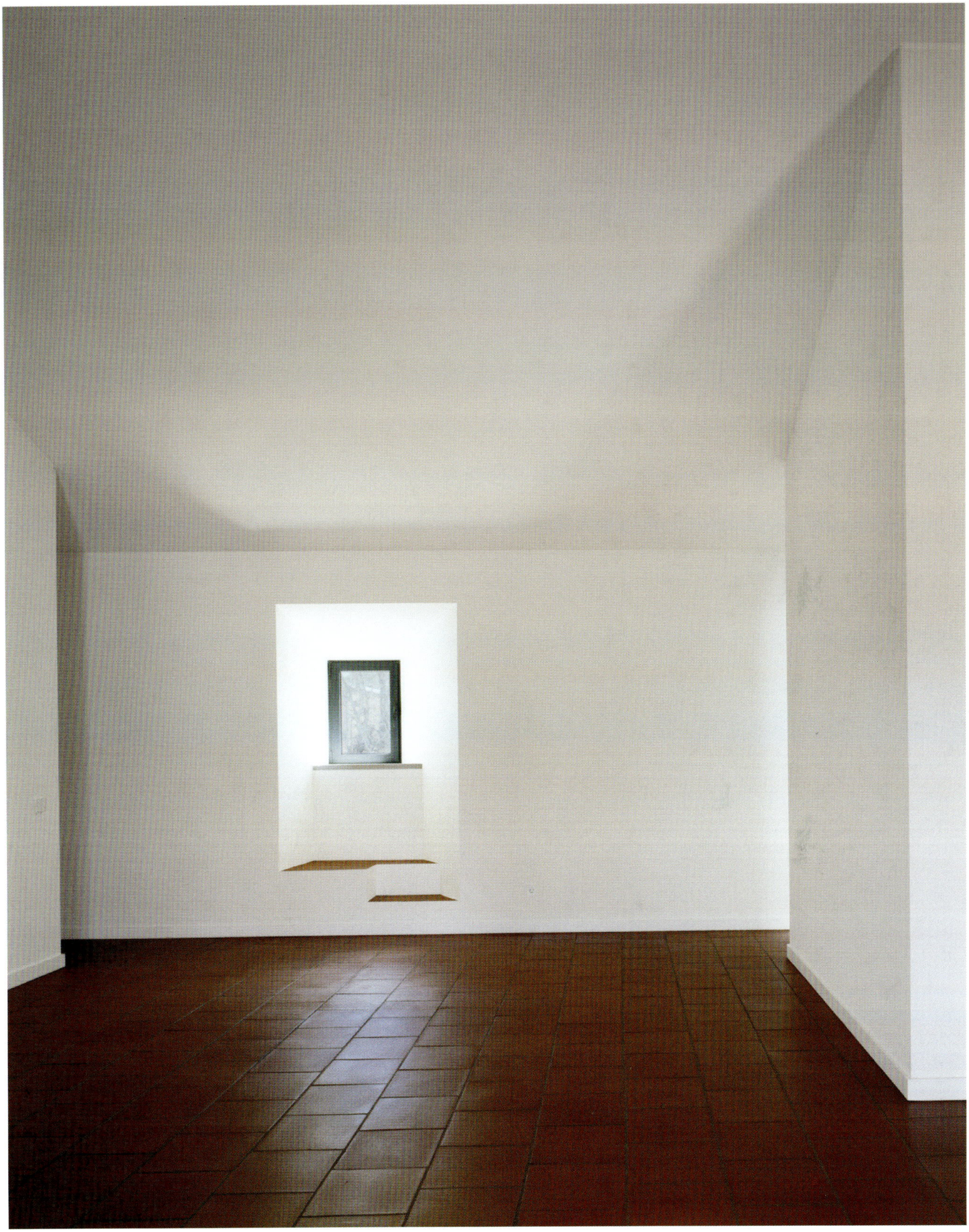

The aim of this project, located in a small village 55 miles from Madrid, was to restore an old rural space consisting of a stable and the remains of a barn, and adapt it for residential use.

House in Horcajuelo de la Sierra

Architect: Esther Maldonado
Photographer © Juan Latova
Location: Horcajuelo de la Sierra, Madrid, Spain
Completion date: 2006

Behind the preservation of the façade of local stone and the tiled roof hides a radical interior transformation; a completely different look altogether, inspired by modern-day urban lofts. A homogenous space has been created through the use of open plan rooms, where areas dedicated both to work and home life co-exist.

The main challenge has been to fuse the existing traditional materials with other contemporary ones, like the central steel structure that constitutes the backbone of the entire space. A single pillar, around which the ground floor is organized, vertically pierces the house behind the wood-burning stove. The flooring has been covered with gray limestone. The original windows have been preserved with the old wooden frames, and other new windows have been added. On the exterior façade the frames have been renovated and sliding shutters lined with steel have been installed. The framework of wooden beams has been reconstructed, replacing the old beams with new ones. Throughout the house the only enclosed spaces are the two bathrooms and the two small dressing rooms. The ground floor plays host to all social functions: in a single room there is the dining area, the living area and kitchen. In summer this floor extends to the exterior, encompassing the large terrace, defined by several low walls, on which the drinking trough has been reconstructed using steel sheets. The upper floor houses all private areas of the home: the bedroom, the bathroom and a work area with a large wooden table, which overlooks the living area.

The photos show the design of the stone façade's preservation, as well as the beams of the windows and doors, to which sliding shutters have been added.

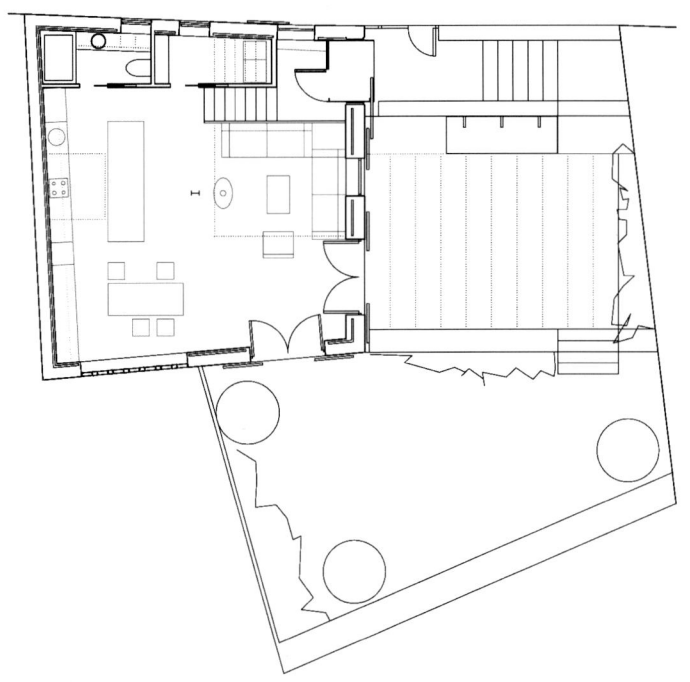

First floor

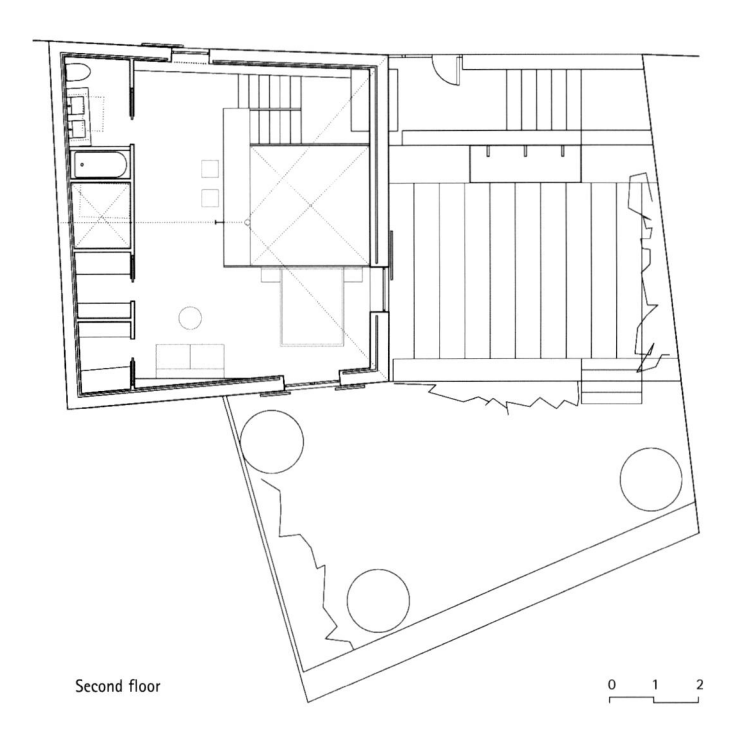

Second floor

0 1 2

House in Horcajuelo de la Sierra 235

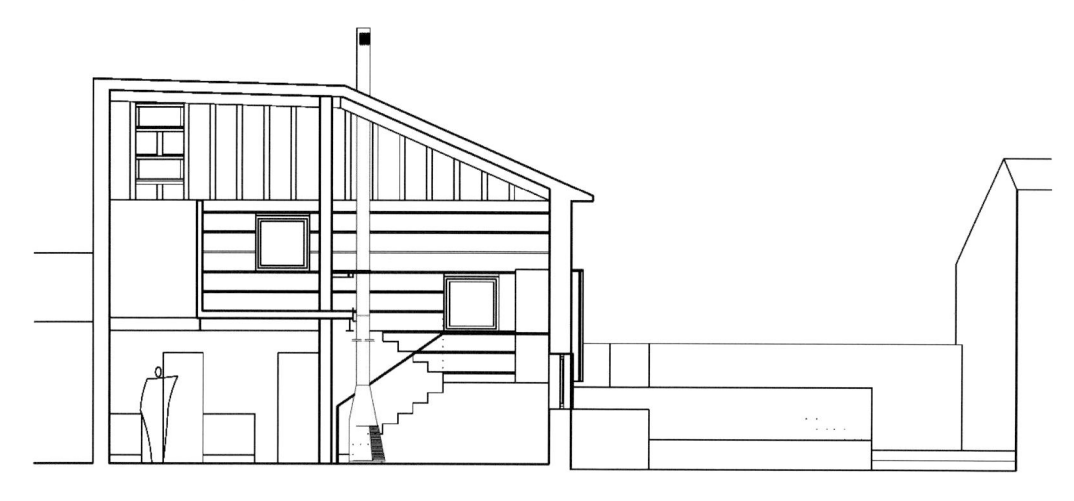

Longitudinal section

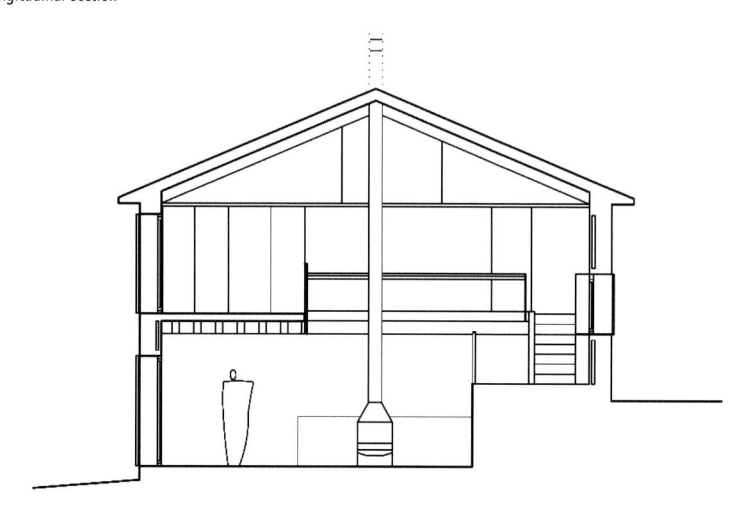

Transversal section

Transversal section

236 House in Horcajuelo de la Sierra

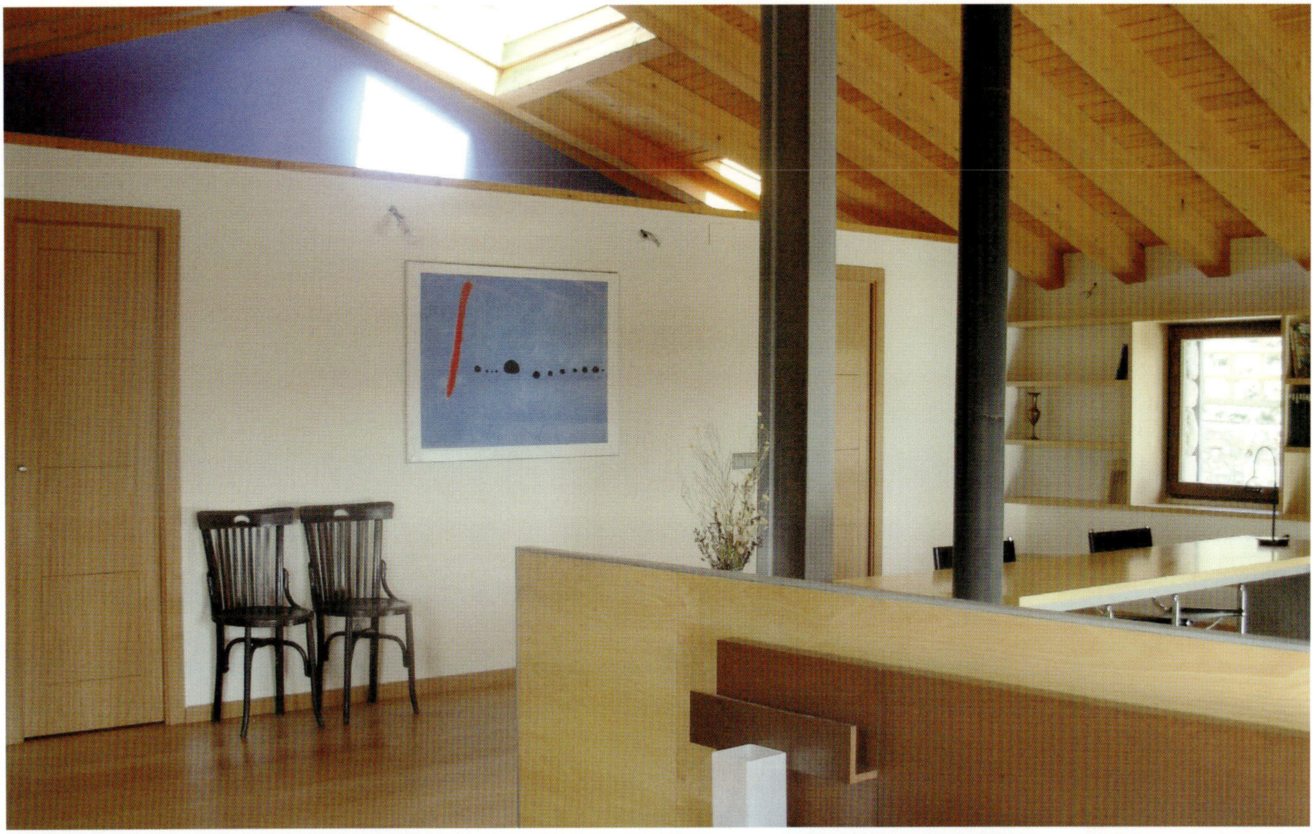

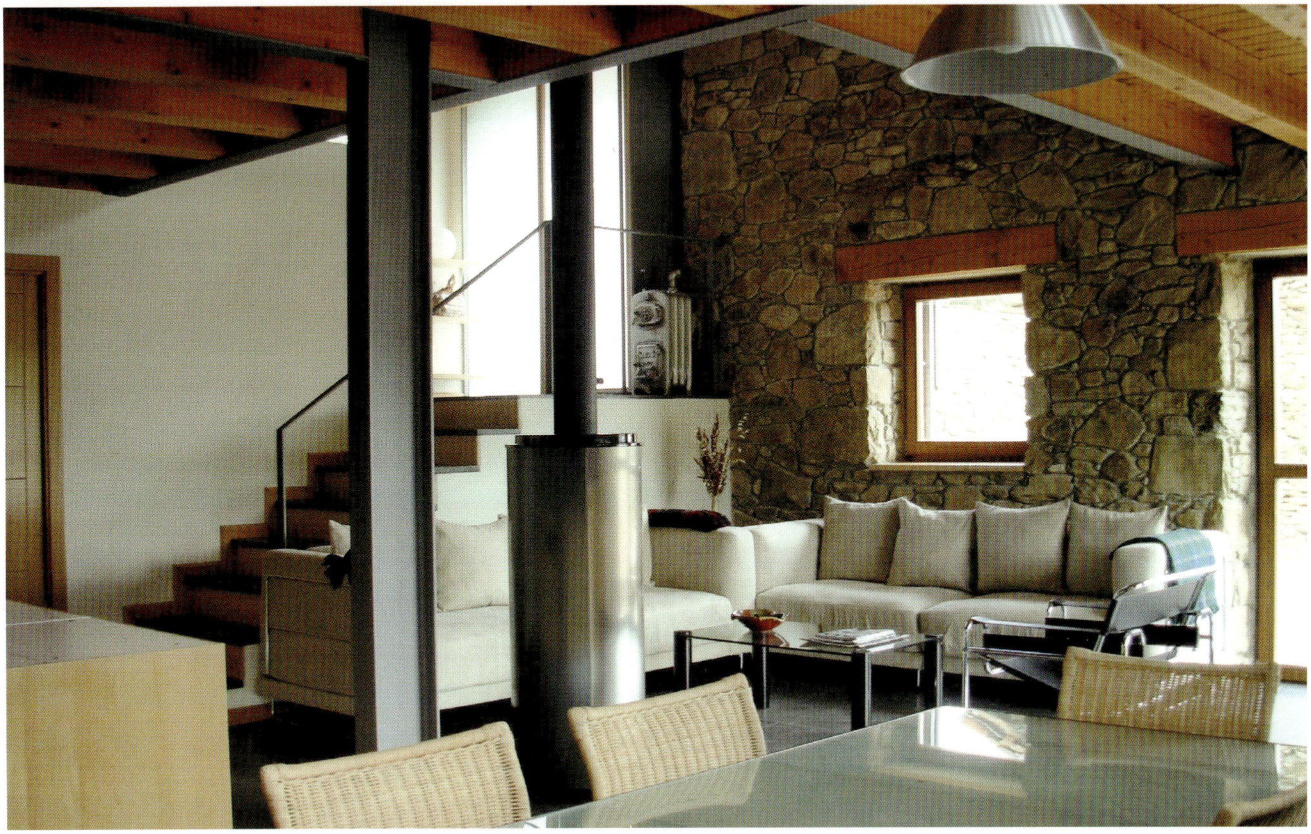

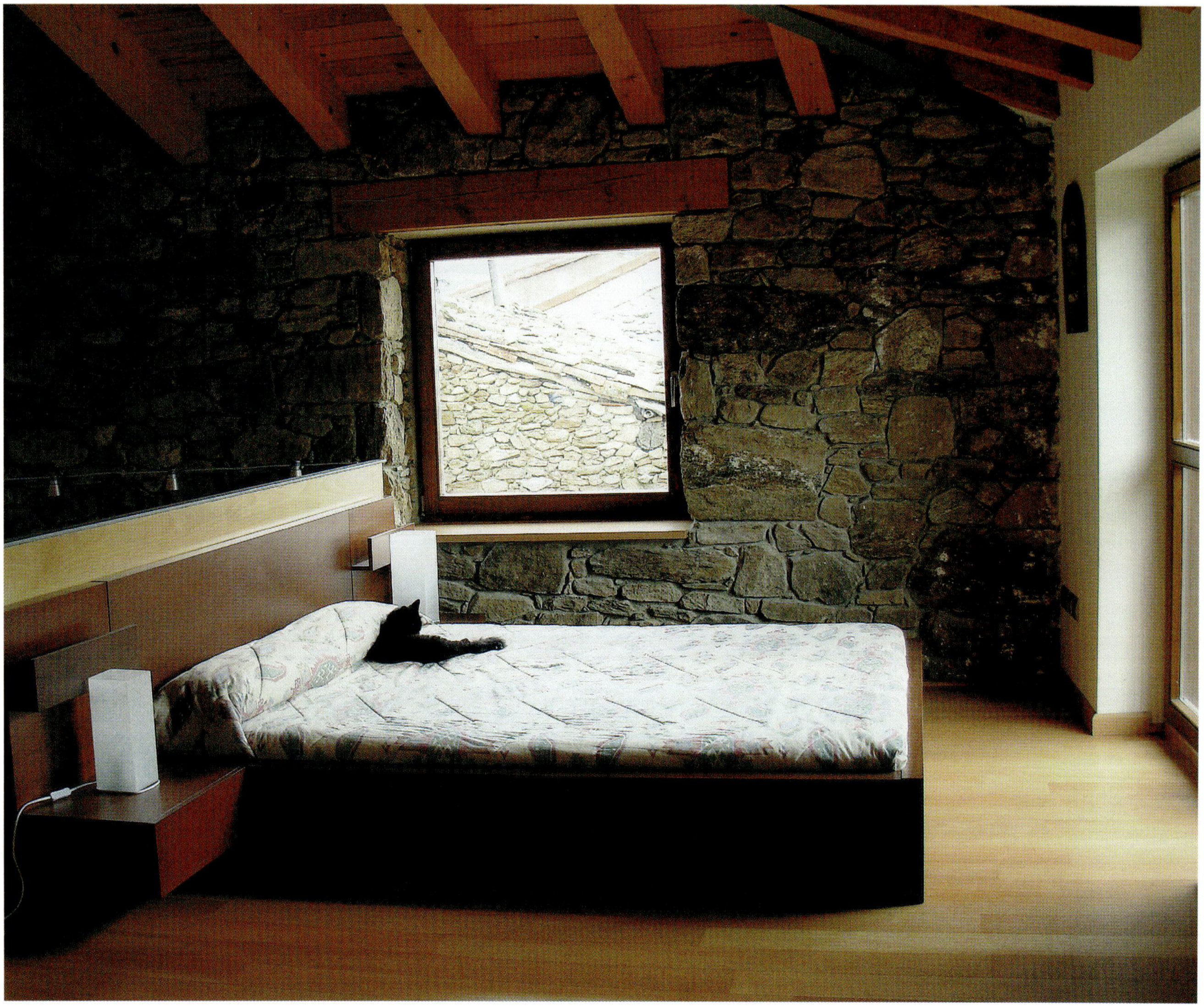

Northeast elevation

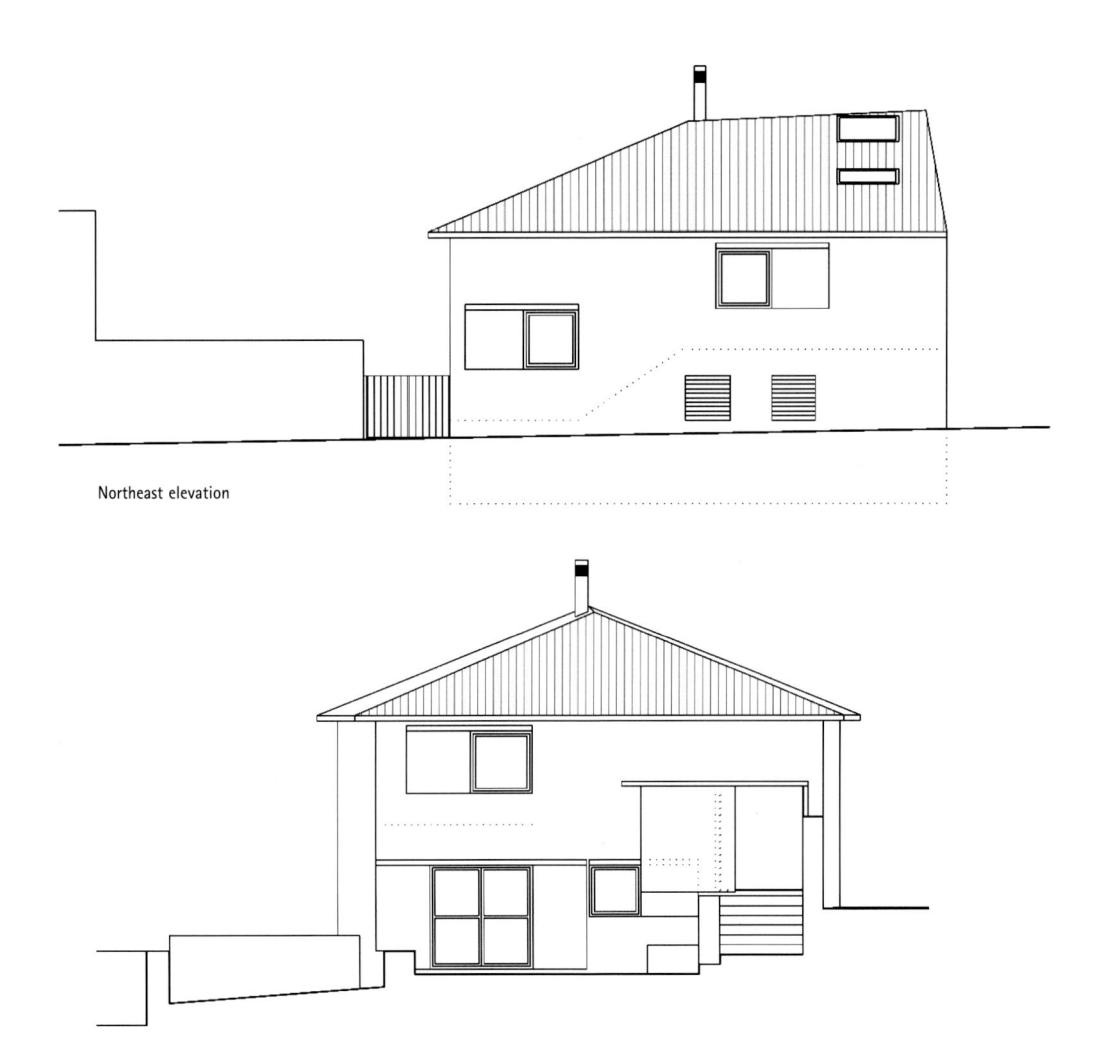

Southeast elevation

Southwest elevation

This property is located a few miles from the town of Hico in Texas. This wild and rocky region has, in recent years, become a refuge for families from Dallas who have restored old cattle farms and transformed them into second homes.

Party Barn and Guesthouse

Architects: Shipley Architects
Photographer © Charles Davis Smith
Location: Hico, TX, United States
Completion date: 2004

This old farm is located two hours South east of Dallas, in an area known as "Texas Hill Country". Before being acquired by its current owners, the main activity on the farm was raising cattle and producing hay. There was also a hencoop, an orchard, silos, a barn, wells and a mill. The Coxes, the current owners, have converted a cattle farm into a retreat. The project consists of an extension and a newly built annex. A 400-ft^2 extension has been built beside the original 800-ft^2 house, which includes a bathroom, a laundry room and a porch that is protected beneath the roof of the original home. The new building was erected just a few feet from the house. It has a surface area of 1100 ft^2 and includes two bedrooms with bathroom, a bedroom with bunk beds, a kitchen and a large central space with a stone fireplace. It has been dubbed the "Party Barn". This place has been built as if it were a pavilion; two sides of the room have sliding glass doors situated beneath the roof of the side porches. In this way the room is connected to an exterior courtyard. The upper half of the exterior walls has been clad in corrugated iron. The lower half is covered by corrugated PVC panels combined with perforated corrugated metal. This combination allows the entry of diffuse light throughout the day. To create a comfortable interior part of the interior walls has been clad in pine panels.

Floor plan

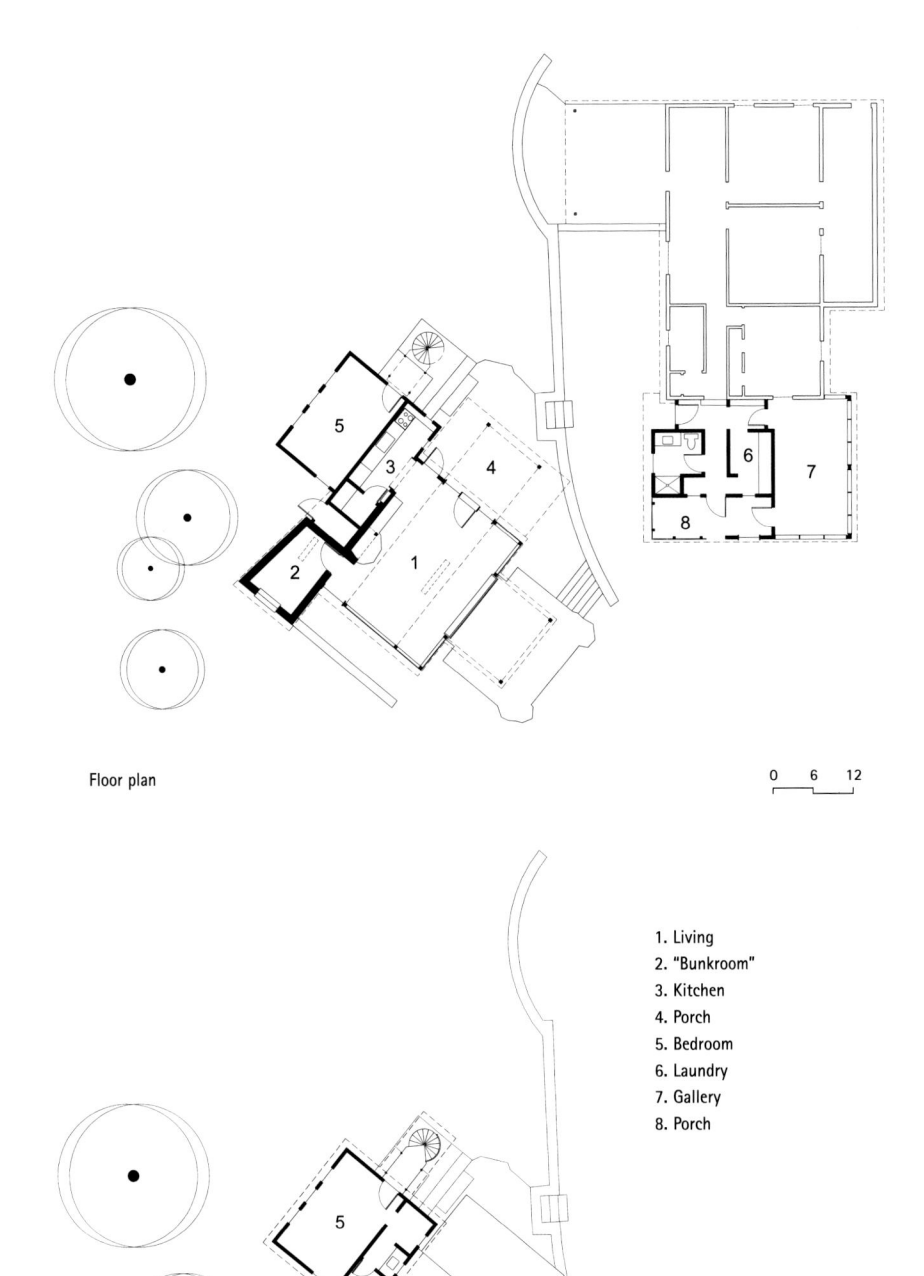

0 6 12

1. Living
2. "Bunkroom"
3. Kitchen
4. Porch
5. Bedroom
6. Laundry
7. Gallery
8. Porch

Second floor

242 Party Barn and Guesthouse

Party Barn and Guesthouse 243

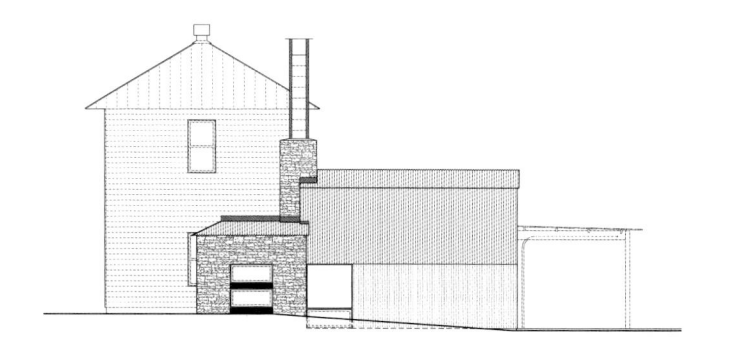

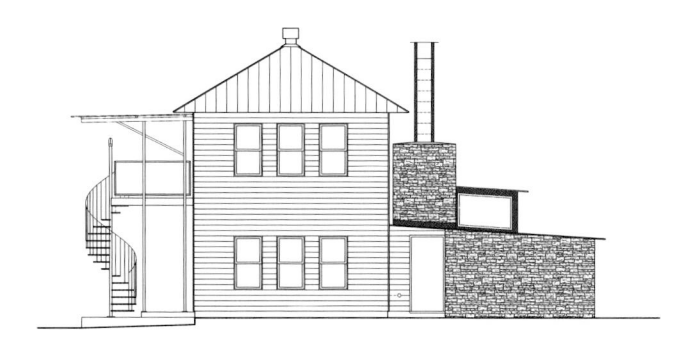

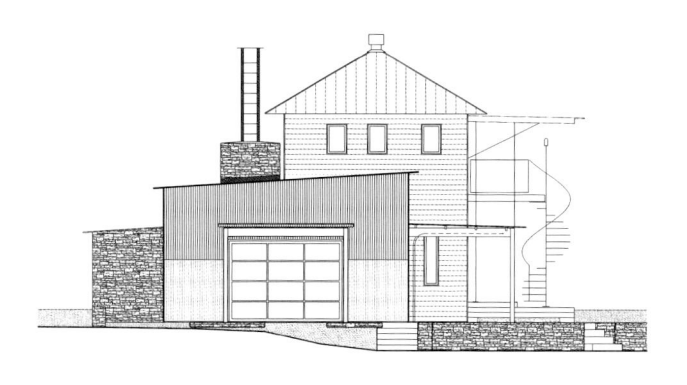

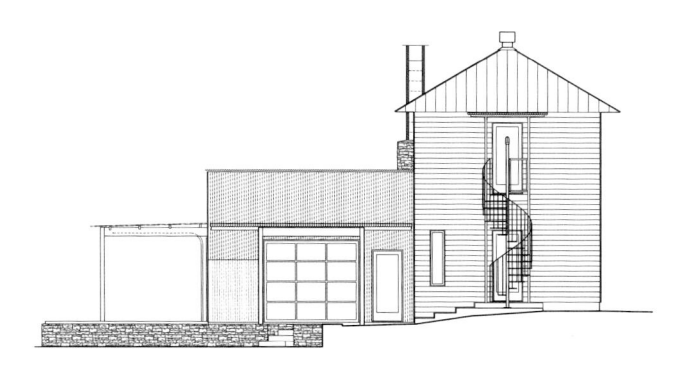

Elevations

The design of the "Party Barn" aims to connect the space with the outside. The glass doors disappear from view once they have been slid beneath the roofs of the porches.

Party Barn and Guesthouse 245

To achieve a warm interior in the large room wooden panels have been used and the fireplace has been clad in stones taken from a nearby stream.

Party Barn and Guesthouse 247

Despite the careful restoration, which has resulted in an elegant second residence, the house, surrounded by nature, maintains the image of peace and tranquility.

Podere 43

Architects: Labics
Photographer © Luigi Filetici
Location: Albinia, Grosseto, Italy
Completion date: 2002

This home forms part of a group of 45 homes built in the 30s with aim of using land once occupied by the nearby salt marshes. The original house, attributed to architect Marcello Piacentini, had three central spaces that acted independently of each other: the farm, the barn and an auxiliary cabin for the farming implements that included a brick oven. A young couple with two children decided to make this old farm their second residence. This place was chosen for family get-togethers and reunions with friends, offering a space where this could take place in a rural and tranquil setting, surrounded by fields. The image of land and water encourages reflection on the physical and symbolic nature of the space. The volume that was originally used as the living space maintains that use, since the couple wanted to conserve the historic character and value of the construction. The barn and the cabin were completely remodeled and transformed respectively into a living room and a guesthouse. The changes were carried out taking into consideration their relationship with the surrounding landscape. The result consisted in a gentle transition between interior and exterior spaces. A very modern interior design and the appropriate choice of materials achieved a harmonious contrast between contemporary and rural styles.

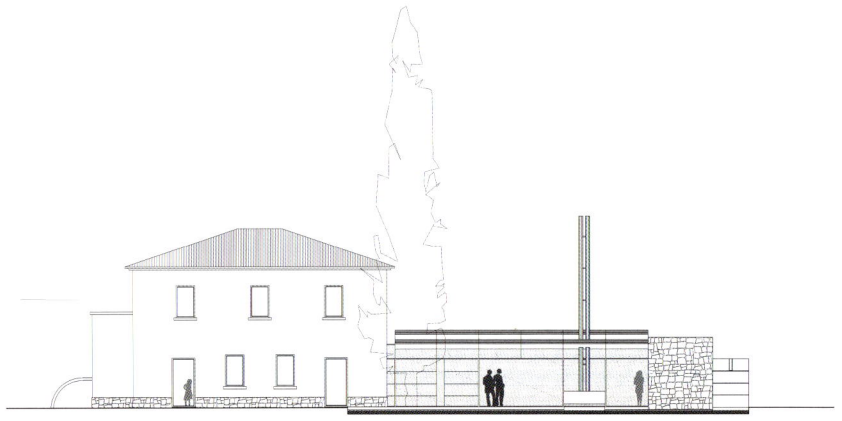

Front elevation

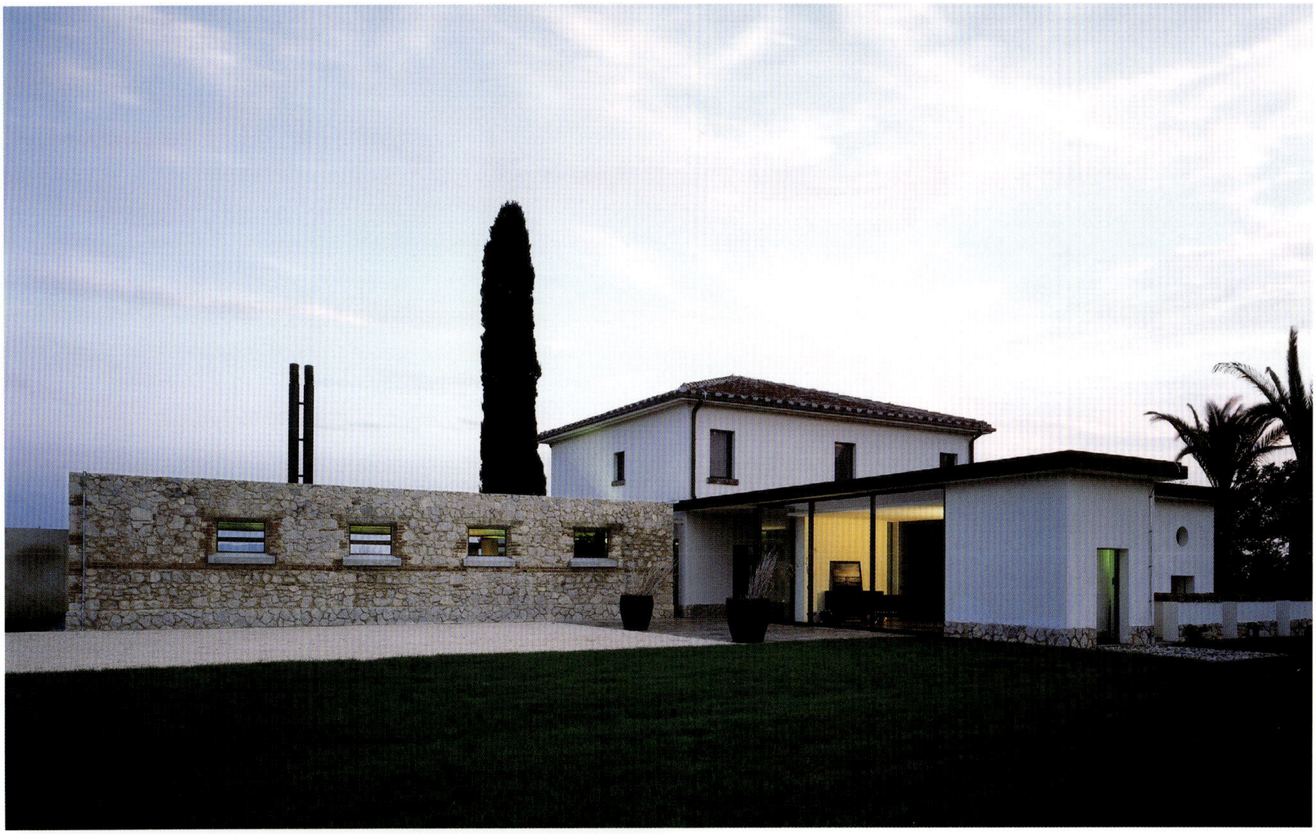

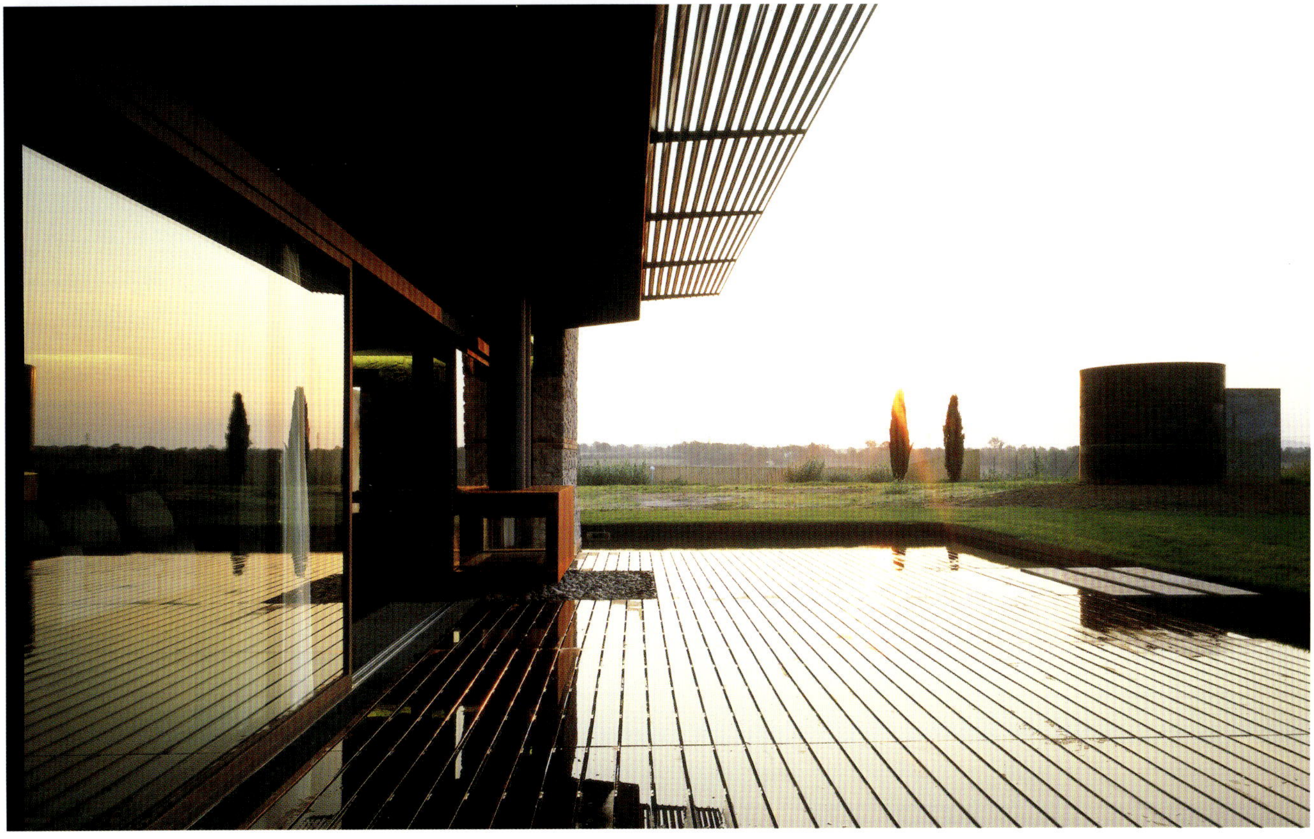

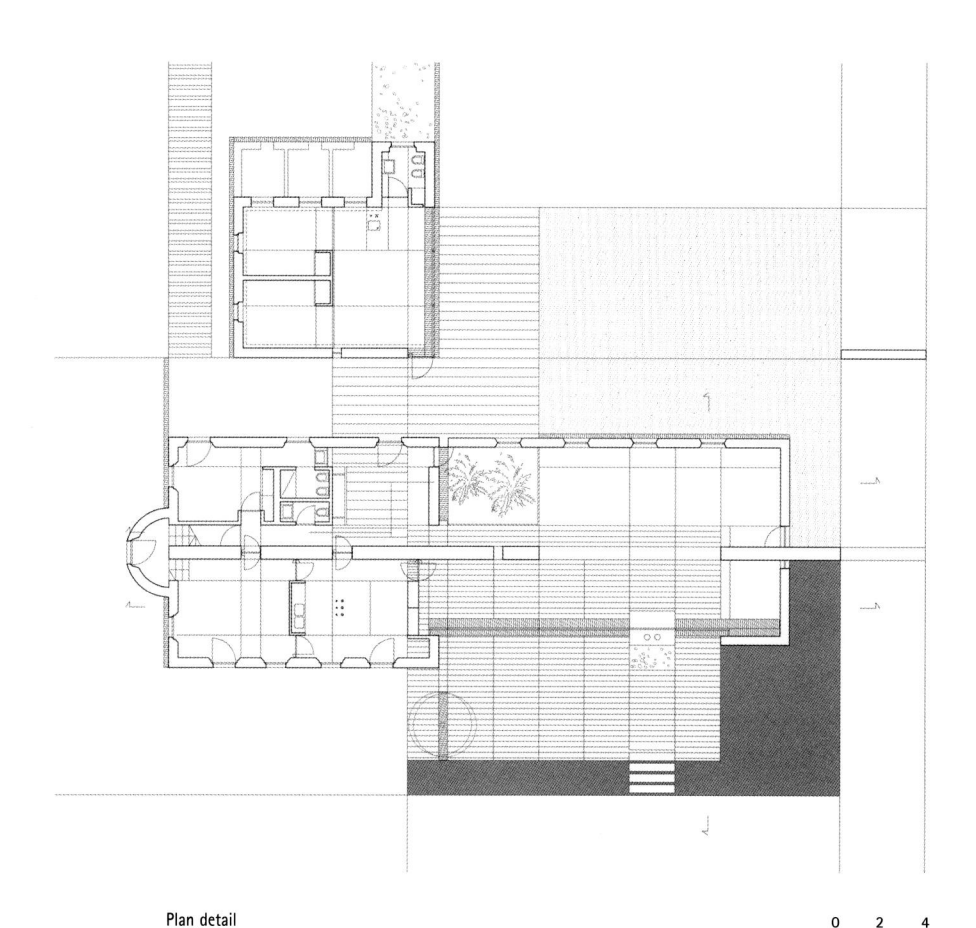

Plan detail

0 2 4

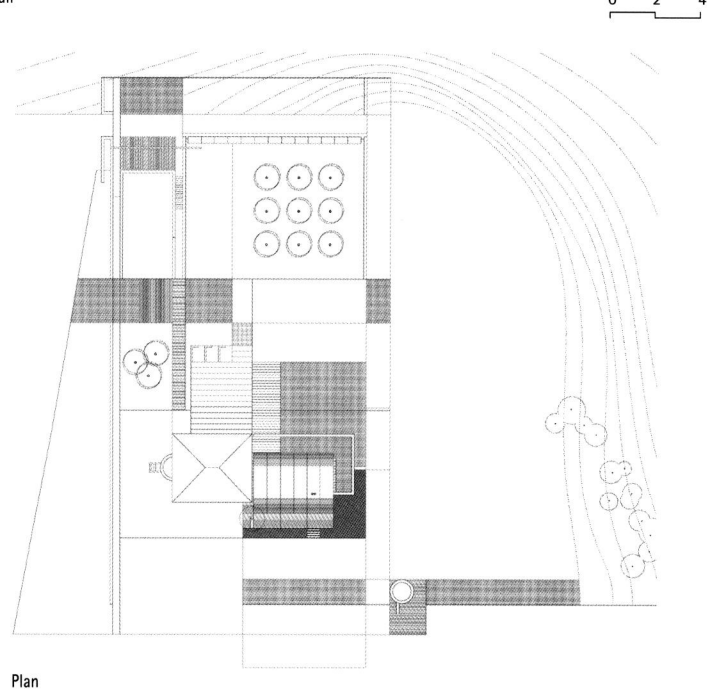

Plan

252 Podere 43

Water partially surrounds the part of the farm that was most modified and is reminiscent of the salt marshes, which occupied this place years before.

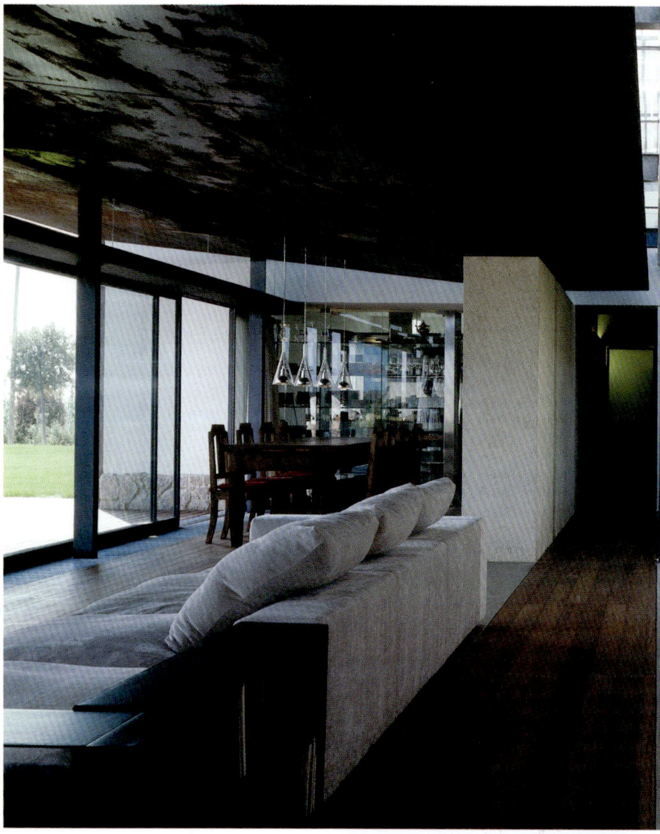

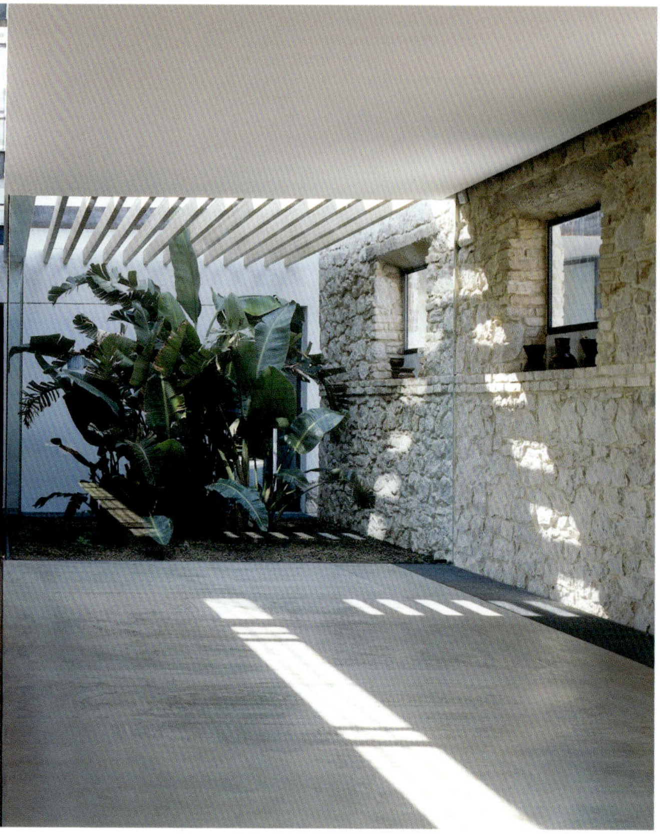

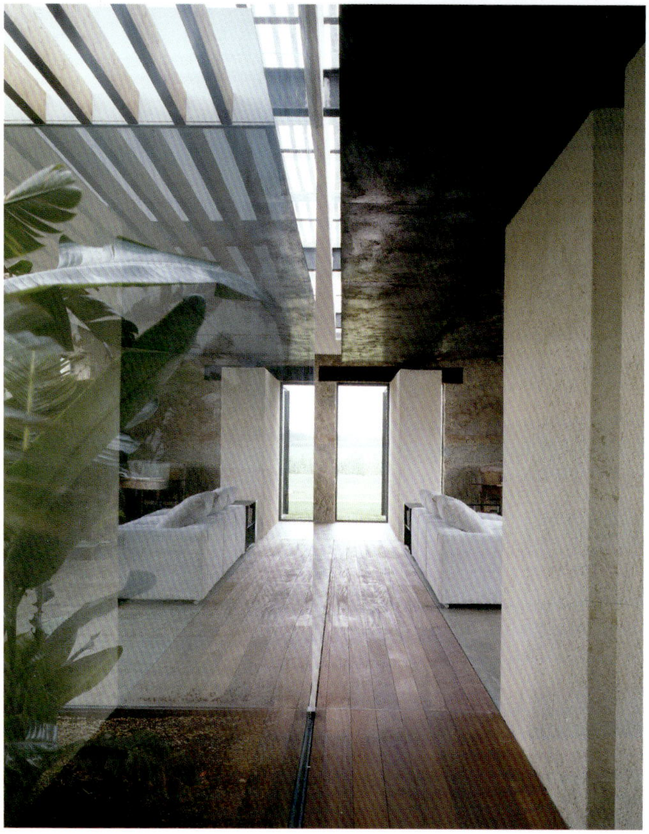

The interior of the old farm has been transformed into a space with modern aesthetics, which connects with the outside thanks to a glass wall.